WRITING IN THE RAIN

WRITING
IN THE
RAIN

STORIES, ESSAYS & POEMS

Howard White

with a foreword by Barry Broadfoot

HARBOUR PUBLISHING

Harbour Publishing Co. Ltd.
Box 219
Madeira Park, BC
V0N 2H0

Cover drawing by Kerry Waghorn
Cover design by Roger Handling
Maps and charts in "Tides" by Roger Handling
Photographs in "William Duncan and the Miracle of Metlakatla"
    courtesy BC Provincial Archives
Drawings in "My Experience with Greatness" by Maurice Spira
Printed and bound in Canada
Typeset in Elante

CANADIAN CATALOGUING IN PUBLICATION DATA

White, Howard, 1945–
    Writing in the rain

    ISBN 1-55017-010-4

    I. Title.
PS8595.H58W7   1990C818'.5408C89-091504-0
PR9199.3.W54W7 1990

CONTENTS

FOREWORD

The Sechelt Peninsula is that smoky blue jut of mainland I see when I look out across Georgia Strait from my window in Nanaimo—and for years I looked out and wondered about a man I heard of over there named Howard White. He was a damn good writer, so my friends told me, and he published a lot of books on an old press he bought for a few hundred bucks, and when the garbage piled up at the dump he got on his bulldozer and shoved it out of sight.

Interesting, I thought. Having learned most of my prejudices about the Canadian book business in Toronto, the mental picture I had of regional writers was of sensitive types sitting around the floors of each others' homes drinking wine and reading their work to each other by candlelight, getting out the odd slim volume which didn't sell beans and engaging in an endless hunt for Canada Council grants. A west coast writer who could do anything as useful as bulldoze his town's garbage seemed at least worth checking up on. I dug around and by God, yes, here was something different. The guy was producing books, a lot of them, and not only that, they were good. The bulldozer was true too.

Howard White grew up right over there in that smoky blue jumble of islands and logging-scarred headlands, a fact which shouldn't be surprising but somehow is. He is just old enough to have caught the tail end of the coast's postwar boom years when every one of its thousand bays had a gyppo camp or cannery in it and the Inside Passage was alive with the famous little steamships of the Union Line and the whole landscape was swarming with pioneers who have now largely disappeared. The elder White was a gyppo logger and the future writer/publisher had a most un-literary beginning, neglecting his grade one correspondence lessons to run the dump winch that tumbled logs into the water from the trucks, beat off wild cows who wanted to eat the camp dynamite cache, and out-bluster randy chokermen who were determined to jump into bed with the babysitter, to name just a few routine distractions. Later the family put down roots in the isolated fishing village of Pender Harbour where White caught up on his lessons enough to get to university and learn that the great outside world didn't hold a candle to the one he'd left behind on the smoky Sechelt coast. In 1970 he moved back to Pender Harbour to start the town's first and last newspaper, which evolved into the legendary BC coast journal *Raincoast Chronicles*, and then into Harbour Publishing. As a publisher-writer White made use of his logging camp upbringing in two ways: he mined it as a source of material for excellent stories like "The Bomb that Mooed" and "The Day Joey Came," and he recalled old skills to hire himself out as a freelance bulldozer driver, thereby subsidizing his cultural enterprises through the early years.

"Oh, yes, Howard White. He's out there on the west coast somewhere, isn't he?" a Toronto publisher said to me recently. To him that was all that need be said. "Out there on the west coast"—the ultimate condescension. It was just this attitude that made it so necessary for Howard White to become printer/publisher/writer instead of simply *writer*, as he probably would have preferred. But if that exigency has diminished his own effect as a writer it has also magnified it by allowing him to recognize the special extra gene writers have and bring it out in others. With his wife Mary he went off in search of the authentic west coast voice the publishing establishment disdained, finding writers with the right stuff and coaxing and bribing and editing their material into books of arresting quality. These books attracted others of their ilk and the Whites through the years nurtured dozens of natural writers who have contributed scores of books on everything from lighthouse keeping to bush flying to whaling.

I could have persisted with my Toronto friend and argued that Howard White and his Harbour Publishing had done more for regional writers, the history of the west coast, its people, its character, its fast-fading uniqueness, than any other publisher in Canada—hell, in North America. May I be allowed one further escalation? In the world. That gumboot fits. I could have said this, but I knew it would be no use. Instead I played the one card I knew would register and pointed out that Harbour's books sell well, astonishingly well, even by Toronto standards. That always gets their attention, and there have been not a few eastern attempts to do Harbour-type books, seldom with much success.

For me the most important thing remains that the writing is so damn good. Both in his own stuff and in his publishing, the influence of White the regional west coast writer is strongly present. He knew there were stories to be told and he knew that anyone who talks a good story has a fair chance of writing it. I can pick up a copy of his *Raincoast Chronicles* and a 100-mph south-easter can be blowing the house inside out and I'll keep reading.

Forewords should be short and here I've gone and shot most of this one talking about Howard White's publishing instead of his writing, but in his case more than in anyone else's I can think of, it's all one seamless web. Start at page one of this book, don't skip a damned word, and you'll find it a rich heady flavourful brew with enough chokerknobs rockcod salal bush steampots and old smells of the coast in it to to keep you coming back, like Oliver, asking, "Can I have some more, sir?"

BARRY BROADFOOT
Nanaimo, BC

PREFACE:
WRITING IN THE RAIN

I've actually done that, write in the rain. I could tell you a lot about it, sitting out on a road grade on a spreading machine waiting for the next turn, hunched over a piece of writing paper folded down to vestpocket size, scratching down thoughts in shorthand as rain drips off the end of your nose, raising a spongy welt on the paper and then the ballpen ink won't stick. At the end of the job I'd have this little pile of exceedingly dirty folded-up notepapers covered with undecipherable chickenscratch. I've got them from the Rainbow Lake oilfields of Northern Alberta and the muddy sidehills of Vancouver Island above Port MacNeill. I've got them from Delta dyke jobs and lots from the garbage dump detail in Pender Harbour. This is where writing has always been for me, wedged uneasily between the world of gravel, logs, ringing phone and the other, equally demanding world inside. Like all interfaces, all borders, it's a precarious place to set up one's shop, but it's also a place where interesting things happen, a frontier.

Such an approach does not lend itself to grand projects, and tends to accumulate a collection of disparate short pieces over the years. I first got the idea of placing scattered shorter writings together in one volume, prose and poetry, published and unpublished, when I saw the Saskatchewan writer Ken Mitchell pull it off a few years ago with his book *Ken Mitchell Country*, and I was

9

reminded again as I meandered delightedly through Garrison Keillor's recent sampler *We Are Still Married*. I don't wish to risk unflattering comparisons between those triumphant achievements and my own gumboot meditations except to say that I share the writers' fascination with regional character, and I pray that fascination will provide some vaguely unifying rationale which would otherwise be missing from the following assortment.

HOWARD WHITE

Pender Harbour, August 1990

OOLACHON GREASE

Oolachon grease gold, you hear about it
how the Tsimshian empire held
the whole coast to ransom for it
brought the poor stick Indians begging
from the interior, beating paths
between the mountains you could
follow in the dark, by nose
the "grease trails" that let the
whiteman in, later on —
a beautiful woman professor told me about it
paler than butter she said,
but like butter without salt
and not at all repugnant to
the European palate
used as a condiment
but I ask you, are empires
sustained by condiments?
It was their oil, for the flame
in the flesh and more
                    I found it finally
in Bella Bella 1976 price $48/gal.
and it smelled like the cracks
between the deck planks of an old fish barge
if you can imagine spreading that

on your bread — quite enough to hurl
the European palate toward the nearest
toilet bowl which is how far
Indian is from White how far
learning is from knowing how
far we are from this ragged place
we've taken from them, for that,
the smell of fish left in the sun
and let go bad, that is the old
smell of the coast, known, as scent
is the final intimacy known of lifelong mates

take that barge plank, let it toss
ten years on the tide, knock on every rock
from Flattery to Yakutat, bake another
ten in the sun, take it rounded like
an Inuit ivory and grey as bone
crack it open and sniff the darker core
and you will know
what Vancouver knew ducking through
his first Nootka door pole, the essence
the odour of the their living here
and however far you are from loving that
is how far you are
                 from arriving

Morts

Up in our neck of the woods these days, fish farming is the thing. It's the big action and the big argument. Basically the people who're making a buck from it like it and everybody else thinks it stinks. Well, everybody agrees it stinks, but the argument sticks on the point of whether or not a little stink and mess might be put up with in the name of a few paying jobs. The jobs are kind of crummy and the pay is poor, but this strip of rock and Christmas trees has been kissing goodbye to jobs for so long there is a whole generation that's never known steady work. Big healthy guys in their mid-twenties still living at home, still driving 1973 Trans Ams. Anything that promises to get their wasting carcasses off the living room sofa and out of the house for a few hours a day has to look pretty good to their families.

But that doesn't apply to me. My sons are still playing peanut hockey. I sit a lot myself, but in front of a computer, not on the sofa. I do better tickling the keyboard of an IBM than I ever did pulling levers on a D-8, much as my old construction buddies find it hard to believe anybody actually gets paid for this kind of thing. And not having to work outside anymore frees me to think kind thoughts about it. I have actually convinced myself that I liked physical work and miss it, and from time to time this leads me to dabble in it. I keep a hand in a small sand and gravel outfit with two other guys and put in the odd shift over the weekend trying to prove I'm as good a man as I ever was.

You might think I run a certain risk by doing this, and you're right.

It was September 1988. Around here it had been a wonderful month—very sunny and dry. The boys over at the water board were issuing handbills banning all sprinkling—even days or odd, before 7 PM or after. They were going up every day to the reservoir with their yardstick and measuring the fall and calculating how many more days of dry spell we could stand before water stopped coming out of all the taps in Pender Harbour. The kids were still swimming in the salt chuck.

This had an implication for the fish farmers. With all the pollen and leaves and dust and other end-of-summer goodies blowing around and stewing up in the warm water, the plankton thought the good times were here again and launched on a record-smashing population bloom. Any time one of these clouds of happy plankton drifted down on a fish farm, the fish choked in the pens. A hundred thousand six-pound salmon die at once, costing someone a million dollars. At first the farmers surreptitiously chucked their "morts" (mortalities) over the side, but when the volume got into the hundreds of pounds, then into the tons, this illegal activity became too obvious. They began burying the morts in limed pits ashore like they were supposed to, but in no time at all every scrap of dirt on the rocky shore became stuffed with dead salmon. Fish tails were sticking out from under every rock and leaf. So the farmers began loading the mushy carcasses into one-ton totes and hauling the totes to the garbage dump, two to a pickup truck. But the morts kept coming, and soon the farmers were out of totes and out of pickups.

This was when I got the call.

They didn't call me to compute. They called to hire our truck, a twelve-yard cornbinder in fair shape for its age.

I don't get many calls about the truck. I am on the phone all day about books, but I don't place much store in that. Getting a call as a truck operator was something special. The regular hauling jobs that came up—clearing lots for new retirement mansions, cleaning ditches for the department of highways—were passed around among the serious sand and gravel operators with never a nod of recognition in our direction. My sand-and gravel partners, when they were around, kept the truck going on projects they always seemed to stir up on their own, but when they were away and I was holding the fort as I was now, the truck sat embarrassingly idle. I felt I was letting our side down, but the construction bunch just didn't want to talk to me. I suppose when any outsider stopping by Blueband Diesel mentioned the possibility of getting our truck on a job, some greasy fellow might say, "I think he's too busy writin' books, ain't he?" there would be sarcastic laughs, and that would be as far as it went.

You better believe I was tickled to be called about the truck.

"Say, you got some kind of a truck dontcha?" the gruff voice demanded.

"Yessir, that we do."

"Well, how would you like to have it up here in the morning?"

I was in the last stages of getting away a contract publishing job worth fifty thousand dollars, and even if they took the truck for a whole day, it couldn't be worth more than two hundred dollars. I was also sick. My padded leather chair was shiny with sweat and my heart was pounding and my mind kept evaporating and blowing out the window. It had gone on too long to be anything usual, and later in the month I would finally drag myself off to the doctor's and discover my metabolic system was going mad under the influence of an overactive thyroid, but at this point I was assuming it was all just something that came with turning forty-two. I could barely hold my pen. At the slightest exertion I would collapse in my chair, panting and shaking.

"Wh—what is it you want hauled?"

"Ha-ha. Whaddya think? Fish!"

"Er, how much?"

"Oh, I dunno, seven-eight totes. There's more comin in all the time."

I knew it was insanity to consider doing this. Nobody who liked me expected it of me, and this guy seemed to be laughing at me even as he asked me to do it. I had made quite a public thing of doubting fish farms and their works, and had every reason to abandon them to their smelly fates, as all the other truckers apparently had. I also didn't have a valid licence. I had a Class 5 licence for driving cars, pickups and mopeds like most people, but for a truck of the cornbinder's size you needed a Class 3. I used to have a truckdriving licence, back when it was called a "C" licence—I was very proud of the fact I took my original driver's test in my dad's ten-yard Dodge tandem when I was a sixteen-year-old kid, but when they went from letters to numbers I somehow got downshifted. I had pointed this out to the Superintendent of Motor Vehicles in numerous letters, claiming protection under the grandfather clause, but so far I was losing the argument. My partners kept telling me to smarten up and go get a new one, but it was a matter of principle for me. I had been stopped by cops once or twice and they hadn't noticed this technicality, but they could. The fine was $2,500, but the real penalty was getting written up in "This Week In Court." It was just another thing that might have tipped the scales toward saying no to the fish plant.

This was just the sort of deal I could never refuse.

"Yeah, I'll be there," I said.

And of course immediately panicked. What am I, nuts, I asked myself. You can't fill a gravel truck with rotten fish. The slime would leak out the crack around the tailgate. But my mind was running ahead of me, patching the holes. I could buy a roll of 6-mill poly and line the box with that, maybe a double layer of it. It still might squeeze out at the back where the crack was an inch wide. Could jam a two-by-four in there, under the poly. What if the tailgate unlatched under the weight and let ten tons of rotten fish out on the road? What would I say to my friends in the Save Our Scenery Society then? But if I pulled the chains tight, it would hold the gate shut even if the latch broke.

Conspiring with the enemy gave me a rare kind of thrill. I was a professional, and when a professional receives an honest request for his services, he answers the call. His personal politics stay out of it. There are limits of course—Eichmann went too far—but this little job wasn't going to affect the fish farm issue one way or another. I would come out of it a man with inside knowledge, a guy of substance—unlike the pencil-necks at SOSS. I would have the wisdom of Tiresias, the old seer with the dugs of a woman and the dork of a man, who lived both sides.

The truck started for me and I made it up the twisty road to the fish plant only half an hour late.

"Hey—you came!" the foreman laughed. He was burly and bearded like an old antarctic whaler and obviously only half expected me to show. "I'll back you in under the crane as soon as Fred gets unloaded." He met my eyes for the first time and his voice relaxed into a friendlier, fellow worker tone. "I . . . I guess loose fish will be okay in that truck, eh . . . ?" It warmed my heart. I didn't expect to see him let his doubts show, not at this stage anyway, but seeing me standing there in front of him, nervous and weak from sweating, I guess it was too much for him. But I was on my way now, I didn't want sympathy.

"Oh yeah, I think so. I got a roll of poly and some boards to seal it up. Long as you don't fill me too full most of it should stick." I don't think my breezy manner convinced him, but it gave him all the excuse he needed to go ahead. He broke into his tough grin again, and clapped me on the shoulder.

"That's the stuff! I knew you could handle it. Back that big bastard in there!"

I wasn't all that smooth with the truck because I had only driven it around the Bluff to blow the airhorn at the schoolkids. I'd never driven it loaded, and I'd never driven any diesel truck with a thirteen-speed transmission before. But I slid it back under the crane without grinding any gears or knocking over any sheds, and got out while they went about filling the cornbinder's twelve-cubic-yard gravel box with rotten fish. I sweatily went over the checklist in my mind. I'd laid the board across the back. I'd cut it two inches too short, but I'd jammed a square rock in the gap. I'd cinched up the chains as tight as I could. Must remember to unhook them before I dump. The poly was laid out and hanging over the sides, with dirt scattered around to hold it in place while they loaded me. I went upstairs for a coffee and leaned over the rail looking down on the operation, trying to look nonchalant. I was smart enough to know that if I hung around where the fish was, I'd end up with my hands in it. My goal was to get home without a single fish scale on me, or on the truck.

They had a bunch of broad-shouldered kids sluffing around and the whaler fingered one up into the gravel box to handle the tote-dumping while he worked the crane. The totes were wooden boxes about a cubic yard big, and they lifted them with a sling around each side. They lowered them into the gravel box, then the kid would take the one sling off and they'd lift one side, spilling the tote over. At the first spill the kid doubled over and lost his breakfast. He crawled over the side, white in the face and refusing further service. The whaler looked around and picked another, bigger kid, a good-natured hulk I knew slightly who was on his first day. He slowly made his way up and got the spilled tote away, moving to a far corner of the box and fanning his nose between lifts. Then I saw why he'd been so slow to get in: he hadn't had time to buy gumboots and he was trying to get by the first day with flimsy plastic overshoes. It wasn't long before a look of horror came on his face and I looked down to see foamy pink fish juice pouring over the top of one overshoe.

He returned a sickly smile, then stepped right out of the shoe, plunging his white sock right into a pool of orange fish muck. He made a pathetic noise, and I put my fist to my forehead for him. I couldn't stand any more, so I went downstairs into the actual fish plant. It was just a big shed on the water's edge with totes piled up against one wall, a walk-in freezer, and across one whole end a long wetbench surrounded by about twenty-five slickered locals all hacking up fish with funny-looking blunt knives. I was surprised to see a lot of people who I knew to be strong critics of fish farms working there, including Cam Fisher, one of the table officers of SOSS.

"I didn't know you worked here," I said, amazed.

"I didn't know you did either," she replied, haughty.

"I guess there's nothing wrong with taking money off them," I said.

"I don't eat their fish, if that's what you mean. You wouldn't catch me dead eating this garbage," she said loudly, her voice ringing around the tin building as she splatted down a ratty looking jack spring and zipped it open without looking. "None of us do."

There were murmurs of shy agreement along the line. Being mostly oldtimers, they felt salmon should be left the way God made them, and not squeezed into pens and force-fed like pâté de foie gras. When I saw Cam roaring at a forklift putting some boxes down in the wrong place, I realized she was actually inside foreman of the joint.

The truck was loaded with eight totes. I climbed up on top of the cab and looked at the damage. The whole gravel box was about half filled with dead fish, all lying this way and that. They didn't look that bad. It stunk a bit, but it was the old smell of the coast. The load looked pretty stable. I folded the edges of the poly over the mess like a Christmas present and chucked some broken pallets on top to hold it down. There was a stream of pinkish juice the diameter of a pencil-lead draining out one corner of the box, but it looked like it was diminishing. There was nothing to do but put the truck in low gear and crawl up the steep driveway. I roared out of the yard and out of their lives into my own, carefully avoiding any jolts that might send dead fish sloshing over the tailgate. I took comfort in the fact this grade was probably the steepest I would have to handle on the trip, and the load made it up with no trouble. I pulled over every ten miles or so to see if anything was amiss, but nothing was. It might have been a load of clean drainrock I had in there. Even the little pencil-leak had disappeared.

It was going so well I decided to take it to the big dump in Sechelt, where it would be less noticeable than at the little Pender Harbour dump and also give me more truck time. It was a bit nervy driving that mess down the busy streets of Sechelt, right under the noses of fish-farming's most dedicated opponents, but I slid through without a turned head, and up the hill to the dump. They had a special sump pit set aside for such unpleasantries, and I had gone to the trouble of clearing the load with the authorities, something nobody else bothered to do. I did this the night before, just in case I needed it. That's how good I was.

I even remembered to undo the chains holding the tailgate shut before I hoisted the dump up. I even fished the broken pallets out of the stew so they wouldn't go into the sump. Not that there would be any harm if they did, I was just wanted to avoid even the chance of trouble. I wanted to be better than good. The exertion of lifting the pallets had me seeing red in a minute — reminding me for the first time I wasn't quite well — and I did get more than a few fish scales on me at last. But nothing serious. There was a man in a trenchcoat across the pit surreptitiously taking pictures of me, probably for the SOSS. I waved at him.

I made it home before 2 PM, hosed down the truck, and went back to my thinking, feeling like a powerful instrument. Some sticky negotiations that had been holding up the fifty grand suddenly opened up for me, and I got on the phone to Ontario to close the deal before the people went out for the weekend, then phoned up the printer, got the price I was looking for from him, and set the deal in motion. I had been putting these closing moves off for weeks, but I'd come home from truckdriving feeling the power.

The next day they called again. I was no less busy and felt no less ill, but agreed to go without hesitation. I made it on time this time. And went straight into the coffee room to wait for them to load. When I came out and looked down, I noticed two things. The truck was a lot fuller than the day before. And the stuff was a lot juicier. I only had about six inches of freeboard between the muck and the top edge of the gravel box. They had not only thrown in eight totes of very dead salmon from the farms, they had added six totes of offal — fish guts — from the processing plant. Old fish guts, which had been sitting around a week or more in warm weather. I didn't like it. They hadn't asked me. But what could I do now? Tell them to spoon it out? I should have stayed outside to watch, and stopped them half full like the first time. I wrapped the plastic around, weighed it down like before, got in low gear, and ground my way up the hill. I stopped at the top to look it over. Nothing had sloshed over the tailgate, although there were twin streams of pink fish juice the thickness of a cigarette squirting out each corner of the tailgate. I couldn't tell if they were diminishing or not, but I could tell they were really rank. This batch was much riper than the first one.

The old coast had never smelled liked this.

I worked my way over the twisty Egmont Road out to the highway, and stopped for a look. The streams of fish juice were still squirting onto the road. The load itself seemed to have leveled off and kind of jelled. But it was all still there. I got under way, keeping a sharp eye behind me in the big side mirrors. A few miles down the highway, I began to notice little splashes of liquid flying out whenever I went around a corner. Then I began to notice it all the time, streamers of spray peeling off behind me as I motored along. A few cars passed the opposite way and I wondered what they saw. If someone came up behind me, they would probably get quite a surprise. I pulled over at the next wide spot.

The upper edges of the gravel box were glistening. The load looked wetter than it had when I started. The jostling of the road seemed to be breaking the stuff down. And somehow the poly had got pulled down into the soup so it was no longer sealing the big crack between the upper edge of the metal and the plank which made up the top eight inches of the gravel box, and every time the stuff surged a little going around a corner, it would splash out through the crack. Very gingerly I pulled myself up alongside the

load and began trying to pull the poly back up where it belonged
without getting any fish on me. I saw both of my knees turn dark
as they touched the wetness. I inserted a couple fingers very
delicately into the reeking muck searching for the edge of the poly
but when I found it I couldn't get a grip. It was very slippery. I had
to thrust both hands in to the wrist and rip hand-holds in the
plastic. By the time I had it pulled up on both sides, my shirt front
and my thighs were saturated with the oil and the stench of rotten
fish. I spent a good many minutes scuffling in the dry grass on the
side of the road trying to clean my shoes, but to little effect. When
I climbed back into the cab, the smell was so strong I had to roll
both windows down. It was so strong I soon lost the ability to smell
anything, only a rawness in my nostrils and a fever on my brain.

Not ten miles further on, I looked in the mirrors and saw
ribbons of spillage once again trailing off behind me on both sides.
My heart sank. I had to go back and put my hands in that rotten
muck again. I looked for another wide shoulder and pulled over.
The whole outside of the truck was now glistening with fish oil.
The streams at the corners of the box had increased to the
thickness of a cigar and had created sizable pools on the ground
just in the first few minutes the truck was stopped.

I was starting to feel I would be lucky to get out of it this time
around. I wished for the first time but not the last that I had turned
off at the road to the Pender Harbour dump several miles back
instead of making for Sechelt as before. I jumped up and plunged
my arms into the gooey mess, no longer having anything to keep
clean, and pulled the plastic cover up. When my eyes came to rest
on the load of fish, I couldn't believe my eyes. When I had first
started out, the load had looked mostly like fish. But as I drove
and the rotting carcasses fell apart under the jostling of the road
and mixed with the gooey offal, it came more to look like fish
purée.

Now it looked like nothing I'd ever seen. I had to shake my head
and blink my eyes. It was like a field of dandelions gone to seed.
The entire fuming mass was bristling with little translucent globes.
Hundreds of little pointy sacs waving in the breeze. It took me a
minute to figure it out. These things were swim bladders. Each
fish has this little bag it can fill with water to regulate its depth,
and they're made out of some tough cellophany stuff that doesn't
rot. As the rest of the fish parts broke down and went to mush,

these little guys had become inflated with gas and floated to the top. It was a most hallucinatory sight, as if the load had suddenly burst into bloom. It disconcerted me. It heightened a sense of unreality that had already gone far enough.

I decided to get back on the road before the puddle of liquid fish under the truck got any bigger. As I drove I began to consider the implications of going through Sechelt with this steaming, dripping mess. Just waiting at the stoplight on Dolphin Street would result in a couple of gallons of rotten fish puree in the middle of the town's busiest intersection. The people in Pronto's restaurant would suddenly lose their appetite. The people in the office of the Happy Shopper, the pro-fishfarm newspaper, would suddenly get a new perspective on the artificial fish issue. People would swarm round. It would be the event of the week.

The streamers of slime were out again. It was happening faster each time as the load became less and less stable. Going around one corner I glanced in the mirror and saw a little slosh of pink go over. If it kept getting looser, I might not be able to drive it at all pretty soon. I slowed down to 20 mph, 10 on corners. I might just make it to Sechelt in time to have it all go over the side — or suppose a pedestrian stepped in front of me and I had to make a hard stop. Tons of reeking pink glop would surge forward and go cascading up over the front of the truck, flattening the jaywalker and plugging every storm sewer for three blocks. The central core would be evacuated for days while cleanup crews worked over-time, all at my expense. Next week, banner headlines: Glop Truck Driver Had Wrong Licence. Court trials. Crippling expense. Disgrace. No one would ever talk to us again.

A car pulled up close behind me, then punched on its brakes and dropped back fifty yards or so.

I decided to turn around and take the load back to the Pender Harbour while I still could. It was no closer by this time, but it would save my having to go through any towns. The problem was to find a place on the narrow, twisting coast highway where I could swing this big bowl of jelly. It had to be level and wide, so I didn't spill the load. . .

Just then I came to the Election Section. The Election Section is a half-mile stretch of bad curves near Secret Cove which the government has been promising to straighten for over ten years. Every election they give the local highways office a few thousand dollars to round up all the local contractors and make a show of doing something, then on the day after the election they're all sent home leaving the stakes to be torn out and the blasting holes to be silted up for another three years. At this point the Vander Zalm government was suffering at the polls so the Election Section was in business again. New clearings had been made on either side of the road and a portable office trailer had been dragged in along with a water truck, and a few government engineers in orange and white pickup trucks. To me it looked like a good place to turn around.

I geared the truck down and slowly reduced my speed to about five mph, then slowly eased the nose of the truck off the pavement into the clearing beside the office trailer. It bumped a little bit harder than I planned, but not very bad. I looked in the mirror and saw a flash of pink.

Lost a little juice, I thought.

I'll get a hemlock branch and go brush off the pavement. I rolled gently to a stop, popped the maxi brake on and opened the door. There were a few fishtails and bits of flesh stuck to the side of the box, which I thought odd.

I walked around the rear end and looked behind.

My heart stopped.

For a hundred feet the highway was covered with fish, fish-heads, fishtails, and bright orange mush. Both lanes were fully involved.

Some of the fish were whoppers.

And the little swim bladders were bobbing everywhere. Thousands of them, dancing, mocking me, in the hot sun. The car that had been following me at a safe distance was now stopped at the edge of the spill, and there was another behind it. I could see the driver shaking his head.

My heart was pounding like a runaway steam locomotive. I didn't know it, but the condition I had was giving me high blood pressure to start with. When I later had it diagnosed, I was solemnly warned to avoid excitement or sudden exertion lest I pop a blood vessel. This kind of stress was no doubt sending my reading off the scale. My ears were ringing. I was seeing red when I turned my head. But somehow I managed to stay upright. I waved the cars through, guiding them along the left hand shoulder, clear of the mess. Then I got the shovel off the truck and started spooning the slop toward the ditch. I worked too fast and exhausted myself in seconds, making no discernible difference to the bubbling mass. Cars kept coming and interrupting me.

Then one of the government engineers showed up. He was a youngish chap wearing an orange plastic hard hat and carrying a clipboard. He had been over on the jobsite somewhere, doing his best to put in hours without any crew or equipment to boss. He kept looking at the road, then at me, then at his clipboard, as if he hoped to get some guidance from it. He didn't know what to say. Nothing like this had ever come up in engineering school. But I could see that he was determined to be uncooperative.

"What are you stopping here for?" he said. "You can't leave that stuff here."

"I just pulled in to turn around and spilled a little. I'm on the way to the dump," I said.

"Well I'm going to have to get some information," he said, rolling up a new page on his clipboard. Just then cars came shooting around the corner from both directions, braking hard as the vista of salmon chowder opened before them. I ran out to flag them through, one at a time. When I finished and picked up my shovel again, the engineer caught up to me with his clipboard.

"I'm going to need some particulars," he said.

"Look," I said, "We're going to have an accident here if we don't get the road clear. Why don't you let me take care of that, then I'll give you all the particulars you want." Another three cars came squealing to a halt and I had to rush over to signal them through. The drivers all looked sour and shook their heads with disapproval at me. I was the focus of all their anti-fish farm feelings. What am I doing here, I wonder, I kept musing. I should be at home quietly clicking my word processor, whispering pleasant assurances to elderly lady poets over the telephone. Will I ever get back there? Will I escape from this mess alive? My blood pressure was setting a new Olympic record.

The engineer had now come up with a new idea, which was to surround the spill with about three dozen fluorescent orange traffic cones. He encircled the spill completely, blocking both lanes off, so that traffic actually had nowhere to go. This created a very dangerous situation, since he made no attempt to guide the traffic, and within minutes I had to run through the muck waving my shovel to prevent a head-on collision between a rusted-out

Volkswagen Beetle and a 36-foot Winnebago-with-everything, both trying to slip by on the far shoulder.

I looked at the engineer. "This is a bit dangerous, don't you think?" I asked.

"I don't want people running through your garbage," he retorted hotly. "I *live* here."

I couldn't quite follow his logic. I guess he was making some oblique reference to the fact fish farmers were outsiders, a lot of them, missing the point I'd lived in the area for 38 years myself. I reckoned if it came to a head-on collision, most people would probably prefer to swerve through the spill and get a little rotten fish on their tires, but I didn't have the breath to argue.

I began looking for something better than the shovel because I wasn't getting anywhere with the cleanup. A snow shovel would have been better, or just a plank I could lay down and push like a bulldozer. Beside the engineer's office-trailer I spotted a heavy wooden rectangle used as a base for portable road signs. I walked over and grabbed it.

"Hey!" the engineer hollered. "We use that. I don't want you getting your, your. . . stuff all over it."

It was like the word fish had suddenly become unmentionable to him.

"I'll clean it up after," I said, walking past him and banging it down on the road. It made a pretty good bulldozer. A little rusty car stopped on the shoulder and a burly kid got out. He walked over to me with a grin on his face.

"You need a hand?" he said.

I couldn't believe my ears.

"Do I ever," I said, "but it ain't very pretty."

"Ha-ha, little bit of rotten fish never killed anybody," he chortled, and grabbed the shovel. Between us we soon had most of the big lumps pushed over into the ditch, leaving only a smeared layer of virulent orange mud over a lane and a half of the road.

"What are we going to do with that?" he asked.

"Dunno," I said. "maybe we could slosh it off with water, if we had water." I remembered the tank-truck parked beside the office trailer and hollered at the engineer.

"What's the chance of getting some water out of that truck?"

"What for?" he said.

"To clean up your road here before this shit gets baked in and you end up breathing it for the rest of the year," I said. That got his attention. He shuffled over to the truck and opened up a hatch alongside the tank.

"What have you got to put it in?" he said dubiously, still clutching his clipboard.

I couldn't believe my eyes. Under the hatch was a high-volume fire pump hooked to a coil of hose.

"Does that pump *run*?" I shouted.

"Of course it runs," he said.

"Well for chrissakes, start it up and hose this road off before somebody gets killed! We could have had this road open half an hour ago with that thing!"

Sulkily, he gave the starter a pull and a two-inch jet of high-pressure water burst from the hose. He kept it himself, not wanting to trust unlettered persons with the operation of a government water hose, and within a few minutes had the road gleaming as blackly as if it was freshly paved. While he was carefully spraying off the sign stand I jumped back in the truck and was out on the road before he noticed. I could see him waving his clipboard in the rearview mirror as I geared into high range.

I figured there had just been time for the first cars that had passed through to reach the police station in Sechelt. Now, if I made straight for the Bluff dump as fast as I could go without spilling any more, I might just make it in half an hour. That would give the cops just time to make it back to the spill—depending how long they spent taking a statement.

I should just be able to make it.

The Indy 500 never seemed so long as that fifteen miles. I had to gear the truck up furiously on every bit of straight-a-way, trying to make time, but brake with enormous care coming into any corners, tender as a waiter with a three-tiered tray full of beer. Another spill of any size would be game over. It didn't help that my hands were shaking with fever and my oily shoes kept wanting to slip off the clutch and brake pedals. I spent as much time looking behind me in the rearview mirrors as I did ahead at the snaking road.

After an eternity I crawled into the dump, drove straight toward the hole up at the far end I'd already picked out in my mind, and put the hoist in gear. The sopping mess slid out the rear into the ground. No constipated sperm whale ever felt greater relief. The evidence was off the truck!

I turned and began rolling down the grade toward the exit.

At that moment a police cruiser came flying into the dump at the head of a huge plume of dust, raring over the potholes like a bucking bronco. It shot past me without making any sort of signal, so I kept on rolling toward the highway and home. The cruiser bounded up to where I'd let off the load, spun around in the gravel, peeled back toward me and put on the siren. I pulled over, popped the maxi and climbed down onto the road.

I was strongly moved to fall down on the ground and pour my sick heart out in the dust, but a tiny voice in the back of my head, barely audible over the pounding of my temples, was whispering, "Don't give it away, don't volunteer anything, act cool, you never know..." The cop walked up looking mean, until he got a whiff of the truck box, which twisted his face up like a prune.

"Wow!" he yelped.

"Bears love it," I laughed. This was a lie, in fact. It was a peculiarity we'd all observed over the past months that the one kind of garbage the dump's considerable scab-ridden army of bears wouldn't go near was fish farm garbage. It was their only taboo.

"Did you just unload a truckload of fish waste in this landfill?" the cop intoned in his cop-like way.

"Can't deny it," I grinned, reeking. "Yes, I did."

"And are you authorized to do that?"

"Yeah, I am," I said. His eyes were watering, and I moved closer to him where the wavy lines coming up off my fishoil-soaked pants would go right up his nose.

"Oh. We were told you weren't..." he said, backing away.

"Well, you just phone the works superintendent at the Regional District and he'll fill you in," I said. I was like ice inside, dreading the next request. If he uttered the words "driver's licence," I would collapse in a heap, my life over. But the wavy lines did their work.

"Okay, well, sorry to bother you," the cop said, and hustled back to the car. I let him go on ahead.

It didn't matter.

It was still the worst day of my life.

'TIRESIAS II

That must be really Interesting, doing the garbage dump
they say. I try to think how.
They tell me I ought to find interesting stuff.
They ask me if I can read the garbage like Christie Logan
Seem to expect me to make prophecies about our civilization
I think over the stuff I see up there.
For a catskinner used to ploughing
the clean and trackless wastes of the north
it is interesting to find Tampax
jammed into the track-adjuster hole
panty-hose wound around the sprockets
bank records impacted into the belly-pan
it is interesting to realize a healthy HD7-G
can stall dead out trying to move a heap
of used Pampers the size of the Community Hall
it is interesting that most people don't seem to care
what the dump guy knows about the bad condition
of their underwear or Mastercard account
while others compulsively set fire
to everything even their dogfood cans
causing the whole dump to flare up
in a pillar of orange and turquoise smoke
that towers over the town like a mushroom cloud
filling the local paper with irate letters

and causing me to get hauled on the carpet to face dumb
dump questions I can't answer
because breathing the virulent fumes
has reduced my voice to a reedy squeak for over a week
it is interesting when the whole five-acre lump
begins to glow like plutonium
and the town's weekly byproduct
of screwtop wine jugs begins to explode
with dull artillery thuds
ripping up through the ground like Titan missiles
and a forty-pounder of Sommet Rouge
smokes past my ear to splash
against the guard behind my unprotected head
giving me brief intimations of mortality—
maybe that's the sort of thing they're looking for.
I have kept my eye open for the dead babies
blackened in the sun finding none
but once there were three bloated sheep, shot in the heads
someone's back-to-the-land project over with a vengeance
and for prophecy it did occur as the Pampers
balled up before me the size of a barn
there could be another population explosion on the way.
This was a year before the sociologists
came out with the same news on TV.

But don't you get some sort of vision of society's underbelly?
You're an archaeologist of the present
can't you describe us by our leavings?
I tell them about the lack of anything old
everything people throw out was new last year
broken-backed sofas the price and size of a compact car
tinselly fabric still gleaming in the sooty firelight
plush carpet smelling of dog more fridges
and automatic washers and electric hot water tanks
than stones in a field   masses of plastic
kindergarten lunchbuckets decorated with last year's TV hit
kitchen gizmos briefly made indispensable by a K-Tel ad
toy bulldozers designed by someone who clearly never saw one
all the inventive genius of America come to rest
in a single heap of anonymous red yellow blue

it is a long, depressing list that adds up, in the end,
to very little
my admirers tend to frown and change the topic
but then us prophets are used to that

THE BOMB THAT MOOED

My father first set foot on Nelson Island some time in 1949, as near as I can figure. To this day I think he may thoroughly regret that move, but none of us kids do. How could we? To him and Mum it was a tough luck show that robbed them of their prime years; to us it is the mold that formed us — to reject it would be to reject a basic part of what we now are.

Charlie Philp was to blame for Greene's Bay. Charlie was a rich guy who lived in Vancouver. He'd been a lowly car salesman at one time but then he got the Mack Truck dealership just as truck logging was sweeping the coast, and made a million. He enjoyed his surplus wealth by funding ambitious young loggers like Dad to go out and set up hard-scratch gyppo shows, then slowly tormenting them into bankruptcy. My dad had just gone through the process with one partner, Eddie Barnes, up in Cardero, before moving to the Fraser Canyon for a season. Now he was coming down and starting over again at Greene's Bay.

The camp itself was already set up when we arrived. It consisted of three small board-and-batten shacks on posts just above tide line and three somewhat more permanent shacks farther up from the beach, located on the west side of the bay beside a waterfall that roared like a rushing freight train all winter and disappeared in the summer.

It was in 1950, on May 24 as I inexplicably recall, that Dad decided to move the rest of the family, consisting of my mother

31

Kay, my eight-year-old sister Marilyn, my five-year-old self, and my three-year-old sister Cindy into camp. We had just moved out of a failed camp at North Bend, after weathering the record-setting winter of 1948 in one of the province's most extreme climates (my father's luck wasn't good, but it was consistent), spent a few months of respite in the comfortable family seat at Abbotsford, then moved with all our effects aboard the fish packer *Moorpack*, owned by the keeper of Pender Harbour's general store, Royal Murdoch.

The house we kids slept in at Greene's Bay was practically at the foot of that waterfall and that eternal roaring still goes on somewhere in the back of my mind; whenever I hear the rush of falling water now it does strange things to me. That house wasn't a part of the camp; it was finished on the outside with real siding and lined inside with birch veneer like a real house in the city, built as a wilderness home by a family named Yates who still owned the twenty-acre preemption on which the camp was situated. All we kids knew of these mysterious Yateses was that they were Christian Scientists; the closets and attic of their abandoned house were packed with innumerable issues, not of the *Christian Science Monitor,* but of a lesser, true-believer publication on octavo-size pages with a vine border framing the covers. Thousands of them.

I suppose Dad chose the Yates house for us because it appeared at first glance to be the most comfortable; it had two private bedrooms, a large living room, kitchen cabinets with doors, an old wood range and hot water, and an inside bathroom with a chemical toilet, all finished in birch plywood; in contrast to the other bunkhouses, which were just bunkhouses, with the usual beaverboard and spiked-to-the-wall orange-crate appointments. But the Yates house was totally accursed. I still dream about it regularly; it provides my subconscious with a purgatory symbol that can't be improved upon. It was always dark, dank and cold. It was built in a kind of muddy hole in one of the few locations with no view of the bay and was so overhung with droopy cedars the sun never shone. It was always wet; glossy magazines left in that house for more than a few days would turn to mush and clothes gathered mildew hanging in the closet. Dampness was endemic. A cool steam wafted over from the waterfall, filtering through trees burdened down with Spanish moss. Periodically the wetness would gather its energies and erupt into the open; during spring and fall rainstorms, an impromptu river might force the back door and flood the whole house to a depth of six inches. I recall being delighted the first time I awoke to find my gumboots bobbing against the wall, then later when the waters subsided discovering the plywood floor blistered into a series of springy hills that made for good jumping until Dad caught us. I remember him looking underneath the house and roaring, "They actually dug the goddamn thing down into a hole! How could anybody be so goddamn stupid as to build a goddamn house in a goddamn mudhole! They must have blasted to get it so bloody low!"

Logging camp kids. Marilyn helps me hold up my first major catch — a dogfish — while Cindy steals the show with a perch.

Everything had been done wrong in that house. Doors opened the wrong way, the steps were pitched to make you trip every time, the water pipes couldn't be made to stop leaking in the summer or freezing in the winter, so they were simply never hooked up. As a result the bathroom was inoperative, the kitchen sink was only good for trapping spiders and the stove couldn't be lit because that would burn out the unused water coil. And yet here were all these good intentions; dish cabinets with glass doors, leaded windows, pretentious archways, laboriously built dry-stone terraces, all useless. It was like an arrested dream. We very much envied the wife of the camp foreman, who occupied the boxy shack on the hill which had none of these pretensions but was warm, dry, functional and commanded a clear view of the bay. The only good thing about the Yates house was that we kids had it all to ourselves, after Mum and Dad moved down the trail to less gracious but more livable quarters in the back of the cookhouse.

At first a teenage girl from Egmont was hired to watch that we didn't stay up all night and make us work at least a few hours a day at our correspondence lessons, but that lasted only until I chanced to observe to my dad one day that the men in the big bunkhouse must be short of blankets or something because one of them was coming over in the dark of night and sharing our babysitter's.

We kids often climbed in with each other when it was cold, so the man's behaviour didn't seem all that unaccountable to me, except for the fact that they were so noisy, and I was surprised by the reaction my casual report of it drew from my parents. They were thoroughly scandalized, but the situation must have been a tricky one. Dad had hired a crew of local boys from Pender Harbour and had already begun to discover some of the reasons more experienced heads had warned him not to do this. One young fisherman had persisted in showing up for work on the rigging crew wearing gumboots, and when the foreman fired him, the entire crew dropped their work without a word and walked down to camp.

When Dad realized what had happened he got one of the men aside and asked why he'd walked out. "Harry's my cousin," the young man said. "If you fire him I gotta leave too. Our family wouldn't like it if I stayed." One by one, the others gave the same reason. To Dad's surprise, it turned out they were all related. Harry got his job back.

They didn't know just how our babysitter and/or her paramour fitted into the local maze of family relations, but there seemed no delicate way of finding out, so Dad came up with a strategy involving me. In the peculiar quavery hush I would come to know better as his talking-about-sex voice, he directed me the next time I heard the lovers carrying on, to barge in and put on a display of childish outrage. This, he calculated, would make the culprits feel so ashamed of themselves they would break it off, or at least become acceptably discreet. The actual words I was coached to say were, "What the hell do you think this is, a whorehouse?" This astonished me because we kids weren't permitted to say even "damn" or "bugger," and I couldn't believe my father was actually coaching me to violate his cardinal rule against bad words. It put me in a quandary I struggled with all day. I was still awake fretting that night when the familiar noises began in the next room, but with my heart in my mouth, I leapt into duty. I stomped down the hall making as much noise as possible, as I had been coached, burst open the door and began my piece:

"What the. . ." At the critical point my nerve failed. "What the *heck* do you think this is, a hoorhouse?" I squealed at the shocked silence. "Hell" was the only part that stopped me. I had no idea what a whorehouse was, so that part didn't trouble me at all.

Dad's ploy worked like a dream. The noises were never heard again; in fact the girl left of her own accord very shortly after for reasons she kept strictly to herself. The only result for me was that all the men in camp suddenly began treating me with new respect.

After the babysitter experience, we kids were left to our own rules, and it is instructive to recall how this worked out. Naturally for the first few weeks we stayed up all night and slept in each morning until Mum had the men away, the dishes washed, the lunches made, and trundled over to shake us out. Likewise, the amount of correspondence lessons completed was negligible, and of course the house was a impenetrable tangle of dirty clothes, cut-up Eaton's catalogues, stepped-on plasticine, peanut butter sandwich remains and dirty milk glasses with clots of "Klim" milk powder doing colourful things in the bottom. But within a reasonably short time we discovered on our own we could not go on this way, and our little system righted itself. We simply learned about ten years earlier than most kids about the basic necessities of looking after yourself on your own, and became a very responsible, self-sufficient, easy-to-look-after little group. My older sister Marilyn even got around to doing her correspondence, and kept her courses up so diligently that when we moved to Pender Harbour some six years later she was able to walk right into junior high school and start knocking over top marks immediately. I didn't fare quite as well. After four years I was still fumbling around in the early stages of grade one, although I had become the camp's regular dump winch operator. My mother finally became so disgusted she completed my grade one course herself in two afternoons, doing the printing exercises with her left hand.

I essentially omitted my first four years of schooling, but I can't say as I have ever missed them. All three of us ultimately graduated from high school and went to university, a relatively rare occurrence in Pender Harbour then, and my younger sister Cindy had the distinction of being invited to attend Simon Fraser University straight out of grade eleven, one of only a few so honoured in the entire province.

When we first moved to Greene's Bay, the camp was called Arbutus Logging and was run by Cam Prior, Harold Pearson, and Graham Whalley. But my father, through a combination of genuine capability and inexhaustible gullibility soon assumed managership, then ownership, changing the name to Jervis Logging (Bob Hallgren, when he was general manager of the giant Rayonier Timber Company, told me Dad was the most versatile all-round logger he ever knew). True to his trusting nature, he took along one of the less qualified employees of the camp, Charlie Trebett, as partner. Charlie claimed to own the camp's yarder as well as knowing everything about running your own show. In the end he was a total disappointment. Not only did he know nothing, the yarder turned out to be on loan from a man named Samson, and then to top things off, he married my mother's younger sister Jean, who came up on a summer visit. The partnership ended in a real honest-to-goodness fistfight down by the light plant, wherein my dad, an old street brawler, landed a haymaker that sent Charlie head over heels right through the salal brush and onto the beach below. The barnacles left him looking like he'd tangled with a bobcat.

Ever since that time, Dad has been down on partners as a general thing. "Don't go into partners," he warns us younger entrepreneurs. "You just do it because you think you can get somebody else to be all the things you aren't but it never works."

We kids loved Greene's Bay, or as we invariably call it, Greenzbay. There was nothing for us there—no schools, no playmates, no television, no radio, not even regular mail or newspapers, but for us it was paradise. We lived basically on our own in the Yates house, our parents were so preoccupied with business. Our entertainments, in spite of the lack of modern amenities, seemed endless. At night we would stay up as long as the light plant stayed on, enjoying movies which consisted of new car ads for '52 Plymouths and Chryslers from the *Saturday Evening Post*, pro-

Greene's Bay in the snow. In the centre is the camp cookhouse and the camp boat Suez *is at the float. The Yates house is off to the right.*

jected on the wall with Marilyn's opaque projector. After lights out she would read to us by flashlight from risqué bestsellers such as Edna Ferber's *Giant* and John Steinbeck's *Cannery Row,* which served us in place of *Mother Goose.*

By day we lived in a world of pretend that with time developed a Byzantine elaborateness. Each of us had one main pretend persona. Marilyn's was Marilyn of the Stores, so named because we originally began by setting up pretend stores stocked with beachcombed bottles and cans. I was a straight-laced masculine hero named Sevward Billington, and tag-along Cindy was a ne'er-do-well named Mrs. Bad Keeky. During much of our waking hours we lived in these made-up roles, snapping out only when confronted by grownups, and frequently branching off into innumerable lesser roles that altogether comprised a pretend world of such highly developed interrelatedness the adults in camp were continually astonished by the glimpses they caught of it.

In the course of our play we transformed the geography of Greenzbay into a fantasyland. Our parents were of the enlightened generation who followed the indulgent dicta of Dr. Spock and went him one better, allowing us the free run of the place as long as we kept our bulging kapok lifejackets—which we seemed to spend most of our waking hours in—firmly buckled in place. We were provided with a rowboat my father had built for us, using plans from *Popular Mechanics*, his hands-down favorite reading material. The skiff was a blue-painted, high-sided, V-bottomed, blunt-nosed thing called a "pram," hand-made out of half-inch plywood, and we wore out one set of oarlock holders after another exploring the local seascape. Across the bay from camp was a sheer bluff which contained a cave with eerie signs of previous occupancy. Part way down the bay toward the north end was an equally evocative abandoned campsite and boat-beaching grid where I found a five-inch barnacle that grownups told me could only have come from the west coast of Vancouver Island. Legend was that this site had been previously occupied by an old hermit who beached his sailboat there. Later another wanderer found it: the legendary Allen Farrell, who built his famous ketch *Native Girl* there some years after we left.

The north end of the bay ended in a mudflat surrounded by green slopes which had been terraced into gardens by some previous wave of settlement. Shortly after we came, two families of early-day hippies named Gregerson and Fraser beached a floathouse on these flats, enlivened by some completely unworkable vision of living off the land. Within six months they were gone, Dave Gregerson to become Pender Harbour's resident dipsomaniac electrician, Fraser I know not where, though I've often wondered.

Coming out of the bay from the north end, on the west side opposite the hermit's boat ways, was the foundation of a log cabin, mysteriously abandoned half-finished, said to be the work of the mythical Yates family. Rounding a bend that led into the waterfall bay where our camp's log dump was, was a low mossy knob which owned a special place in our hearts because it was where the otter herd in its annual migratory visit set up a slide like a group of touring acrobats and enthralled us for an unforgettable afternoon. Directly in front of this mossy dome was "The Reef." The reef served two essential functions. One, it anchored the standing boom to which our camp's booming ground was tied. Two, it provided the camp with its chief summer entertainment—watching yachts smash into it, then blither about like chickens with their heads cut off. It's a particularly treacherous rock in that it is surrounded entirely by steep-to shores, and is therefore unsuspected. In our day its insidiousness was increased by a six-foot boulder perched at its centre, but in recent years some civic-minded towboater booms to have rolled this into the deeps. The reef was a favorite visiting spot at low tide, serving as a mock Treasure Island as well as a bounteous source of every subtidal life form from foot-long foot-shaped oysters and eating crab on down to clams, blennies, anemones and fat juicy sea worms that made you feel sick just to look at them.

Going farther out the bay past the camp, on your right you had, first of all, Chair Bay. I forget why it was called that. Either we found a driftwood chair there or it looked to one of us at one time like a chair in its overall shape. The main feature it had, besides an enormous house-sized boulder with a stagnant green rain pool on top, was a flat shingly beach, the only decent one in the bay, which made it good for two things: wading at high tide when the rocks warmed the water, and collecting driftwood. Chair Bay supplied us with most of the rusty tins, glass bottles and rimracked condoms that stocked the shelves of our make-believe general stores. The most prized items were the most exotic, such as aerosol cans of whipping cream with elaborate plastic trigger-tops, which would fetch at least fifty prime salal-leaf dollars, or items with unmarred labels, or anything plastic, which in the fifties was still a rare and magical substance. Opposite Chair Bay was Cover Point, a low, smooth nose of granite that faded out into the sea in a very gradual slope so that the water always seemed to be very gently lapping it. Cover Point was also a nice place to swim, its wave-worn stone was so warm and smooth to the foot, but it was even more notable for its tidal pools populated with large hermit crabs. Hermit crabs, after otters, are perhaps west coast nature's most comical creatures, and we spent days howling at the antics of those unfortunates we captured and took home in jars. They proved ideal pets, surviving no end of clumsy attention and carrying on their bizarre underwater antics unbothered.

Cover Point was really the last named geographical area we regularly frequented. The little bay in its crook was called Maple Bay, for the huge overhanging maple which papered the water with bright leaves each fall, shore to shore, and the little angular bay adjacent, Mud Bay, because of the unpleasant muddy bottom which was pocked little volcano-shaped mounds of sand we always thought must signify a robust population of clams, though all we ever found were icky sea worms, dig furiously as we might. At the very mouth of Greene's Bay on the left was Eagle Point, a forbidding place so named because of the gnarled snag there which, we felt sure, must be just the place for an eagle to roost, though I can't remember seeing one. On the right was the Crag, an old dead snag that had the profile of a pterodactyl and stood ominous guard over the Greene's Bay entrance until very recent times, when it finally crashed to the beach.

I knew only that the owner of this plane was some important man who gave me a candy bar. Years later I found out it was airline president Jim Spilsbury and repaid him by writing his life story.

Unlike settlers up on the Blind Bay side of the island, down at Greene's Bay we felt virtually without neighbours. Technically speaking we had some, the Henrys. The Henrys were an old-world Finnish couple and I think the term my father used for them was "hard-bitten." They had the old cannery site in the little hole-in-the-wall just to the right as you came out of the bay. They called this little lagoon, which becomes landlocked at about half-tide, Hidden Basin, in memory of their first homesite up at Hidden Bay, which they had left some years earlier following persecution by the unreasonable people who lived up there—as they explained it.

In any case, the Henrys managed to find a rather favoured location for their second Nelson Island home. Unlike the big bay we occupied, it got sun, it had a bit of flat land where they could run their solitary brush-fed cow, and there were still a number of cannery cabins scattered along the beach bluffs which the Henrys promptly organized into a sort of low-budget summer resort, mainly for Finn millworkers from Fraser Mills. It was actually this piece of land which had been owned by the Greenes for whom the main bay was named. I never did learn much of this pioneer except that he took out a large tract some time before the first World War and he must have leased it to the cannery, because after the market for canned protein collapsed at the war's end, Greene regained possession of the cannery site as well as the large two-storey, twelve-foot by thirty-foot cannery building itself, which he turned into a shingle mill in partnership with a Vancouver millwright named George McConnell, Ian McKechnie and another man named Sensen. This venture soon failed for lack of raw cedar to saw and ended in litigation between the partners — as, my father would be quick to point out, most partnerships do. Eventually the main cannery building burned, and when we were there the only sign of it was a scattering of barnacled, sea-worn bricks on the beach. Of the cannery operation itself I have never been able to find any written record. Jim Warnock of Pender Harbour tells me it was owned by a man named Windsor, who called it the Windsor Cannery and originally set it up in Bargain Harbour before moving to Nelson Island to be nearer the big humpback run up Jervis Inlet. McKechnie says that when he went to work as a millhand there in 1923 there was still stationery headed Cliff-Lomond Packing Co. drifting about the premises. His theory is that there never was enough high-grade fish to support a cannery in the area and that the cannery was only set up to cash in on the wartime market, when you could can "anything that swam."

What this sketchy early history does indicate is a pattern of failure and abandonment—a pattern that persisted through our experience, and ultimately through the Henrys', although in our time they seemed to have secured a pretty sound foothold. As Finns tend to be, the Henrys were inexhaustibly hard-working, especially Mrs. Henry. Boats leaving camp at daybreak would always discover her out before them, jigging for cod off the bay mouth in one of the curiously designed sampan-like boats they used. During the spring she toiled until dusk in the large garden they had built up on a rock knoll near their house, laboriously packing soil in pails and fertilizing it with starfish, dogfish and seaweed until it blossomed into a heartbreaking jungle of fruits, berries and vegetables — heartbreaking because, gawk and drool as we might, we can-fed urchins never got to sample a bit of it. Every scrap of food Mrs. Henry could lay her hands on went into jars to feed her summer guests. Again following the typical Finnish stereotype, everything about the Henrys' place was sparkling clean, orderly and well kept. The house itself was quite striking, with large windows, crisp white-painted shingle siding, a bright green tiled roof in the shape of a curved arch and odd projections at each of the four corners where the eaves continued clear down to the ground, the way we always assumed all the houses in Finland must be, though now I suspect it was just another of Captain Henry's quirks. In the midst of all that enclosing coniferous jungle, they maintained a neat lawn with trimmed shrubbery and charming flower plots that gave the place the aspect of a toy village in the Alps, or in Finland I suppose. It was a kind of magic realm all of its own to us kids, just because its civilized charm was such a contrast to the bunkhouse and bulldozer universe we occupied, but on the few occasions we were admitted to the house, with its fragile furnishing, porcelain trinkets and unearthly cleanness, we felt suffocated.

The locals warned Dad that the two old Finns were "mesatchie" — a reputation resulting no doubt from their dispute in Hidden Bay — so, true to his perverse nature, he set out to win them over. This proved less than simple. Some of those old first generation Finns had a very hard face which they turned to the non-Finnish world, a peculiar expression which seemed so blanched of feeling as to be completely intimidating, and this was the face we would be met with on any attempt to stop the Henrys for a chat on the Irvine's Landing dock, or to drop in on them for a casual visit. One's business would be crisply asked, and there being none of note, no quarter would be given. The seven-mile trip to Pender Harbour and back was a day's undertaking in those slow-moving days, particularly with the Henry's snail-like little sampans, but all overtures toward collaborating on shopping runs were dismissed without consideration. The initial attempt to deliver their accumulated winter mail was received with something akin to shock, and resulted in the postmaster being rudely dressed down and ordered not to allow it again.

They were also extremely jealous of the boundaries of their large tract of mostly useless bush and would be seen lurking behind the trees whenever logging operations came anywhere remotely near the vicinity. If we kids ventured out that way in our rowboat we would be shooed home, and once when some of the men fired a shotgun at some mallards they were stalking down the beach from the Henrys, the old lady popped out of a crevice in the rock and gave them such a ferocious tongue-lashing they retreated without attempting to retrieve the good-sized drake they'd hit. They had been unable to determine whether Mrs. Henry was upset by the noise, didn't approve of killing, or just wanted to chase them off so she could put the duck in her jars.

There were two cracks in the Henrys' heavily armoured independence, however: their cow, and the internal combustion engine. Old Otto was a deep sea master mariner but his experience was all in sail and he had never really gotten the hang of gas engines. Since in the summer they depended on their boat to meet guests coming up on the Gulf Line steamers to Pender Harbour, this was a serious problem, and finally one morning Mrs. Henry appeared at our wharf in a dreadful state, pleading for help. She had the better English of the two and was normally quite comprehensible, but when she got worked up, you had to filter out a lot of Finn to get what she was saying. This Dad couldn't quite manage, but it was clear enough the problem was over at their place, so he towed the old girl home with our camp boat, a coffin-like ex-rumrunner entitled the *Suez,* and found the old captain almost dead of exhaustion from heaving on this one-cylinder Easthope in the sampan. He was just purple and gasping and his hands were raw to the point of being bloody. A quick check showed the gas line to be running rusty water, and after draining the tank and cleaning the carburetor, the engine ran like it was intended to. The old boy was effusive in his thanks, and Mrs. Henry insisted Dad accept a King George dollar bill, neatly folded in thirds. She was so upset when he declined that he offered to take "something for the wife" from their garden, and came home with four carrots and a bit of lettuce.

The trouble with the Henrys' cow was it was Canadian. They wanted a Finnish cow as frugal and orderly as they were, but this cow was haywire. For one thing it gave too much milk, and always at the wrong time, so she always had lots when there were no guests to feed and none when there were lots. This led to her next actual attempt to acknowledge our neighbourly existence, which took the form of her approaching my mother with an offer to provide the camp with fresh milk. Mum of course happily agreed, even when it turned out the old lady wanted the same price per ounce as canned milk at Murdoch's store. Mum took it and even kept taking it after we discovered it was so queer-tasting, a result of her cow's peculiar diet of seaweed and salal brush — that no one would drink it, so anxious was she to establish something approaching a normal human relationship with her only neighbour.

The other thing about Mrs. Henry's cow that helped bring us together was its propensity for wandering. There was no real road connecting our two places, they wouldn't let Dad make one, and Mrs. Henry desperately tried to keep it fenced and roped in, but that cow was over at our place every time you turned around. I don't know why. It just hung around. I think maybe it longed to hear its own language spoken. We kids naturally liked it and made a big fuss over it and snuck it pocketfuls of rolled oats, but Mom and Dad made a neighbourly effort to send it home. Dad was afraid a logging truck would run over it and he'd have to pay Mrs. Henry its worth in T-bone steaks at Murdoch's Store. The trouble was, it was very hard to get home. It would get bogged down in swamps, jam its head between close-spaced saplings and get stuck trying to climb over fallen logs, bawling and thrashing as spike knots dug into its udder. We could never figure out how it got around on its own or why it was never killed by a cougar, or one of the area's numerous pit-lampers.

Its greatest caper was the time it ate the dynamite. Dad was a bit sensitive about the dynamite because by law it was supposed to be kept locked up in a special airtight magazine built out of six-inch by six-inch timbers, while he had it stashed in a flimsy open lean-to just up the road from the shop. On top of this, you were supposed to destroy dynamite after a certain date because it becomes unstable and dangerous to handle, but he could never bring himself to just burn dynamite he'd paid good money for. Eventually ours got so old and cranky they were all afraid to go within a hundred feet of the magazine, let alone use the stuff. This was when Mrs. Henry's cow was discovered standing by the road chewing away on a stick of twenty-percent stumping powder as contentedly as Fidel Castro munching a Havana cigar. Closer inspection revealed that the beast had been living for some days at the magazine, stomping boxes open and eating case after case of dynamite, evidently enjoying the piquant taste of saltpeter-and-nitroglycerine-soaked sawdust.

"Holy jumped-up, bald-headed, bare-assed, black-balled Mexican Christ!" my father shouted, twisting his cap around on his head as the implications of the discovery sunk in. "Nobody touch that cow!"

The creek is froze up, Dad's back has a kink in it again, Mum's expecting again and there's no logs in the boom, but it was a great life for kids.

"One hiccup and we're goners," observed Jack Spence, the sardonic foreman. "Can you imagine what a time the cops would have trying to figure it out? Just a crater full of guts, hooves and hardhats."

They were afraid it would go home and blow up in Mrs. Henry's barn, or else the dynamite would get into the milk and poison half the crew of Fraser Mills. Finally they decided to drive it way to hell and gone up the logging road where it would take two weeks to get home, by which time it should have cleaned its system out. But nobody wanted to go close enough to tie a rope around its neck, so they hit on the idea of getting behind it with the logging truck and scaring it up the road with the air horn. With everyone else cowering down behind stumps, Tom Grey eased slowly up in the truck, but at the first blast the unsuspecting animal shot into the brush like a goosed kangaroo and was gone. We all spent the following week with one ear tuned for large blasts, actual or verbal, emanating from the Henry's direction, but the case of the bomb that mooed closed without further incident.

The next thing I remember about that cow was Dad killing it. I think the suspense got to Mrs. Henry, after so many years of sitting home fretting about losing all that potential bottled beef to a marauding cougar, and eventually she prevailed upon Dad, who she had somehow found out was a trained butcher, to do the thing in. Being of the opinion that it was never too soon to start disabusing his male heirs of any innate squeamishness about blood and gore, Dad took me along to "help." I remember there being a parental discussion on the matter, where it was concluded this would be good for me, so the event took on a ritual air. This was augmented by the careful laying out of tools, the erection of the hanging beam, and by Mrs. Henry's hysteria. Even before we arrived her face had the wrung-out, red-eyed look of a person suffering through a death in the close family. However this was equalled by another kind of excitement, at the veritable bonanza of bottled provisions which were about to land in her lap, and she couldn't pull herself away until the fatal moment was upon us, and then only with the odd request we summon her immediately the deed was done. Then she struggled off, wringing her hands, to hide in the house. Dad cocked his head in the direction of her retreat to make sure I learned my lesson.

"What's wrong with Mrs. Henry, Dad?" I said.

"Well, son, she's like most people," he intoned. "They can't bear the sight of blood, but they like to eat meat. That's why there has to be men like you and me around to look after them."

Then he told me to put down a handful of hay under the hanging beam and when the cow walked over to it and lowered its head to munch he quietly suggested I hand him the ballpeen hammer we'd brought along in our bucket. I fetched it and he delivered the cow an easy thud on the back of its head, collapsing it in a heap exactly on the spot he wanted to hang it from for skinning and splitting.

"Gee, is Mrs. Henry's cow dead now, Dad?" I said. It didn't seem like much of a spectacle, for all the buildup there'd been.

"That's all there is to it, son. Farmers, you'll see 'em get the animal rearing all around beating on its nose with a claw hammer, but this is the way a butcher does it."

Coming from the Fraser Valley, Dad always used farmers as the example of people who did everything haywire, although after he'd been up the coast for a few years he began to cite fishermen instead of farmers. I grew up thinking of both the way prairie wasps think of Ukrainians. It wasn't until I was fully grown I heard fishermen refer to gyppo loggers in the same spirit.

I looked at Mrs. Henry's cow lying there whole, unmarred, as unchanged as if it were asleep, except for the odd finality of its stillness, and found death didn't impress me at all. Then Dad reached down and drew our butcher knife across the cow's silken brown throat and my heart stopped as an ocean of blood burst out over the dry fir needles.

"Take a stick and draw a groove in the ground so it'll drain over there and we don't walk in it," Dad said. But I was transfixed. At this point Mrs. Henry came puffing up the trail. "Is it done? Is it done?" she kept calling, not wanting to get too close in case it wasn't. Then she followed my pale stare to the blood.

"Ohhh! I wanted you to call me." She produced an enamel milk pitcher and stared from it to the brilliant puddle now dispersing amongst black fir tree roots and spongy moss.

"I . . . I wanted to keep the blood," she stammered. "We always keep it, in the old country . . ." And then she knelt with the pitcher to her cow's clotted jugular, but the flow had stopped. This was too much for me.

"What's she doing, Daddy?" I shrieked, jumping up and down. "You told me she couldn't stand blood and now she's going to drink it!"

I survived their pained explanation and the full spectacle of slaughter as it unfolded before my now thoroughly impressed eyes. Mine, but not Mrs. Henry's. Her squeamishness forgotten, she fastened herself to my father's elbow, snatching every scrap and drip for her jars. The stupendous eruption of guts did not faze her; she hungrily seized upon the tripe, lights, brains, heart, hustling them off to the kitchen and returning quickly for more.

"What's that?" she would demand in the angry-seeming way

that was more her normal tone, with that singular Finnish blanch
beginning to seize her features, as Dad went to throw another
piece on the compost pile.

"Bung," he said.

"What?"

"Bung."

"What's it good for?"

"Well, Scotchmen use it for haggis. . ."

"Give it here!"

Dad gave it.

"What's that?"

"Bladder."

"What's it good for?"

"Well, when we were kids we used to blow it up and play football
with it. . ."

For his efforts Dad was allowed to take home a roast of his
choice, so he cut out what should have been the choicest sirloin —
she didn't know one cut from another anyway — and amid much
festive feeling and dynamite belch and exploding oven jokes, the
camp crew sat down to eat it that Sunday, but true to form, Mrs.
Henry's cow was completely inedible.

Captain Otto Henry was a good deal older than his wife and
once you learned how to decipher his mangled English, actually
proved the more sociable of the two. Once or twice when Mrs.
Henry was off on one of her occasional trips to Vancouver, Dad
and some of the guys went over with a bottle and even discovered
the old guy to be a bit of a rounder. He could laugh, tell stories,
and his history was fascinating. Finland had built up a merchant
navy early in the century by buying richer countries' mothballed
sailing fleets and crewing them with destitute farm boys who
worked under seventeenth-century conditions. Captain Henry
had begun as a cabin boy on one of these ships, and told horrific
tales of the hardships the Finn sailors suffered from hard work,
bad conditions and harsh discipline.

One of young Otto's tasks was to take care of the raisins — raisins were the one luxury on the ship's menu — and while he had
the raisin locker open to squish weevils and count out portions,
he was under orders, under pain of the lash, to keep continuously
whistling.

Despite the hardship of life in his native land, Captain Henry never ceased to be homesick for it and scornful of his adopted one. His dream was not only to once again see the old sod, or old tundra as it were, but to build himself a fine little ship that would take him back to all the wondrous places he'd seen in his youth and provide him a long retirement of leisurely drifting on the tide. The whole time we were on Nelson Island, Captain Henry worked on this perfect vessel as assiduously as his wife did her jars. It took shape in a shed a few hundred feet down the beach from the house, but so painstakingly was he piecing this last command together, double-planking it with yellow cedar over oak ribs and teak fittings, that the progress from year to year was barely perceptible. It was a very strange-looking ship, for a dream boat, about thirty-six feet and rather tubby, with a long foredeck and a high house amidships with tiny round windows. Of course, it was designed to sail, I'm not sure he even planned to bore the keel.

The end of the story goes without saying. Not too long after we left in 1954, victims of the Social Credit government's policy of closing the woods to small free enterprise and delivering it over to the big monopolies, Captain Henry, who must have been eighty, died with his little ship still on dry land. I went up to look

Wrestling gas drums was one of the constants of gyppo life. Here Charlie Trebett loads empties onto the Moorpak *while Aunt Jean stands ready to grab a ride to town.*

at it and noted that he had gotten as far as painting a name on the bows — *Esto Utopia*. I once thought *Esto Utopia* to be a marvellous piece of arcana evoking a special Finnish Valhalla but my friend Raimo Savolainen tells me it was just the English word *utopia* paired with an acronym made of the Henry's two anglicised names, Esther and Otto. A few years later Mrs. Henry sold it to a fisherman who cut off the outlandish house, bobbed the stout mast, painted out the *Utopia* and converted it into a very prosaic gillnetter called simply the *Esto*. I never saw it tied up to the Whiskey Slough fish barge without stopping to marvel at its romantic history, but its new owner only complained of its screwball design and the rot in its timbers.

By the late fifties, Greene's Bay had thus won its sunless, rockbound solitude back to itself once again, and buried another generation of settlers' dreams. My parents never forgave it and remember the period only with bitterness. As for us kids, it has remained a place of dreams, and my dreams of it are the pleasantest I have. Every time I dream about it, I resolve to go back for a visit, and at least once a year Marilyn and I do. But it gives us a funny feeling. The falls are still there, and Dad's old log dump, but all trace of the camp is gone. Even the one permanent structure, the Yates house, has been so thoroughly consumed by salal and elderberry we can never agree exactly where it was. The great looming bluffs across the bay are gone, replaced by an unimposing low hump, and nothing seems mythic at all. I swear someone has moved the reef a hundred feet closer to the shore where the otters used to romp, and somehow changed the way it looks. There are traces of the intervening decades — the burned-out hulk of a west coast troller, Clarence Cook's old *Morien II*, below the falls, and around in Mud Bay a tug in similar condition, I think the *Viking Prince*. Over in Hidden Bay, Henry's successor, an even bigger Finn dreamer named Ken Viitanen, who spent several years there trying to grow exotic hothouse orchids for worldwide distribution, has vanished without a trace, although his son-in-law Walter Ibey continued to boom salvage logs in the main bay for years. The Henry's house is gone too, having burned in disgrace during the hippy era, which brought the most recent wave of dreamers to Greene's Bay. Thirteen of them went together and bought the old Yates property, but already the little

shacks they dotted through the woods have been left for the
ravens.

THE DAY JOEY CAME

Dinah had a chair pulled backwards up to the cookhouse window and she was kneeling out on her elbows. "The tide's almost up to the floor," she said. Sammy was kneeling on the bench at the end of the table playing with plasticine.

The bay was so full the water was touching the brush all the way around the shore and the bluffs across from the camp you could barely see for rain and mist. Outside, the broken evestrough was plopping rainwater into the chuck and somewhere else a great big drip was hitting one of the washtubs: ting-tang, ting-tang, tong! Raindrops were scooting down the windows like tree roots and the glass was misted over from the roasting pan on the stove opening its lid like an oyster and blowing out big whooshes. It was almost as dark as nighttime.

"Mummy, will you please make some homemade bread today?" I said.

"If I get time, dear," she said.

I was at the other end of the table drawing boats. A great big tugboat making piles of black smoke and a bow wave big as Niagara Falls. All the boats I drew had big bow waves and big stern waves. Daddy always said making big waves was cowboy stuff and good boats like Archie Nichol's could skim the water like a seagull, but I liked big waves.

I drew a picture of the Clarke truck. That was our big logging truck and it was always broke down. It was homemade and for power it had two Chrysler Crowns side by side, so I made one that had two Easthopes in it instead of Chrysler Crowns. That was so it would never break down. We had an Easthope on our boom winch and it never broke down.

"Frankie's drawing logging trucks," Sammy said.

"You better put that plasticine away before Daddy comes home and catches you," Mommy said. Sammy was rolling the plasticine into snakes, rubbing her hand back and forth on the table real fast till the snakes got long pointed tails that whipped around and snapped off. Then she made a jacket of it around a pencil and rolled it till the jacket was big and loose. She had plasticine all stuck to the table and the bench and her hands.

"You're getting the colours mixed up!" I said.

"I am not," she said.

Me and Dinah tried to keep the colours in separate balls but Sammy always got it into one big ball the colour of mud, like when you mixed all the poster paints together. Then the ball would shrink smaller and smaller till we were out of plasticine again, like it had evaporated. I never did figure out where plasticine went to and I never figured out where the fuzzballs came from. The fuzzballs were under Daddy's big easy chair and he'd get mad and make Mummy sweep 'em all up but pretty soon they'd be back like tumbling tumbleweeds scooting around, and Dad'd be mad again. He got even madder at plasticine because it got stuck to the floor. All around the table there'd be flat circles of plasticine squashed onto the floor and he'd yell for Mummy to scrape 'em up with the pancake flipper and tell up the next time he saw plasticine in the cookhouse it was going straight out the window, but Mummy always bought us new stuff and when you used it your hands would get nice and clean and smell all day like plasticine. Me and Dinah would make the new cars out of the Saturday Evening Post and good airplanes with windows and rivets showing even, except the wings always sagged, and Sammy'd whimper that we were taking too much plasticine, but all she could make was snakes.

"Mr. Black is back," Dinah said. We all went over to look out the window.

"Quiet Sammy," I said, "You'll scare 'im."

"I will not," she said, and pushed in front of me.

"Over there, under the gangplank," Dinah said. You could just see a black shadow on the bottom. Mr. Black was a black stranger fish who came every year to our beach and rested on the bottom just below the low tide line. He wouldn't bite any kind of bait and Daddy said he must be an Alaska Black Cod.

"Must be wintertime in Alaska," I said.

"Gangway!" Mummy called out and came between us with a bunch of peelings in a basin. The rockcod all took off, then when the peelings settled down they came twitching back from rock to rock and started gobbling and tearing, stirring up the bottom.

"Here comes Bulldog," Dinah said. Bulldog was a big black and white rockcod that chased the other guys away and we could never get him to bite either. He'd grab a bacon chunk if you dropped it down but not if it was on a hook. He was mean but smart too. The littler cods were so dumb we could catch them anytime, but we never bothered fishing unless there was some big stranger fish around. I caught a big lingcod out the window one time, and one time we looked out and saw something that looked like somebody'd dumped a tub full of deer guts kinda melting along over the garbage and after a while Dinah figured out it was an octopus. Dad and Jack Cummings came with a pike pole and stabbed it but the old octopus just wrapped an arm around and around the pike pole, lifted both of 'em up and scooted away. That's how strong octopusses are.

There was a bunch of clumping on the porch and Sammy grabbed her plasticine and ran into the back room but there was a big lump of it where she was sitting with cloth marks pressed into it and other bits scattered around so I yelled at her and she was back digging at it with a knife when Daddy banged the door open and said, "Lil, will you throw something down on the floor?" The porch didn't have any roof and he didn't want to stand out in the rain to take off his cork boots. Charlie and Tommy Gray and Ivan Purdy were with him, and Charlie said, "I hope the coffee pot's on," but it wasn't. Mom busted open a cardboard box for them to walk over to the table on but Ivan Purdy's corks stuck to it because they were new, so he took two big tip-toe steps out on the linoleum. The corks made a sticky sound and Mummy gave him a cross look.

Charlie rubbed Sammy on the hair and said, "How's Mrs. Bad Keeky today?" Mrs. Bad Keeky and Mrs. Good Keeky were two pretend characters of hers and the men always joked about it because they thought she was cute but she was just little.

"Mrs. Keeky's asleep in her house," Sammy said.

"She better wake up, it's time to put supper on," Ivan Purdy said.

"She's gointa wake up in a minute and put supper on," Sammy said.

"Where is this house of hers, I don't think I've seen it," Tommy Gray said.

"That's because it's over in Chair Bay," Sammy said.

"Chair Bay, where's that?" Charlie asked.

"That's around the first point where that reef comes out," I said.

"How come you call it Chair Bay?" asked Ivan Purdy.

"Dinah named it that," I said. "She named everything."

Dinah kept looking out the window because she didn't like to pretend in front of grownups anymore. Lately she didn't want to pretend much with me and Sammy either. She was starting to have private stuff and be by herself a lot. Mummy said it was because she was a big girl now, but she wasn't that big, and besides I didn't see why we couldn't have just as much fun as always.

"Did the fallers stay out in the woods, Bud?" Mummy said.

"Yeah, we came down with the load," he said. "They'll be here pretty quick."

He saw the plasticine but didn't say anything. He never got mad where there was people around.

"Would you put some coffee on, Lil," he said. He was a little bit mad that it wasn't ready already or he would have said Love.

"I thought you looked more like Good Keeky today," Tommy Gray said, bending down to Sammy who was still digging at the plasticine.

I pushed my drawings over to him. "See my boat drawings?" I said. They started looking them all over real interested which made me start to have a swelled head. Whenever somebody like that started to pay attention to me thousands of tiny tickles would rush up the back of my neck to my head like little bubbles when you bang a glass of 7-Up. It felt better than just about anything.

"By God that's a good one of the old truck," Charlie said. "What's this here on the front?"

"I put Easthope motors on it so it won't break down all the

time," I said. That made them laugh, "There you are Bud, maybe that's your answer." Dad grinned a little and said, "Yeah, we'll never be short of answers as long's we got Frankie around."

"This boy of yours is quite the artist, Mrs. White," Tommy Gray said. He was the only one who kept calling Mum Mrs. White. Dad always said he was a real little gentleman.

"The way you can draw you should be a naval architect and design boats for people. Then you'd make lots of money," he said.

"Frankie doesn't want to make a lot of money. What would he do with a lot of money?" Charlie said.

Charlie always treated me like a little kid. He never let me hold a sharp knife or walk on the boom. Daddy would even have log rolling contests with me and get me to run the dump winch when there was no men around. He'd say I was as good as having another man in camp, and my head'd swell for two days. Even Dinah couldn't do things like that.

"If I made a lot of money," I said, trying to sound as much as I could like Daddy, "I'd pay off all the bills so a guy could get some sleep at night around here." The men laughed longer at that than anything, and Charlie banged the table and said, "By God Bud, you've done a good job on this kid," but I could tell by Daddy's look I'd done it wrong again.

"You kids pick up this mess and go into the back room," he said. "Lil, is that coffee on?"

I hated it in the back room. It was dark and cold and Dinah wasn't there. She got to help Mum in the kitchen. Dad went out and started the light plant because it was so dark and Sammy started whining to go see movies. Dinah had a projector that showed pictures on the wall and whenever the light plant was on we'd get it out and shine pictures of new 1952 Packards with jet holes along the side and Tugboat Annie pictures from the Saturday Evening Post. Sometimes we'd shine a new Fox and Crow comic book and Dinah would read it out like a real movie. But that was way over at the Yates house where us kids slept and it was raining outside. Besides it was no fun doing anything with Sammy. She was too dumb. The only fun I had was with Dinah. She was about the smartest girl in British Columbia and she was my best friend.

"You're as dumb as a bum," I said to Sammy.

"You said a bad word. I'm going to tell Mummy."

"A bum is an old man," I said. She ran for the door but I grabbed her and she started hollering. I let her go but the talking in the kitchen stopped and I heard Mum say to Dinah, "Maybe you better take the kids over to the Yates house till the men have eaten."

The hard raining was ending and the chuck wasn't in grey patches anymore, it was glassy black with just light pinpricks like cork boot prints on the ripples. The tide was changing and there was a crooked line of driftwood right across the bay.

"Let's go over to the Yates house and show movies," I said to Dinah.

"Yeah, let's," Sammy said.

"No, you have to stay here and have your afternoon nap," I said.

"I had it already," she said.

"You never did," I said.

"She can come," Dinah said. Whatever Dinah said we did because we wanted her to play with us. We never did what Mum said.

There was a bright flash like a tugboat searchlight at the window and sunlight came shooting in yellow stripes of turning dust just like when it shone down between the wharf planks fishing perch, lighting up the teredo dust that was sifting down.

"Sunshine!" Sammy squealed.

"Now we can't show movies," I said.

The men were still sitting around the table drinking coffee and arguing. Dad was leaning forward pointing at Charlie saying, "Say you're a Chinaman now Charlie, just for a minute," and Charlie was making a funny face saying, "A Chinaman, eh? I'm no good with chopsticks..." and Ivan was pulling on Daddy's shoulder saying, "No, no, Bud, look here..."

Outside one whole side of the sky was crackling saltchuck blue and the side that was still black you could tell was losing out. The wharf was steaming already and the air was so sharp with the smell of elderflowers it hurt your nose. It was like a different day. It was fresh like morning and the sun hurt our eyes.

"We should row out to Chair Bay and see if anything good drifted in," Dinah said.

"I'm going to come!" Sammy said.

"You don't have your life jacket," I said, but she ran into the cookhouse to get it.

Chair Bay was the best place to look for junk that drifted in because it was the only place in Greene's Bay—except Cover Point—that had a flat beach. The shore everywhere else was either straight bluff or else big boulders and things didn't get hung up easy. Chair Bay also had a huge granite boulder to climb up on with a brown rain pool on top and behind that a tallgrass flat and lots of good places to play. We all ran down the float and piled into the dinghy.

"I'll be Dinah of the Stores and you be Sevward Billington," Dinah said. They were my favorite characters because Seward Billington was sort of Dinah of the Stores' boyfriend. "And say this is a two-hundred foot luxury cruising yacht that I own and you're my guests," she said.

"Well this is a very nice ship you have here, Dinah," I said in my Seward Billington voice. "How did you get ahold of it, because as I recall last time we were speaking, you were broke."

"Who should I be?" Sammy said.

"You be the motor," I said.

"You be my handmaiden, Mamie," Dinah said. It didn't matter because whatever Sammy tried to be she always came out Mrs. Bad Keeky.

"I said how did you get the boat and you haven't answered yet," I said in my real voice.

"I know," Dinah said in her real voice, then put on her Dinah of the Stores voice. "Well, I certainly wasn't broke and I think it's most rude of you to bring it up, but since you did, I will say that I've had some rather good luck with my oilwell explorations and in fact there have been two gushers on some property I hold up near Goose Lake this week."

"I'm very glad to hear that," Seward Billington said. "I'm doing pretty good myself since I just put in about a hundred sections of number one fir from my show up by the shop there and I think I'll get me a fancy ship like this myself when I get back from this here luxury cruise we're on."

"I'm going to get one two times as big as you guyses," Sammy said in her Keeky voice.

"You can't do that!" I said. "Ol' Keeky can't be a millionaire!"

"She can too, if you guys can," Sammy said.

"How'd she get it then? You've got to have a proper way."

"She went around her house cleaning up and got all the money out from under the cushion on the easy chair and off the window sills, so there!" Sammy said.

"Ha!" I said, "That wouldn't even come to one dollar!"

"I hear a boat," Dinah said for real and held the oars up to listen.

"It's not the Suez," I said, "It's a Chrysler Crown though."

"Maybe it's Ed Wray. It's sure close to the shore," The boat came out from behind the point under the leaning snag where the eagles always sat and it was Archibalds, from the next camp down Agamemnon Channel. As it went by us they slowed down and waved there was a big boy standing in the back. "Hey, that must be Joey," I said. Archibalds had a big boy who went to boarding school in the city that we'd never seen before.

"We better go back to camp," I said when we could hear them going in reverse at the wharf.

"To see him?" Dinah said. "He's creepy. I don't want to see him."

I didn't see how she could tell that from far away.

"Mrs. Archibald said she was going to bring Joey up to play with me sometime, so I have to go back," I said.

It was funny for Dinah to be that way because we always went to meet anybody who came in on a boat, especially if there were kids on it. When we got to the wharf they were all up on the cookhouse walk talking and laughing with Mummy and Daddy and the men, and the boy was with them. Mrs. Archibald saw us and started screeching in her real pointy voice, "Oh there they are! Hello there children. Come up and meet Joey!" But Dinah turned and went towards the Yates house, scooting along with her head down and her arms folded across her front.

He was away bigger than me and after Mrs. Archibald said our names to each other and told us to go off and play but not to get where we couldn't hear her if she called, we just kind of stood around and it wasn't till the grownups went inside we said anything.

"Let's get outta here," he said. "I need a drag."

"What did you say?" I said.

"A fag...a smoke..." he said, holding a flat tailormade cupped in his hand so I could see.

"Do...you smoke?" I said.

"Yeah, but my old lady don't know and I don't want her to find out. My old lady's a bitch."

"Is...is she?" I said. I never thought I'd hear anyone call their own mum a word like that.

We went along the boardwalk past the storeroom and toolshed and onto the trail up around the Little Bunkhouse, curling around the cliff where the Big Dome stuck out and past the light plant.

"This is a keen trail," he said, tripping on a root, "It's just like Lynn Canyon Park. Have you got any keen sights to see around here?"

"What's keen?" I said.

"Boy, you ain't too hep are you?" he said. "Keen is... nifty...sharp...fun?"

"Oh sure," I said. "We got lots of stuff like that."

"Keen," he said. "Wait'll I get a light and let's go see some of it."

I took him to see the rivers behind the Yates house where the rain had built up some new sand bars with little feather designs like brown frost on the mud full of gold flecks, but he thought that was dumb. Then I took him to see the monkey tree behind the Yates house, a crooked cedar tree that hung out of a cliff like a camel's neck with branches looping down curled up at the ends like monkey tails, but he said there were lots of real monkey trees in the city and they weren't anything like that.

We went back to the float and I took him all the stuff we collected in our pretend store at Chair Bay and the hermit crab pools at Cover Point. I kept going further and further looking for something he'd think would really be keen. Finally we went right around Eagle Point under the snag that looked like a nightmare bird to Mrs. Henry's stumpranch to see their cow, but it just got worse and worse.

"What's so great about that cow," he said. "In Richmond there's more cows than there is seagulls. I wanna go back to your camp. My mom might be looking for me."

I was ashamed because I didn't know anything keen. We'd been out so long by the time we got back to the wharf the sun was going down, burning a hole like a welding flash in the mountain, but the grownups were still inside laughing and drinking beer so we started walking back over towards the Yates house. I was trying my hardest to think of something to do, then I remembered before he came thinking of going up to look for the grape hyacinth, so I led him up to the top terrace of the old rock garden. Sure enough there was one out, poking up through the crabgrass and marestail.

"You brought me up here to see a stinking flower?" he said.

"It's the grape hyacinth," I said. I thought the grape hyacinth must be the keenest thing in the world, with its little purple balls like toy grapes. "It comes here every year, just by itself."

"Big deal!" he said, "Don't you do anything around here besides sniff posies and play stinkfinger with your little sister?" He got out the butt of his flat cigarette.

"Do you ever pretend?" I said.

"Pretend, what the hell's that," he said, making the cigarette bounce between his lips. The smoke went in his eyes and he squinted them just like a grownup.

"Pretend..." I said, "Go around and pretend you're made up characters..."

"No, is that what you do?" he said, like it was the stupidest thing he had ever heard. "That's for little kids." He held the cigarette out to tap the ash off, but it was too short and fell on the ground. The way he swore scared me. He was madder than just at it.

"Look out, you're stepping on the grape hyacinth," I said as his boot touched the purple flower.

"Big deal," he said and stomped it flat. I couldn't believe it and jumped up, opening and closing my mouth without any words coming out.

"You shouldn't of done that..." I said.

"Why?" he said with a mean grin.

"It was my Mum's..." I said.

"Well how'll she know who did it," he said, "Unless you tell her? This isn't a garden anyways, it's just a weed patch."

"You shouldn't a done it," I said, bending down to try and fix it. "I liked it."

The little grapes were smashed open and bleeding purple blood, such a beautiful dark purple a lump came up in my throat and I had to close my eyes. If I started crying I wouldn't be able to stop.

"Where's that broad?" he said.

"What broad?"

"That ginch — girl, you dipstick. I saw a girl come in with you in the rowboat, an older one. Is she your sister too?"

"That's Dinah," I said.

"Dinah, like Dinah Shore?" he said laughing. "How old is she?"

"Twelve."

"Twelve! Wow, are you sure? She's really stacked for twelve. I'm twelve and nunna the broads in my class are that stacked."

"She'll be thirteen on July seventh," I said.

"Hey, izzat right?" he said. "I'm eight days oldern her. Where is she?"

"Probably up in her tree reading," I said. "Over by the waterfall."

"In her tree! What a blast! You guys are really bizarre. Let's go bug her." I didn't know quite what to say. It gave me kind of a funny feeling to hear anybody talking that way about Dinah but I was glad to find something keen before he got any madder. He made me feel all cold and strange inside.

We crawled up through the bushes on the cliff where we could look down at the big maple where Dinah was sitting with her book picking lint off her blouse.

"Wow, she's stacked!" he whispered. "Have you ever seen her boobs? You must've."

"You mean breasts?" I said. I could tell what that meant. He nodded, grinning. "Nope, ever since she got 'em she doesn't bath with us anymore," I said.

"Wow, I'd sure like to bath with her," he said. "Have you ever felt 'em?"

"I punched one of 'em when she wouldn't let me read her Katy Keene comic," I said.

"Didja? What was it like?"

"Good. She just kind of crumbled up and dropped the comic on the ground. I got in heck after though."

"No, you ding-a-ling! I mean, what did it *feel* like? The boob."

"Like a sea anemone kinda. Squishy."

"Keen," he said, "That's really keen." My head started to swell a little.

"Holler and tell her to come and play hide and seek." he said.

"Hey Dinah, Joey wants ya to come and play hide 'n seek," I yelled, and she looked startled.

"You moron!" he said, grabbing my shoulder. "I'll tear your head off. Don't say I want her to. Say you want her to."

"No Joey doesn't wantcha to, I wantcha to," I hollered again and Joey got so mad I got ready to run. I knew he couldn't catch me in the bush.

"Well I don't want to play hide and seek with either of you," Dinah said. "I would appreciate it if you just left me alone."

Joey pulled loose a piece of moss and heaved it down at her. It smashed up in the branches and dirt dropped on her.

"Go away and leave me alone!" she screamed. It was funny, because I'd played worse tricks on her before and she didn't get that mad. It was something to do with Joey but I didn't know what.

"You throw one," Joey said, handing me a clump of juicy moss. It hit the same place as his. Dinah jumped up and started climbing fast down the tree. We threw some more, but we could see she was going to get away before we could get down off the bluff.

"Let's cut her off so she can't get back to the grownups," he said, and we started crashing through the salal, running with our arms and our legs almost like swimming, and getting almost as wet too. We got to the trail a little bit after Dinah but we were closer to the cookhouse so she turned and ran back towards the Yates house. There were no locks on the Yates house, but she jammed a table knife in the crack and it took us a few minutes to bash it out. She ran out the back door and up the trail towards Mum's vegetable garden. Joey stumbled on a boulder and hit the funny bone of his knee and by the time it stopped we couldn't see her anywhere. The path to the garden went up a dry creek through a thick stand of alder trees for about ten minutes, then opened into a big clearing of green grass. The sun was almost down and the shade made the wetness of the brush so cold my teeth started clicking. The garden was in the middle of the clearing, with a tall wall of skinny poles with points at the tops to keep out deer. Part of the back wall was a tall hollow stump so brown and buggy its bark had all fallen off from us kids playing around it.

"I bet she's hiding in there," I said. We walked up to it and the hole at the bottom was covered with a board. "She's in there," I whispered.

"Tell her we'll quit if she'll come out and play hide and seek," Joey whispered.

There was no answer. We stood there and looked at the stump. We kicked at the board but she had it jammed good. Joey tried climbing up but just got orange goo all over his good clothes. "I've got matches. Maybe we could light a fire and smoke her out," he said, but I knew there was nothing dry enough to make a fire with. I had an idea I didn't want to tell him, but I got afraid he'd get mad again. I grabbed a handful of grass, pulled up a sod, and lobbed it up on top of the stump. It went down the hole.

"Hey!" Joey said, and we started tearing up sods and lobbing them in, yelling and making Indian noises till there were hardly any good sods left. Then I heard a funny noise.

"Hey stop," I said. "I heard something."

We held still and listened.

There was crying, coming out of the stump.

"Let's quit now," I said. In an eyeblink it had gone from where you could see to where it was all dark shapes you couldn't tell how far you were away from. I felt scared in a very weird way. I'd never made Dinah cry before.

"Are there any cougars or bears around here?" Joey said. He was just a voice coming out of the dark.

"No, not very many," I said. I could hear him brushing off his shirt.

"I better get back," he said. "I'll be in hell." His voice was sorta shaking and he started running and stumbling down the crunchy gravel. I was starting to get the feeling of something more happening than just what happened. The dark shape of the stump was gone into the dark of the forest and the sad sad crying just seemed to be coming from everywhere. I tried to think but I just didn't know. I couldn't believe I'd gone on some stranger boy's side and ruined my best friend in the world.

I closed my eyes and opened them. It was so dark it didn't make any difference. I didn't feel like I was where I was. It was like it was all a dream, like the real day ended when it was dark before and the men came home, and Joey coming was all a dream, only I couldn't wake out of it. Things wouldn't go back the same.

TIDES

Think of the towboats out on the straits, stretching a distant even thread of motor noise through the night. They work the tide shift. Think of the weary gillnetter rolling in his bunk, setting the alarm for the change of tide. Think of the Haida clamdigger hunched over a cloudy hole in the glassy plain of a Queen Charlotte Island sandflat, breakers roaring in the distance and a briny wind cutting through neoprene layers right to the numb core of her bones. As winter progresses she will hunch in the blue dawn, then the bright noon, then the moonlight again, as the tides command. They work in the tides' time.

Tide. The word has been in steady use since the Saxons. They said *tid*, and it meant time as well. Tide was time to them. They too lived with their backs to the land, their eyes to the sea.

"Time and tide wait for no man." King Canute. Scylla and Charybdis. The image of the whirlpool, or maelstrom, or vortex, recurring over and over as a symbol of the extremity of experience.

Out there in the corner of the third eye, the tides have influenced our culture more than we know.

Here on this coast the Indians knew, with a thoroughness only a people whose lives had pulsed in the tides' time for ten thousand years could know. The perpetual dependable shifting of the water was one of the groundswell rhythms of coast mythology and in the most basic stories of creation and transformation the tide is always present, changing the scene, moving the plot along. In a typical Salish flood myth it's not the rain that drives the native Noah to the dry peak of Anchor Mountain, but the wrathful flood tide.

Most coast oldtimers, approached cold for some comment on the tides will say something like, "Tides! You want to know about tides! Well, she comes in and she goes out. That's about all I can tell you. She comes in and she goes out."

But just at the mention of the word you will probably detect a faraway look in the corner of his eye, the sort of transfixed look you find in the eye of a troller whose boat and bodily form have just come into dock but whose mind remains hooked into some deep mystery back in the Gulf. The tides of this coast, upon which fishing of all things depends, is an inexhaustible study, drawing the thoughts of many different shades of men to a same transparent fineness.

Most people, faced with making some sense of the tidal mystery, will invoke the hidden astronomical machinery of the sun and moon. Admittedly this is where it starts, although finally it's only a minor part of the explanation.

The sun and moon pull on the earth and it swells a little on both sides. Not the sea only; air and land also. It has been calculated that Moscow rises and falls twenty inches each time the moon goes by. The sky tide is estimated in miles, and jostles the atmosphere in ways that are well known to farmers and fishermen and recently to scientists as well.

The sea tide is comparatively slight, averaging perhaps two feet in the open ocean, a very faint bulge held fixed by the moon as the earth slides around underneath it.

This would quite neatly explain the occurrence of one tide per day, one rise and one fall twelve hours apart. But as anyone who's copper-painted a boat on a beaching grid knows, you frequently only get six hours — or less — to do your job. You beach on the high tide at, say, 7 AM, the boat is high and dry by 1 PM and by 8 PM that evening it's floating again. And if you didn't quite finish re-caulking that bad seam, you may get chance to finish up at 2 AM the following morning, when the tide is out again. So life experience tells us there are usually two tides a day, with four changes — two rises and two falls. Why is this?

I have found that hardly anyone can answer this most basic

tidal question — not the most barnacled old salt, not the most loquacious and reflective lightkeeper — unless they have made a specific study of the subject.

I have often heard it argued the first tide is caused by the moon and the second by the sun, but such is not the case. The sun does influence the tide, but its influence is sufficiently fainter than the moon's it can only increase or decrease the moon tide — it hasn't the power to override it.

The actual explanation of the diurnal (twice-a-day) tide I find myself having to accept on faith, because it's never seemed quite obvious to me in common sense terms.

It goes like this: when the pull of the moon causes the ocean to bulge up toward it, a corresponding bulge just naturally happens on the other side of the world. Is this the equal and opposite reaction? An astronomer could explain it — hell, a highschool physics student might explain it — but I can't. What I am here to tell you is that the tidal bulge created by the moon is double-ended like a hen's egg, with one end toward the moon and one away from it.

To extend this ovular image to its logical limit, the earth rests inside its envelope of sea like the yolk inside its envelope of white. If you hard-boil that egg, shell it and slice it lengthwise, think how it looks. A white oval with a yellow circle in the middle. At the ends the egg-white is thick and in the middle it's thin. In earth terms the thick represents high tide and the thin low tide. If you were to rotate that yolk inside the white as the earth rotates under the moon's pull, you can imagine how in the course of one revolution a given spot on the turning yolk would pass through a zone of thick white and a zone of thin, then another zone of thick and another zone of thin. This is what the earth does in the course of one daily rotation.

If you haven't got it now, give it up. It doesn't matter anyway.

During the equinox when the sun and moon are straight out off the equator the two daily tides are more nearly equal in size, but as sun and moon range north or south of the equator, most extreme during the solstice, they pull the bulges askew so we pass through the thick middle of one and only the thin edge of the other. This is when you hear fishermen speak of the "big tide" and the "little tide."

FULL MOON · HIGH TIDE
(WINTER SOLSTICE)

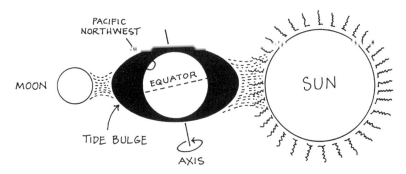

Since the moon is on an elliptical orbit it varies in distance from the earth, with corresponding changes in its gravitational pull, and this causes long-term variations in the range of the tides. Another thing that causes long-term variations is the relation of the sun and moon to each other. During the new and full phases they pull in line, creating "spring tides," and during the quarters they pull against each other, producing "neap tides."

These astronomical motions are extremely regular. If that's all there was to it the whole world would read its tides from the *Farmer's Almanac,* which in fact started out as a primitive sort of tide book in the sixteenth century.

Hydrographers have a saying: all tides are local. There are so many local factors that affect tidal behaviour the neat graph

LAST QUARTER · NEAP TIDE

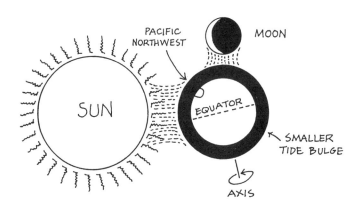

rhythms of sun and moon become lost in a scribble; if it has final order there hasn't been a computer made that can begin to crack it.

There's wind. In 1943 the Masset clamdiggers' co-op almost went broke because a hard onshore wind kept the surf from baring North Beach all winter, and in 1953 North Sea gales boosted Dutch tides thirty feet, breaking miles of dyke and drowning two thousand people. Tides are continually delayed and hastened, increased and diminished by strong winds. On this coast it can be generally stated that a hard southeaster will push the tide up and hold it up, and a hard westerly will have the opposite effect.

But mostly there's land. Theoretically tidal range decreases with latitude, but Frobisher Bay in the Canadian Arctic has ranges of thirty-five feet, second highest in the world, owing to its scoop-like shape, and the world's largest tidal whirlpool is off Lofoten Island in the Norwegian Arctic. Fundy and Nantucket are less than two hundred miles apart but the one has fifty-foot tides and the other two-foot — all effects of local geography. There are parts of the world like Chile and Western Africa where the coast is so straight and rational tides can almost be calculated from the calendar, but they are the antithesis of BC. The northwest coast is the most intricate in the world, as involuted and inscrutable almost as the brain itself. Even water has a difficult time finding all its crevices, and ends up in a continual frothing confusion. West coast tides abandon the most fundamental laws of tidal action, devoid of any logic but their own.

Oceanographers have built contour models acres in size, pumped water in and out for months on end and produced armfuls of theories but in Georgia Strait tides make and break up to a week out of phase with the moon; in an area that is supposed to be semi-diurnal Victoria has diurnal tides twenty days of the month and no one knows why.

The tide tables are offered as simple observations, compiled through years of watching by such notably un-theoretical folk as the Bill Logans of Clo-oose, who took readings in the late twenties that were used to establish the current tables for Nitinat Bar. "We'd walk over to the Bar with a stopwatch and time high and low slack, all hours of the day and night, all kinds of weather. It was a couple miles, I guess. We were pretty spry then."

The BC coast is basically in two parts, with huge islands on either hand, Vancouver south and the Queen Charlottes north. Stormy, exposed Cape Caution, with its cold blue beach sand ground fine as flour, marks the mid-point. In the lee of the islands are the vast protected water of Hecate Straits above and Georgia-Johnstone-Queen Charlotte Straits below. Then there are the inlets, basically thirteen major systems, and four further series of inlets on the outsides of the islands, the great lagoon of Masset Inlet in the centre of Graham Island like the hole in a doughnut, and a multitude of lesser inlets, arms, bays, channels and islands any direction you turn.

As the 1.5-foot ocean tide, moving in from the southwest, strikes the Vancouver Island shore simultaneously from Nitinat to Cape Scott, it slops up to an average height of ten feet. At Port Alberni, at the head of broad-mouthed Barclay Sound and long-stemmed Alberni Canal, it's twelve feet. This funnel effect was particularly evident during the Alaskan tidal wave of 1962, which passed with little notice at Tofino on the outer coast but caused heavy flooding at Port Alberni.

The tidal swell actually jars Vancouver Island on its base. The earthquake seismograph at Beacon Hill each day records the slightest backward movement of the shore as the tide comes in, and the slightest outward movement as it retreats.

The tide enters the Strait of Georgia by curling around Cape Flattery and running southeast down Juan de Fuca Strait. This reverse turn is not easily accomplished and those prone to think of severe tidal turbulence as a property of constricted inland channels might be surprised to find fierce rips and overfalls out here miles into the open ocean from Cape Flattery. The same thing happens where the tide enters around the north end of the Island, off Cape Scott. And nearly out of sight of Cape Knox at the top end of the Queen Charlottes, where the stream is turned down Dixon Entrance, there are overfalls steep enough to capsize large boats. Moving oceans don't change course very gracefully.

On the west coast of the Charlottes the tide is also in the ten-foot range, but arrives a half-hour later than at Vancouver Island.

The tide progresses very slowly down the sixty-mile length of Juan de Fuca Strait, filtering tediously through the narrow passes of the Gulf Islands, and arrives in Georgia Strait delayed a full six hours. But once the tidal swell reaches this regular, open basin it

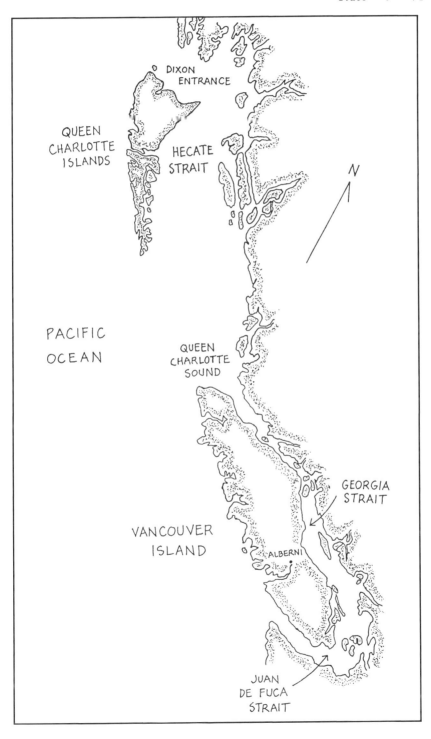

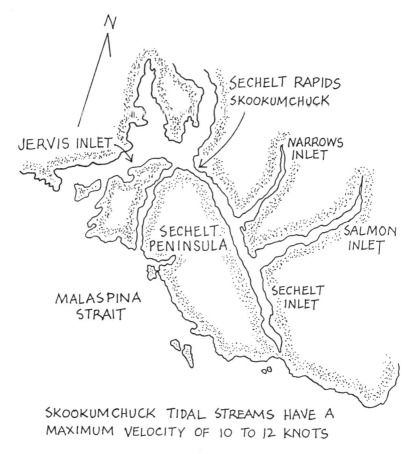

SKOOKUMCHUCK TIDAL STREAMS HAVE A
MAXIMUM VELOCITY OF 10 TO 12 KNOTS

covers the full 130-mile length in thirty minutes without great variation in range or current; Powell River, Nanaimo and Pender Harbour can all use the Point Atkinson table in the tide book. In Vancouver Harbour however, less than two miles east of Point Atkinson, a separate table is required. Vancouver is inside the narrow neck of Burrard Inlet, and any inlet with a constriction at its mouth has tides distinctly its own. The floods tend to be later and smaller. At Holberg, at the end of constricted Quatsino Inlet, the tide comes forty-five minutes later than at Clayoquot just outside, and at Porpoise Bay below Sechelt Inlet's notorious Skookumchuck Rapids high tide is two hours and thirteen minutes later and 6.4 feet smaller than at Sechelt a few thousand feet of low isthmus away on Georgia Strait.

There are all degrees of landlocked inlets on the coast, from

Burrard, Princess Louisa, Sechelt, Drury and Draney Inlets with their increasingly small necks, to Nitinat Lake on the west coast of the Island where the seas of the open Pacific have pushed up a gravel bar that partially dries at low tide, to big lagoons like Von Donop's on Cortes Island or Bradley Lagoon in Blunden Harbour with its reversing salt water waterfall, to Powell Lake at Powell River, which hasn't had a tide since the ice age but is said to still hold salt water in its lower depths.

The most outrageous bottleneck on the coast is probably Nakwakto Narrows near Cape Caution, which drains a system of four inlets — seven hundred miles of shoreline all told — through a passage barely a thousand feet wide. There is a small streamlined island in the middle of the narrows called Tremble Island, that is reputed to shake so perceptibly the trees dance in a big tide. It may be the swiftest tidal rapids in the world, achieving velocities of twenty-four knots, but for all its thunder and whirling spume it never manages to get the water in Seymour Inlet down more than about four feet before the outside tide, which has a fourteen-foot range, meets it on the return and sets it roaring back in again.

At the heads of deep-mouthed inlets tides have greater than normal range and occur almost simultaneously with outside tides. Whaletown on Cortes Island is fifty-two miles from the head of Bute Inlet, but the time difference for high water is only three minutes and for low, nine minutes. The range, following the tendency of the tidal swell to surge up as it runs inland, increases by two to twelve percent. In the big northern inlets much the same picture holds true.

As the coast divides basically into two regions, so in turn does

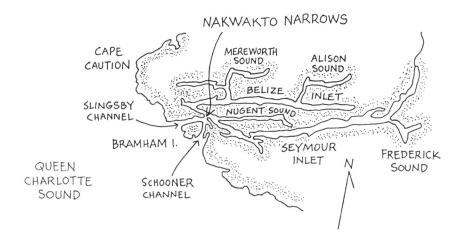

the south region itself. Vancouver Island is shaped like a Haida longhouse, gable on, with its roof peak pressing the mainland shore near the top of Georgia Strait. This gives the inland waters very generally the shape of an hourglass, with the broad expanses of Georgia and Queen Charlotte Straits at either end narrowing into Johnstone Strait, then nearly pinching right off as the roof peak jams Quadra and Sonora Islands against the mouth of Bute Inlet. The tidal stream which enters around the north end of the Island flushes down Queen Charlotte and Johnstone Straits with relatively little impediment until it crashes into Sonora and Quadra Islands here at the pinch in the hourglass. By the time it has boiled through the great rapids of Seymour Narrows, the Hole in the Wall and the Yacultas, this northern tide is almost the same "age" as the south stream, which it meets about seven miles farther down.

Savary Island, a wispy crescent of sand with crisp white beaches and fir trees that arc out over the waters like palms, rests here in the calm eye of the tides and Bill Ashworth of the old Royal Savary Arms, used to attract visitors by eulogizing the unnaturally gentle climate this favoured position endows, advertising year round golf (played on the sand) and periodically greeting visitors in lei and hula skirt. More precisely in the middle of the two streams is rocky Mittlenatch Island towards the Island side, and it too breathes a kind of halcyon air, serving as the night roost and nesting ground for thousands of the Gulf's seagulls.

It's a different story just up the way at Cape Mudge. There the wide swift river of Discovery Pass piles into the Gulf in a mass of rips that constitutes one of the most un-serene pieces of water on the Inside Passage, particularly in a southeast blow. A lump hardly big enough to slop your coffee on the ebb tide, when the tide turns will rear up in a short high sea that has been the end of more than one unwary vessel. Still, those blessed with local knowledge can sometimes skirt over towards Wilby Shoal and ride the big back eddy all the way into Quathiaski Cove for a level coffee and another serious look at the tide book before heading into Seymour Narrows.

North of the pinch in Johnstone Strait is another bad place for mixing wind and tide. A big flood may run south at four knots, and a southeast wind coming up the strait will brush up a short high chop that can make your small boat skipper wish he was back in the dust bowl.

But anyone who heads up there in a southeaster pretty well deserves what he gets; the more innocent predicament is to be caught in Johnstone Strait with an ebb running up against a westerly, which is just as wicked. "Westerlies bring clear weather of course," said John Daly, "so in the morning you'll think ah, what a lovely day, and set out on the flood tide, then by noon it changes and suddenly you're in trouble. In Johnstone Strait there's not many places to hide either, except on the bottom, and there's lots of company down there."

North of Cape Caution the tides work in different ways. The ocean tidal swell washing in through Queen Charlotte Sound fills the deep inlets like Smiths and Rivers, Dean and Burke in the same way as the deep inlets to the south, but the open-ended channels tend to fill from both ends with tidal streams meeting in the middle. Tides in Grenville Channel, that straight-walled sixty-mile alleyway approaching Prince Rupert from the south, meet either at Morning Point or Evening Point depending on season and weather. What is considered very smart is to reach Evening Point at high water slack so that you have the flood pushing you in and the ebb pulling you out.

The main factor that shapes tidal behaviour on the north coast is Hecate Strait. Because at the lower end it's eighty miles wide and two hundred fathoms deep and at the top end forty miles wide and ten fathoms deep — the classic scoop shape of Fundy or Frobisher, the tidal swell surges from about fifteen feet at Bella Bella up to twenty-six feet at Prince Rupert.

According to Daly: "You get the lowest low tides, minus tides, in the middle of the day during the summer, which works out to be just the time we're up there packing gear and grub up and down those ramps. It's climbing a ladder, not walking a ramp."

Water is such nervous, twitchy stuff. How much so you don't always realize because it's clear and you can't see what it's doing, but mark it with something, look at a mud puddle with a little trickle entering it and see the fantastic ceremony and brown filigree that attends the slightest movement, and the histrionic way moving water reacts to the slightest irregularity in its path, enacting all implications, so many swirls and counterswirls it would take a week to catalogue just what happens in one mud puddle.

Then think of this coast, as intricate as life itself, seventeen thousand miles compressed to five hundred, and the water swirling back and forth multiplying complexity by complexity—of course no one understands the tides, not in the way you could write about anyway.

To the people who live and work on the sea falls the task of knowing the entire spectrum of tidal motions, currents, and eddies and rips that are as significant to fishermen and towboaters as the qualities of soils and contours of land to the farmer, though perhaps it's felt more than known. This obscure and subjective science is often referred to in official circles with certain grudging respect as "local knowledge."

Second-generation Vancouver towboater Bill Cates remembered the hazards created by the tides at first narrows: "There is a condition near Prospect Point that I think I ought to call attention to. This is the meeting of the back eddy with the ebb stream. As a big ebb pours out under the Lions Gate Bridge, a strong back eddy is formed which runs along the shore from Siwash Rock towards Prospect Point.

"It is customary for boats entering Vancouver Harbour to take advantage of this eddy and get as close to Prospect Point as possible before entering the ebb stream.

"The danger lies in the fact that the vessel is approaching the point with about a two-knot current in her favour, when suddenly she is struck on the starboard bow by an adverse stream of about six knots and thrown halfway across the narrows directly into the path of outgoing traffic.

"When a tug has scows or a car barge this ebb stream is doubly dangerous, as the tug enters the stream first and is swept westward while the tow continues east. The towline will come slack at first, then tighten with a snap. Several tugs have been capsized by this happening.

"On coming in the harbour the south shore of course is favoured. There is not much eddy until the Harris house is passed, five hundred yards east of the bridge. After the house is passed an eddy forms in by Lumberman's Arch and extends in to Brockton

Point, but care must be taken as there are large boulders in the area.

"When leaving Vancouver Harbour, especially with a tow, it is good to buck out against the last of the flood. The first of the ebb then sweeps close along the south shore to Siwash Rock and in no time you are at Ferguson Point where the guns were placed during the war. This condition, unless the ebb is very small, only lasts a short while and is much more pronounced when it is raining and the Capilano River is high. As soon as the ebb stream reaches any strength, the eddy I was talking about forms and then it would be impossible to tow a boom southwest from Prospect Point.

"My father used to tell me how the steamer *Beaver*, the first steamer on the coast, was wrecked just south of Prospect Bluff. She was a side wheeler, with her rudder placed in the same position as on an ordinary vessel. With her speed of four knots it meant the rudder had very little effect. My father also said that on this trip the crew were sober and therefore not normal. However, she came slowly out of the narrows and to dodge the tide rip the captain swung her bow to the south. As soon as the back eddy struck her bow she swung around and ran ashore just west of Prospect Point. I don't think any attempt was made to salvage her.

"The tide will change from a strong ebb to full slack in a matter of about twenty minutes. Right after low water slack by the tide book a line will form across the channel. There will be a rippling foamy edge appear along this line and all water in this area will start eastward. This is the first of the flood."

And on it goes, a clockwork universe of eddies within eddies, a study not of one lifetime but many, always changing but, as the wise realize, forever doing the same things.

"It is a strange fact that after a tide[*] peaks, although it still has a large range, it will not develop the same fierce currents as a tide that is making. My father showed me this when I was a small boy . . .

---

[*] Coast people have almost as many meanings for tide as Eskimos have for snow. A man may say he is waiting for a clamdigging tide and mean the simple going down of the water, or he may say there's a lot of tide in Alert Bay and mean a lot of current. In this case Captain Cates means a tidal cycle, building up to a peak height and then falling off over a period of many days.

The Yaculta Rapids (pronounced *Yooclataw*) run between Sonora Island and Stuart Island off the mouth of Bute Inlet. They are longer and rougher and twistier than Seymour Narrows on the Vancouver Island side but they have the great advantage of better protection at the south end, which makes them the choice of anyone who has reason to avoid the volatile seas off Cape Mudge.

There are two parts to the Yacultas, the rapids between the Dent Islands and the rapids between the Gillard Islands. Boats travel due north up Calm Channel, then enter Gillard Pass by making a hard left turn heading due west between the Gillard Islands. The Dent Islands are passed either by turning ninety degrees right up Tugboat Pass, between the islands, or by heading straight into Dent Rapids along the Sonora shore. Tugboat Pass is about seven hundred feet wide and the other slightly more. The stream runs eight or nine knots in the passes and breaks up in huge rips and forty-foot whirlpools on the downstream side.

The waters between the two rapids are further confused by the fact that Bute Inlet dumps a lot of boiling water in through Arran Rapids on the east side, which runs nine or ten knots and has a man-eating reputation.

The people who get the most ulcers out of these rapids are undoubtedly the towboat men, who face the regular problem of herding frail and ponderous log booms from the northern logging camps down to the mills in the south. Barges and the practice of bundling logs have taken much of the pain out of it today but until the late fifties it was all flat booms. Dozens of small tugboat companies were competing with each other for myriads of little gyppos that blighted the hills around Minstrel Island and up Knight Inlet like a great scrofulous plague. There was a steady stream of booms making south and the Yacultas were like a revolving door on $1.49 Day.

Captain Hec Fisher, who put in a half-century or so on that route, once said the classic approach was to arrive off Henry Point, a mile above Little Dent, an hour and twenty minutes before low slack. That way the tide was running against you but not too hard, and as it eased off you could sneak up so when slack came you'd be as close in to the pass as you could get.

Still there was no chance of making both rapids in one jump, unless it was a minuscule tide. You'd tie up at Mermaid Bay on the south side of Big Dent and wait for the next low slack twelve

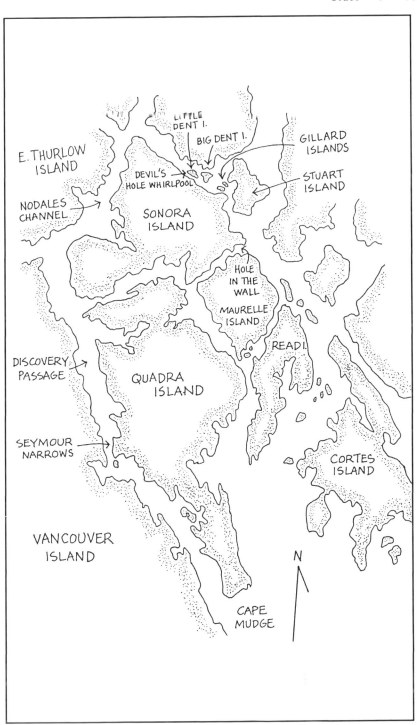

hours later. There would be a high slack within six hours but you couldn't move on that because you couldn't get through before it turned and started hauling you back.

Day after day there would be four and five boats waiting over in Mermaid Bay.

"Well it's a dangerous situation you are because everybody's trying to make slack water, but you can't all be there at the same time. Somebody's going to be late.

"Whoever's got the most power to buck up, he's going to get out first. But the next guy, he's got to think pretty careful what he's doing, because you always overtake the guy ahead of you, the tide's always stronger behind, and if you get too close you can't keep out of each other's way. But if you wait too long you're going to end up in white water."

Why skippers get grey. Do you let the other guy get a tide up on you and get back up north before you so he can poach on your carefully hoarded camps, or do you head in late and risk a forty-thousand-dollar boom?

"I went through there with the *Active* one time," says Captain Jack Ryall, another half-century man, "and hell, I took a whole side of the damn boom out and just about took the winch off. Right at Gillard Island light."

There were many options, depending on your power, the size of your tow, and whether it's half-sunk pulp from some ass-out-of-his-pants barefoot gyppo who doesn't believe in boomchains or nice peelers put together just like the *Kon-Tiki*, but mostly it was a matter of time and tide, and as you churned down Cordero Channel you'd be phoning ahead and watching the water and putting all these things together in your head trying to find the easy combination. Sometimes instead of bucking into Mermaid Bay you could slip in on the last of the flood and save six hours right there. To really frost the poker players in at Mermaid you could smokestack 'er right across their noses and over through Arran Rapids.

"Say you're coming through on the last of the flood. Well by the time you get to Mermaid Bay you only need another twenty minutes tide and bang, you're through Arran Rapids. Mind you've got that long pull around the backside of Stuart Island but then you're twelve hours ahead of the guy that stopped at Mermaid.

"Now not everybody could *do* that. It's a straight shot but there's a bad rip, it breaks up very bad on the flood, on the other end, on the Bute side, there's some bad holes there."

If you made it, it was a real notch on your pole but if you missed and had to call the other guys in to help save your boom they would keep you hanging your head a long time. Still, the man who would gamble on the tides like that would be thought more of than the Mother Gooses who always took two days to get through.

There were a few like Ryall who used the Hole in the Wall a lot. If they could see a traffic jam shaping up at Mermaid they'd turn off into Nodales Channel, go down Discovery Passage, cut back through Okisollo Channel and duck out through the Hole in a twenty-mile U-shaped bypass. The hitch was running the Hole, a narrow rock-studded alley with sheer seventeen-hundred-foot walls and twelve-knot rapids. It was four miles long and a boom three sections wide would just fit.

"What you'd generally do was take the last of the flood, just enough tide to get through. That way it would be slack when you got down to the lower rapids and you could buck the rest of the way out."

"You could tell by the rocks how you were doing. You'd know the rocks — one would always look like a snag but it was always a rock. Another would look like someone's face you know, lying down. Well if the tip of the nose is just braiding the surface of the water you're okay, but if it's out down to the oysters you better give 'er everything she's got, otherwise you're never going to make it.

"You hit it wrong sometimes, you're too early, and suddenly it's all white water and there's nothing to do but try and steer it through. There are places you know you gotta stay away from, other places it can't hit no way 'cause there's back eddies and you're flyin' around like mad trying to stay out of trouble because once that boom hits the beach, why everything's crackin' and flyin', chains are pullin' out of the ends of sticks and you got logs all over the place, it's not a very happy situation.

"Taking chances. It's always from taking a chance. You're late on the tide. You should of stopped. You say, oh I'll make it, I'll make it."

A lot of skippers wouldn't go near the Hole but Ryall says it's one of those things that looked bad but once you got to know it it was all in a day's work.

Hec Fisher towed through Nakwakto for fifteen years and felt the same way about it.

"There's no worst places really. It's more what you know best is easiest."

Salmon don't like to buck the tide. The only time they will do this is when they're late returning to the spawning ground, pushed to it by that terrific instinct. Once at the river of course they will not only buck heavy currents, they will swim up waterfalls. But in the sea they move with the tide, favouring back eddies around points and in rapids to make the easiest headway. When the tide turns against them often they'll lay up in a bay till it changes. They follow the contour of the land. That's why you always see the net boats hounding the beaches, sometimes stringing a gillnet parallel to the shore to catch the fish weaving in and out.

The trollers, too, watch the swirls and counterswirls of coastal waters with a keen eye. They spend their days searching out rips, psyching out unseen bottoms, watching for signs of feed. He spends his days hunting it, talking of it incessantly, claiming to see vast quantities where the normal eye sees nothing.

"Feed goes where the tide goes. If you're bucking the tide your lure's bucking the tide and that looks artificial. Salmon won't bite that, salmon aren't stupid."

So if you can figure out where currents are meeting and bunching the feed all up like they bunch the scattered drift up sometimes on the surface, you'll find the fish because they know how to find it too. Trollers hardly notice what the part of the coast looks like that's sticking out of the water, except when they want to take a fix on a good new hole. They spend all their time piecing together this dream of the part that's underneath, plotting it all out in their little black books.

Generally they hunt for upwellings or rips. Anywhere there's a lot of tide, generally there's a lot of sea life, a lot of feed and a lot of herring hanging around the feed and a lot of spring and coho hanging around the herring. Places like Seymour Narrows and the Skookumchuck have a lot of ling and grey and rock cod too. The best time for the Chuck, say the cod men, is two hours before and two hours after slack.

The best fishing is often two to three days after the highest or lowest tides. You set a gillnet an hour and a half before slack at least.

"There is a breeze always comes up at the change of tide. With a flood you'll get a southeast and a northwest with an ebb. We call it the tide wind. You look over at the treetops and it's dead calm, but there's a little breeze on the water."

Then there's the wind tide. A good wind will build up a surface current of two or three knots. It's a bugger when you're trolling, you can't slow the boat down. Makes you go too fast.

You catch more fish on a flood tide. Humpies swim ahead of a rip. Dogs follow. Cohos swim in a rip.

An old Swede told me wherever there's a rip, there's coho. They swim in the back eddies that form along each side of the rip.

"I remember vun time I vas op Camaano Sound. I vasn't catching a ting! It vas getting late in de day and I figured I'd about had it but I saw one fish yump so I tot vell I make vun more set den I have a good rest. So I set de net and go below. It vas dead calm and I vas cooking someting and I remember I heard blip, blip, blip . . . blip, blip, blip, and I vondered now vat de hell is dat. So I goes op on deck and oh my yumpin' yeesus, here's a grrreat big rip yust strrreaming out of Surf Inlet. Vas de change of tide you see. Vell, *yunk!* you should haf seen de yunk dat rip was full of—vood and sticks and kelp and bark yust sticking out of it. I couldn't see my net for de yunk. Vell I figure I lost my net for shure. I vas so mad I say to hell vit it and go back below. I stay dere awhile, trying to read, trying to sleep, till finally I figured, maybe I'll pull it in for de cork line.

"So I go back on de deck. I could only see a few corks, dey were dese old plastic kind yust shrunk op like prunes. The net vas pulled out so much, I tell you dat net must haf gone halfway to China. I pull on her and man is she *heavy.* Vell dat net was yust *full* of northern coho. Dey vas in dat rip."

"I never did know too much about navigation," said Jimmy Sewid, at one time one of the most successful fishermen in BC, "but I was very familiar with the tides. You have to be very careful with the tides. Most of the time I just looked at the water to tell the direction it was going to change. All the tides were different and I knew them all. They were all in my head."

Jack Ryall: "You get to know a place, you'd just know it, that's all."

Jimmy Sewid: "It's all in my head."

At a certain stage words can do no more than point in the direction of what is unsayable. It's like when you've been some place in the city, not long enough for your waking mind to absorb the location but long enough for this other part of your mind to get an impression so you say, "I don't know where it is but if I see it I'll recognize it." Or sometimes you'll be walking in the woods and you'll think hey, this looks familiar, I've been here before, there should be a little hollow stump right over there. So you go over and there it is, but when you were there before or for what, you have no idea.

If someone came up and asked you how you knew, what would you say? I just know. It comes in from that foggy accurate part of the mind too-rational people don't use because they can't prove it's there but good fishermen, towboat skippers, nuclear physicists and poker players rely on it for all the important things. It's a kind of consciousness this coast of endless intricacy enforces upon those who come to bargain with it for their livelihoods, and marks them with a deepness.

"When the tide is ebbing," says Captain Cates, "all the creatures of the sea become listless. The crabs which you may catch in forty to fifty feet of water and which have been coming constantly to bait during the flood tide will cease to feed during the ebb. It seems queer that they would know the difference in that depth of water but such is the case. Even although the tide is still high and the flats are well covered, all the crabs and small fish will disappear as soon as the ebb starts.

"Along the edge of the receding sea the ducks and gulls feed and the herons wade out quietly on their long legs to catch the small retreating fish with a lightning dart of their long pointed beaks.

"Now as a big ebb reaches near its extreme low, a tension seems to come into the air. I have asked many sailors and they say they can feel it. Certainly the fish and birds and crabs know the flood is coming. A little before low water all these creatures reappear and become very active. Any fisherman will tell you that low slack is the time to catch salmon as they race around in the little eddies and snap up smaller fish. All along the shore gulls swoop and dive, for there is renewed life in the sea. The old Indians smile and say *kwa-'kwatts,* the tide is rising.

"As the tide reaches its crest, the tension eases and peace seems to come to the shore of the inlet. In the summer this is usually in the evening and an old Indian friend of mine used to say, 'Take your white man's pleasures and give me a nice *snaaquaylsh* [dugout] and let me paddle far up the sloughs where the smell of the salt grass fills the air and I can see the flounders scooting away in the clear water and hear the birds in the trees along the shore singing their sleepy evening song. There is no peace like the peace of *Kwahaluis,* the full of the tide.' "

WILLIAM DUNCAN AND THE MIRACLE OF METLAKATLA

Metlakatla today is a sleepy little Indian reserve across the bay from Prince Rupert, BC. A nondescript cluster of bungalows surrounding a modest wooden church and heavily overgrown by verdant rainforest vegetation, there seems nothing to distinguish it. Only a handful of families remain, and outside the immediate area, hardly anyone knows the name. But in the latter half of the nineteenth century, before there was a Prince Rupert or even a Vancouver, and the Province of British Columbia ranked as the most remote outpost of all Queen Victoria's vast empire, Metlakatla was a household word in England and a cause célèbre in the United States, far better known to the outside world than the Province of British Columbia itself. It was, along with the Niagara Falls and the Grand Canyon, one of the things not to be missed by rich Victorian travellers on safari to the new world.

What was the attraction? Lady Dufferin, the Governor-General's wife, toured British Columbia with her husband in 1874. After leaving Victoria aboard the HMS *Amethyst* for a voyage along the coast in August, the vice-regal party travelled up bleak, windswept inlets devoid of human habitation and among maze-like tangles of islands until it seemed they were moving down a long, bleak corridor of time itself, dropping backward into some primeval age when the earth was devoid of sentient life. On the 19th of August, greatly disheartened by the remoteness they felt

from civilization, they arrived at Metlakatla. Lady Dufferin could scarcely believe her eyes:

> The population is 1200. Its residents have a rifle com-pany of 40 men, a brass band, a two-gun battery and a large co-operative store where almost anything obtainable in Victoria can be bought.
>
> We were received with displays of bunting from various points and a five-gun salute from the battery, with Yankee Doodle and Dixie from the band. The Union Jack was flying. The church is architecturally pretentious and can seat 1200 persons. It has a belfry and spire, vestibule, gallery across the front end, groined arches and pulpit carved by hand, organ and choir, Brussels carpet in the aisles, stained glass windows and all the appointments of a first-class sanctuary; and it is wholly the local residents handiwork.
>
> This well-ordered community occupies shingled and clap-board dwelling houses of uniform size, 25 x 50 feet, with enclosed flower gardens and macamdamized side-walks, 10 feet wide, along the entire length of the street.
>
> These people have also a large town hall or assembly

room of the same capacity as the church, used for councils, meetings and for a drill room. It is warmed by three great fires placed in the centre of the building and lighted by side lamps. The people dress very tastefully and I am not sure but that they have the latest fashions. The women weave cloth for garments, and the pretty islets just offshore are virtual floating gardens which afford fruit and vegetables in abundance.

A breathtaking dream-city in the midst of the most boundless, most unrelieved wilderness in the Empire, Metlakatla boasted besides the church and houses, a school, a jail, a dog pound, a fire hall, and in a row of waterfront buildings, a sawmill, a tannery, soap and textile factories, printing presses for a newspaper, and a salmon cannery. Still more improbable than the physical appointments of this shining city were its occupants. On Sundays they could be observed promenading in their fashionable gowns and high-collared shirts along the main street of this village they themselves had built, from a distance resembling some dignified group of Sunday strollers back in London's St. James Square. But a closer look at the broad, dark faces beneath the frilly bonnets and crisp top hats of these unlikely gentlefolk revealed they were each and every one members of the Tsimshian Indian tribes who had occupied the surrounding wilderness since time immemorial, and whose relatives back in Port Simpson were still devoted to the ceremonial eating of human flesh.

The only European in Metlakatla and the inspiration behind this entire "miracle" as it was invariably called, was a diminutive missionary from Yorkshire named William Duncan. A former leather salesman who didn't complete his missionary training and never did become an ordained minister, Duncan was always a charming host to his distinguished visitors and loved to regale them with tales of how his decorous, industrious Metlakatlans used to behave before he arrived in their rambling village near the Hudson's Bay Company fort at Port Simpson to civilize them:

> One day we were called upon to witness a terrible scene. An old chief, in cool blood, ordered a slave to be dragged to the beach, murdered, and thrown into the water.
> Immediately after, I saw crowds of people running out

of houses near to where the corpse was thrown, and forming themselves into groups at a good distance away. This, I learnt, was from fear of what was to follow.

Presently two bands of furious wretches appeared, each headed by a man in a state of nudity. They gave vent to the most unearthly sounds, and the two naked men made themselves look as unearthly as possible, proceeding in a creeping kind of a stoop, and stepping like two proud horses.

For some time they pretended to be seeking the body, and the instant they came where it lay they commenced screaming and rushing around like so many angry wolves. Finally they seized it, dragged it out of the water, and laid it on the beach, where I was told the naked men would commence tearing it to pieces with their teeth. The two bands of men immediately surrounded them, and so hid their horrid work. In a few minutes the crowd broke again into two, when each of the naked cannibals appeared with half of the body in his hands. Separating a few yards, they commenced amid horrid yells, their still more horrid feast. The sight was too terrible to behold. I left the gallery with a depressed heart. My only consolation I found to be in prayer and the blessed promises of God.

Duncan had come among the Tsimshian in 1857, a time when the European population of the region that would become British Columbia comprised some four hundred hardy souls, virtually all men, who found their infant society dwarfed by a robust and aggressive Indian nation numbering over sixty thousand. Ship hijackings and small ambushes were still common on the coast but the threat of more widespread resistance to the white intrusion was kept under control by British gunboats, which patrolled the coast bombarding the Indians' exposed shorefront villages at the slightest hint of trouble. This made for an uneasy peace. The Indians of the coast were forced to acknowledge that whites were superior in military technology, but not in anything else. In spirit they remained unconquered.

In 1857 the Tsimshian were at their zenith. The rich Skeena valley was organized into a vast fur-gathering network controlled by the powerful Port Simpson chiefs. Indian traders from other

CHURCH, METLAHCATLAH.

tribes, such as the Haida, could approach the Fort only after paying tribute to the Tsimshian chiefs, who blocked the way. The Tsimshian rose to previously unimagined heights of wealth and power. Their "cedar metropolis" surrounding the HBC fort was the largest and most opulent Indian village the coast had ever seen. Winter ceremonials were mounted with greater elaborateness and went on longer than ever before. Potlatching—the ceremonial giving away of wealth—reached a peak that scandalised the parsimonious Scotsmen administering the territory for the fur companies.

Wealth and concentrated population put new strains on Tsimshian society and brought new problems. Drunkenness and armed intertribal warfare increased with the growing power and independence of the Tsimshian leaders. So did resentment against the whites. Shortly before Duncan's arrival the Hudson's Bay Company factor, MacNeill, complained that his canoe had on two different occasions been fired upon by Legaic, the supreme chief of all the Tsimshians. The attacks had gone no further, in spite of the crowd cheering Legaic on, and the point had evidently been simply to show defiance, but it was taken as an ill omen. On another occasion shortly after, Legaic shot a Haida trader dead just as he was being admitted into the Hudson's Bay fort. Here again the hostilities went no further, but the Indians' increasingly hostile mood did not sit well with their would-be superiors.

In the winter of 1854, the six-gun paddle sloop HMS *Virago* visited Port Simpson in a show of gunboat diplomacy. Her master, Captain James C. Prevost, found things quiet enough to be able to beach his vessel for repairs needed since accidentally discovering Virago Rock three weeks earlier, and in the course of his stay came up with a typically Victorian idea for getting to the root of Port Simpson's problems. He would have a missionary brought in to capture the native's souls for Christianity and win their hearts for the Great Cause of Empire.

Back in London, Prevost found the Church Missionary Society less than enthusiastic about spending money on the "sheep in the wilderness" of this farflung corner of British North America, but he pressed his cause and finally won permission to take an undergraduate missionary back with him on his return. This was William Duncan.

Duncan was twenty-five. He came from a poor family in Yorkshire and had become an outstanding success in business before joining the mission service in a spur-of-the-moment decision. He had little more notion of where it was he'd volunteered to serve than the Sunday School children who would later read of his exploits. When he tried to buy life insurance, no company would have him. The territory he was bound for didn't even have an agreed-upon name. It was the least populated and most isolated possession in the entire British Empire.

Victoria in 1857 was just a cluster of log shacks surrounded by mud. James Douglas, the territory's ranking official as chief factor of the Hudson's Bay Company, at first refused to allow Duncan to venture further into the coastal wilderness. "It is worth your life to go among those bloodthirsty savages," he is reported to have said, although his own wife was the daughter of a full-blooded Indian from northern BC. He offered Duncan the choice of remaining in Victoria to minister to natives encamped there, but the young man was resolute: either he would be allowed to go to his original destination at Port Simpson, or he would return to England. Like many others to follow, Douglas was forced to submit to the little missionary's iron will, but he ordered him to stay within the confines of the fort once he reached Port Simpson. Duncan obeyed — for a while.

Duncan had been led to believe by Prevost and others that the Tsimshian would be to some degree open to his teaching. Perhaps they would have been if, like later missionaries, he had been willing to respect native traditions, working slowly through the mediums of education and medical aid to build trust between the cultures. But Duncan was never one to make things easy for himself, or anyone else.

According to the anthropologist Wilson Duff, "Duncan was the personification of the missionaries of the time; he had immense faith and courage, and the gigantic audacity required to move uninvited into a large community of foreign and hostile people and single handedly assume absolute control and reshape their lives." Duncan would have nothing but total capitulation from the Tsimshian. He was as anxious to get their bare feet into English shoes as he was to get their souls into Anglican heaven, and spent much time in those early months trying to train them (unsuccessfully) in the wearing of "the Yorkshire clog." When he discovered native women pressing oil out of the carcasses of putrid oolachon fish by leaning on them with their bare breasts (tradition forbade the use of hands), he wouldn't rest until he had devised a mechanical press. It went against his mercantile nature to give away free schooling without getting immediate converts in return, but grudgingly, he did it. He held out the promise of teaching the Tsimshian all the advantages of modern European society, and tirelessly drilled himself in the Tsimshian language to facilitate this work, but he denounced traditional native culture in every detail and insisted all who joined his mission sign a petition agreeing:

> To cease calling in conjurers when sick
> To cease giving away property for display
> To attend religious instruction
> To send their children to the mission school
> To give up Indian deviltry.

The proud and aggressive Tsimshian chiefs were less willing to bow down before this diminutive loner than they had before the traders or the commanders of warships. The traders commanded great wealth and the warships had terrifying destructive power, but the white preacher appeared to them a sort of bogus medicine man without medicine. Like all coast tribes the Tsimshian respected above all else the power to conjure spirits, and understood it as the ability to induce illness in enemies. Virtually all illness was understood by them as spiritual disorder. Duncan came to understand this, and it made him cautious in dispensing medical assistance, lest a failed effort bring charges against him of practising "bad medicine," or conjuring evil spirits.

And yet while Duncan seemed to have less power than any of the authorities with whom the Indians dealt, he made the most extreme demands upon them: that they accept as wrong the only way of life they had ever known and throw it off in favour of the one Duncan prescribed. Understandably, he became the focus of all their pent-up hostility toward the white race.

Duncan did succeed in winning some converts, mostly among social outcasts who had nothing to lose by adopting a new way of life, and established a school to which many of the local children came. In June 1859, an old chief named Neyastodoh said many of his people were willing to turn their children over to him to bring up in the new ways, but urged the missionary to take them to a peaceful place away from the fort. The obvious place was the winter home they had all shared before moving to the fort — Metlakatla.

Violence in Port Simpson reached new levels in the fall of 1859. A man named Cushwaht had threatened to kill Duncan after being bitten by the school dog, and attacked the schoolhouse with an axe, breaking all the windows. When another young man irritated a chief at a drinking party, the chief shot the young man's brother. A round of shooting flared around the school, and two more were killed. The shootings continued at Cushwaht's house, killing two women.

Duncan was forced to consider more seriously the old chief's suggestion he move his flock to the safety of Metlakatla, fifteen miles away, but his efforts at conversion had still made little progress in mainstream Tsimshian society, and his pride wouldn't let him give up. Duncan was having constant confrontations with Indian leaders. It came to a head one day when Legaic, the chief of all the chiefs, requested that Duncan allow a school holiday during an important ceremonial to mark his daughter's coming to womanhood. Duncan refused. The chief's tearful wife then pleaded that Duncan allow just one hour's recess, but he again refused.

Then she begged him at least not to ring the school bell, since that would break the spell of the ceremonies.

"No, I cannot do that," Duncan replied. "If I did not ring the bell, the scholars would think there was no school."

"Well, could you ring it softly, not so hard?" the woman begged.

"No," said Duncan, "if I ring it at all I shall have to ring it so it can be heard." The wife of the chief left weeping, and according to Duncan's biographer John Arctander, "He was inclined to think it was ringing a little louder that day, if anything. And no one who knows Mr. Duncan will doubt that for a minute."

Shortly after, Legaic burst into the schoolhouse with a knife, shouting that he had killed men before and now Duncan was going to pay for his interference. A group of followers cheered him on. The hot-headed Cushwaht yelled, "Kill him! Cut off his head! I'll kick it along the beach!" Legaic was one of the most wealthy and powerful men on the west coast, a man who kept a vast fur-gathering empire and the Hudson's Bay Company under his control by the sheer force of his personality, but in William Duncan he met his match. The Tsimshian people, as Duncan later explained to Arctander, placed great emphasis on self-control. They felt free to kill an enemy who cowered, but not one who showed no fear, because his "soul was on top." Duncan had a will of steel. He never flinched in his confrontations, and didn't now. Calmly, he said, "Legaic, you are a bad man." Legaic backed down, and after "blowing off steam," left the schoolhouse. Soon he returned, half-coherently trying to persuade Duncan he was not a bad man by showing him letters of reference which had been given to him by various traders.

Legaic never regained his former cockiness, and his position among the Tsimshian tribes diminished.

The winter of 1861 was a bleak one for Duncan. The camp was full of violence, and his work had come to a dead end. Winter ceremonials were more prevalent than at any time since his arrival. His arch-enemies, the medicine men, were redoubling their efforts against his mission. He had a resurgence of lung congestion, possibly tubercular, and began coughing blood. At the same time Loocoal, one of the medicine men, made a kind of voodoo using one of Duncan's castoff collars, and a conviction spread through town that Duncan was dying under Loocoal's spell. He half believed it himself. "I live among the dying and I am dying," he wrote in his journal.

At this point only a miracle could have carried Duncan to victory over the forces arrayed against him, and the way he later reported it, just such a miracle occurred. Within weeks he was able to report that once proud Port Simpson families were coming to him in canoe loads, begging to be baptized. Instead of setting up his peaceful village with a few dozen converts, he would boast hundreds.

The event that transformed Duncan's fortunes was one of the worst disasters in BC history: the smallpox epidemic of 1862.

It started in Victoria in March when an American miner disembarked from a San Francisco ship with an advanced case of the disease. Duncan was still stalling his move to Metlakatla, but a dugout from Victoria brought news of the outbreak to Port Simpson on May 17, and he threw his moving plans into high gear. He also took care of other business. "It was evidently my duty to see and warn the Indians. I therefore spent the next few days in assembling and addressing each tribe."

By his own admission he neglected to tell them smallpox was an infectious disease passed from one person to the other by close

contact. He knew the effectiveness of quarantine, because a short time later he enforced it strictly at Metlakatla. But he did not go from house to house informing the Tsimshian they could escape the coming disease by taking refuge in their remote summer villages, as the Tlingit had done in the epidemic of 1832. What Duncan did instead was to urge all villagers one last time to give up Indian ways and "quickly surrender themselves to God." He left them with a warning God's punishment was nigh. In the ensuing weeks Port Simpson was decimated by smallpox, which, according to their understanding of the world, they thought to be caused by hostile spiritual power. The most obvious source of such power would have seemed to be Duncan. Duncan encouraged this belief by speaking of the plague only as a direct act of God—his God, not theirs.

"Your excellency is aware of the dreadful plague of smallpox with which it pleased the Almighty God to visit the Indian of this coast last year," he wrote to Governor James Douglas the following year, "While I am sorry indeed to inform your Excellency that 500 have fallen at Fort Simpson, I have gratefully to acknowledge God's sparing mercy to us as a village. We had only five fatal cases." Duncan fails to acknowledge another force at work—science, in the form of smallpox vaccinations, which he gave to his followers but not to those who rejected Christianity. A passage from Duncan's plague year journal reveals the degree to which Duncan caused the epidemic to be seen as a test pitting his system of belief against the medicine men's: "One of the tribes which had adopted heathenism to the full, went for a long time unscathed, and this filled their conjurers with pride and boasting words, and caused much perplexity in the minds of those who had partly shaken off heathen superstition; but in the end this tribe suffered more than any other, and their refuge was proven to be the refuge of lies."

Duncan had pitted his God against theirs at the outset of the scourge, saying all who didn't follow him immediately would be struck down. According to their own system of belief, the Tsimshian had no choice but to grant total, devastating victory to the spiritual powers in Duncan's command, over those in the medicine men's command. One of the first families to come begging to be baptised at Metlakatla was that of Legaic. "We have fallen down and have no breath to answer you," the crestfallen chiefs told Duncan. "Do your will." The wonder is that even after this awesome demonstration of spiritual thunder, some Tsimshians still didn't submit. A hard core of Duncan-haters remained in Port Simpson, defiant in the face of mass death.

With an army of Tsimshian workers now under his command, Duncan's dream city rose quickly out of the peaceful earth at his new location. They were, after all, a society of skilled woodworkers, and caught on quickly to the new style of building that Duncan and an occasional itinerant carpenter showed them. Their new lives filled them with fervour, and after the factories were successfully established, they acquired a ship of their own and went into competition with the trading schooners. Duncan's mercantile impulses incited him to develop the village supply centre into a trading post, and he built up such a robust fur trade, he ran his old friends at the Hudson's Bay Company off the north coast. When his competition fought back by using rum as a trade item, he sought and received a magistrate's commission and clapped them in jail. By the 1870s Duncan personally dominated the business life and the spiritual life, as well as arbitrating law, for the entire northern coast of British Columbia. His work made him renowned around the globe, and the Metlakatla treasury swelled with the profits of Legaic's old fur trading empire.

Duncan had to control everything. Israel Wood Powell, the Indian Commissioner of the the new Canadian government, duly praised Duncan's achievements when he visited in 1879, but noted with some misgiving, "his individuality seems to me to pervade everything connected with the town." It was an irony that while Duncan had done more than anyone to demonstrate the genius of the Tsimshian people, in his own mind he was convinced they were no more than children, and never would be able to assume responsible control of their lives. Accordingly, he retained absolute control of the community, even raising the young women in his own home.

The Church Missionary Society periodically sent out other missionaries to give Duncan assistance, but none could survive Duncan's strict regime, and each left before long. As the years passed, the Anglican Church itself underwent change, and by the late seventies a new "High Church" leadership inspired by the Oxford Movement began stressing a more purely spiritual role for Anglican missionaries, discarding the "Low Church" approach of evangelicals like Duncan, with their emphasis on secular activities. This change put Duncan at odds with his church superiors, who ordered him to become ordained, reduce his business activities and spend more effort on religious ritual. But Duncan was a confirmed low churchman as well as being gigantically stubborn, and the two sides were soon involved in all-out war.

The church appointed a bishop, William Ridley, to take charge at Metlakatla, and soon the model village was a polarized camp. Neither man was willing to recognize the authority of the other. Ridley claimed dominion over the church buildings, and Duncan the store, cannery, sawmill and civic buildings. Duncan had Ridley supporters clapped in jail. Ridley had himself appointed magistrate and attempted to arrest Duncan supporters. Every tiny aspect of community life became the source of dispute. The most famous altercation, which became so serious a warship was finally called in to restore order, started in a squabble over a toy drum.

When the government stepped in on the side of the church and ordered Duncan evicted from federal lands, he went to court to prove the land was really owned by the Indians, not the government — the first statement of native land claims heard in a Canadian court. Duncan lost his case.

Rejected by his church and dispossessed by law, almost anyone else in Duncan's position would have given up, but his next move proved him one of the most singlemindedly determined men ever to set foot on Canadian soil. Through friends in the US he won permission from the American government to settle his followers on Annette Island, just across the Alaska border some eighty miles from Metlakatla. On August 7, 1887 Duncan and 821 of Metlakatla's 940 citizens migrated from Canada, landing on a remote and uncleared beach to start a new life in a new country.

Cold and hunger plagued the fledgling community as the homesick Tsimshians shivered in makeshift bark huts the first winter, but soon a sawmill was established, then the first houses and public buildings, and within a year the miracle that was Metlakatla, BC began to recreate itself at New Metlakatla, Alaska. A handsome church was erected, and by 1890 a cannery was operating at the new townsite. Eventually the second Metlakatla outshone the original, which ran downhill rapidly after the exodus of Duncan's followers. A fire completed its slide into oblivion in 1901.

Despite the ease with which the physical setting of the model village was recreated, Duncan and his group were never completely happy in Alaska. Part of the reason was that the Tsimshian never felt entirely at home across the border in the land of their old enemies, the Tlingit, and partly it was because, away from their old familiar hunting, fishing, and trapping grounds, they found the living harder. But the biggest problem was living under the iron hand of the aging Duncan, who instead of relinquishing his control over daily affairs of the colony as his charges became more adept, became ever more authoritarian. Although the Tsimshian workers were compelled to stay in the community working for lower pay than they could have earned in surrounding canneries and sawmills, Duncan refused to make them partners in the all-encompassing Metlakatla Commercial Company, which remained substantially his own private property. He also refused to give an open accounting of the community business's financial affairs, or make any firm commitment as to the final disposition of the considerable wealth their joint activities had accumulated. He stolidly refused to make loans or in any way subsidize local enterprises, even for the most deserving projects, claiming that such assistance would discourage native self-sufficiency.

Duncan's attitude created resentment in many followers, and through the 1890s and early 1900s he was faced with numerous petitions and revolts among his own people. One of most revealing struggles was the one with Edward Marsden, son of his first true convert and longtime Man Friday, Samuel Marsden. The young Marsden, although a promising student, was urged by Duncan to remain in his service at New Metlakatla instead of going to university in the US. The younger man respectfully declined to follow this strange advice. After enrolling in law and religious studies at Lane Theological Seminary in Cincinnati in 1895, Marsden wrote Duncan asking for a loan of $50 to buy textbooks. "You do know me very well," he concluded, "and if anyone will be faithful to you in your closing years, it is the writer, who has always respected you and praised your name and good work." Duncan refused the money, writing, "I can see no use in your studying abstruse theological questions which may only, after all, unhinge your mind and impede your usefulness...I think any well-educated man should be able to read up as much law as he would require in a community like ours."

At this point Duncan converted a devoted supporter and heir-apparent into a nemesis. "I have been very faithful to you in spite of your seeming distrust of me and my work," Marsden shot back. "But now, since my patience can no longer hold out, I think it is wise for me to say something about it. If I indulge in the idea that learning and the spread of knowledge among the Indian race are the means by which [we] can be lifted up...I am not mistaken." He speculated Duncan's opposition to his law studies stemmed from "fear of being compelled to respect true justice in

your relation as an employer with my people." After being ordained as a Presbyterian minister, Marsden returned to Alaska, but not to Metlakatla. Instead, he settled at nearby Saxman where he ran a kind of "administration-in-exile" to Duncan, supporting the growing resistance to the old missionary's despotic methods both among Indian and white. On August 5, 1915, the US government intervened in the growing controversy and seized all property owned in Metlakatla by Duncan's company, leaving him nothing. Duncan, isolated and practically friendless, died in 1918, rueing the day he left British Columbia.

Of all the pioneer missionaries, none achieved the fame and influence of Duncan, and none have suffered such loss of reputation. Once a household word, his name is now known only to history specialists, who view him askance. Part of the reason is the equivocal nature of his influence. In the words of the anthropologist Philip Drucker, "He left a deeper mark than any single person on North Pacific Coast Indian history." But was this great influence for good or evil, in that mostly sad history? On the plus side is the modern Alaskan town of New Metlakatla, one of the most prosperous, attractive and pious aboriginal communities in the world. On the minus side is his complete insensitivity to Tsimshian cultural values and the ruthlessness with which he forced his own bleak Victorian materialism upon them. His defenders point to the trim lawns, fresh-painted homes and flush bank accounts of New Metlakatla and say the end justifies the means, adding it's too bad all the Indians of the coast didn't have a Victorian despot in their past to engrave the Protestant work ethic on their souls. His detractors counter that there is enough of the Protestant work ethic in today's world, and not enough of the unique northwest coast native culture Duncan more than any other one person helped to stamp out. It's a question of values, but whichever set you believe there's no denying that William Duncan, the little Yorkshire orphan who stared down the most powerful Indian chiefs in the northwest, possessed one of the most potent spirits ever to flourish on the BC coast, in native times or white.

THE HANDKERCHIEF ANGLE

I've sat down with some pretty fancy people now,
not royalty maybe but millionaires for sure
famous-in-Canada writers, members of parliament,
some regular staff members of the *New Yorker*,
the president of a major regional airline,
a well-remembered former NHL regular,
not quite the international jet set
but plenty enough to make the cookhouse gang
back in Greene's Bay feel smug about
predicting a great future for me
when I was five
but for all I seem to be able to get by
at these Manhattan cocktail parties
I can't escape those cookhouse years
everybody must see it and I ponder
just what it is makes me so different.
Today I think it might be handkerchiefs.
I don't use handkerchiefs. I have tried
but I don't have the habit
and it just seems too late in life to get it.
On the other hand I notice
almost everyone else I meet does, even
the revolutionary poet who refuses to use capitals
the oiler on the *Queen of Coquitlam*

and the hitchhiking skidrow bum.
I trace my history back, searching
for the reason. How did I miss out?
Back in camp the men all blew their nose
by pinching one side closed
and giving 'er shit on the other side.
It works better than it sounds.
I can see them thoughtfully digging out
hard stuff with a black-nailed pinky
as they took instructions from the super.
When they got what they were after
they'd roll it into a little ball
and tweak it over their shoulder.
Inside if there wasn't a snoose can handy
it would get wiped on a thigh but only
in the politest company would you see it
dropped into a shirt pocket.
This was my finishing school
and all considering I've survived it well
except for that one time at the Media Club
banquet in the Quarry House
where I forgot myself and pulled out a real
nugget while we were all sitting there waiting
to see if I beat out the editor of *Vancouver Life*
for first in the Prose Feature category
and went to tweak it under the table
but somehow it ended up on the mayor's glasses...

MINSTREL

By 1974 the raincoast thing was already starting to wear thin. We'd put out four issues of the magazine that was supposed to rescue the coast from oblivion and I wasn't sure whether it was doing that or pulling me into oblivion with it.

It had gone over well. The first issue had sold three thousand copies, the second five thousand and the third ten thousand. We had no trouble finding more stories about failed homesteads on northern islands where wild cattle still roamed the beaches eating seaweed, scientific hermits up remote inlets who ground their own high-powered telescopes but still couldn't find anything to look at except the trees across the water, haunted hydroelectric dams nobody remembers building, etc. But the more I insisted this was all special and unique the more I wondered if it really was.

I had grown up in the last days of the old coast when every bay had a gyppo booming logs and life followed the cycle of the weekly steamer call, but it had never seemed special to me then. It had seemed a half-existence outside the real march of the twentieth century, a backwater my whole growing-up was aimed at escaping. It wasn't until I did escape, and spent a harrowing decade in the city discovering what a half-existence really was, that the coast began to take on this golden glow, a place of legend. But after two years devoted to extolling that quality without actually seeing proof, I was beginning to grow weary of the sound of my own voice trying to convince myself. I hated myself every time I used the word "legend."

Mary, my partner in this quest for the holy grail of regional character, had never believed it in the first place and suffered less from doubt. She had been captivated by the sheer novelty of publishing a magazine, but that was wearing down, too. The spaces between issues were getting bigger.

Joe Simson, the ultimate history fan. PHOTO COURTESY JOHN SIMSON.

I don't suppose I confided any of this doubt to Joe Simson, because we didn't talk about things like that. Joe was a history buff. His "pappy," as he said, had been postmaster of the village of Granville and one of the founders of the Vancouver business community, and in his declining years Joe had devoted himself to remembering his beginnings. When our first issue appeared he had sent us a letter containing several corrections penciled in large printing on lined paper torn from a scribbler, and a cheque for a hundred dollars. As we kept on, the notes kept on, along with the cheques. One day he drove into our yard in his jeep, a lean, handsome man of seventy-four with curly white hair and glasses that made his eyes appear monstrous.

"You're not getting out enough," he told us gruffly, looking around at our cramped pink house trailer with its black soot-stains.

"You better take my boat and get out and see some of this stuff you're writing about or it'll all turn into empty words."

I am sure if it had been put to us any other way by anyone else, we would have said we were too busy working on issue four. But we had come to think of Joe as our patron saint, and he was serious about this. Besides, Joe's boat was gorgeous.

The *Beaver* V was a thirty-foot double-ender powered by a 10-14

The Easthope-powered Beaver V. PHOTO COURTESY JOHN SIMSON

Easthope. It had been built in 1948 and Joe bought it from a fisherman in Secret Cove, moving the motor back into the fish hold to make more room inside. He kept it as a kind of floating museum exhibit, lavishing it with hired care. It was a classic one-man troller, one of the last around, and certainly the best preserved, with one of the very last operating Easthope motors. Everything was heavy-duty, newly painted and in perfect working order. It was the perfect vessel in which to go searching for the lost soul of the coast.

We declared a two-week research period and loaded our stuff aboard. In those days getting ready for a two-week excursion took us about three-quarters of an hour. I took the *Beaver* V around to the government wharf in Madeira, hoping some of the oldtime wharf rats would be there. They were our worst critics. They were outraged at my presumption, as a mere second-generation Pender Harbourite, trying to pass myself off as some sort of expert on their coast. They looked upon the magazine as a particularly obnoxious way of bilking money out of the government. But I knew the sound of the old Easthope, the beating pulse of the pre-war fishing fleet, would cut through and tug at their heartstrings.

There was only one at the dock, an old cod fisherman named Elmer Pottle, slouching in his wheelhouse doorway. I saw his head craning toward the sound of the Easthope, but he looked back down when he saw me. He didn't come over to catch my rope and ignored the trouble I had landing, but slid over later. "Can't resist," I chortled to myself.

"Two-banger, eh?" he said in a tolerably friendly way. "Easthope or Palmer?"

"Easthope. A 10-14."

"Oh, a 10-14, is it," he said with a slight sneer that told me real oldtimers never referred to them that way. He cocked his head listening to the whoof-chuff, whoof-chuff of the idling motor.

"Well I wouldn't go too far without lookin' at them valves if I was you."

With that he shuffled back to his doorway. It occurred to me that it was only to deliver that gloomy prognosis that he had bothered to rouse himself. I had no idea whether he could tell the valves were bad from the sound it made. There was no place you could take an Easthope anymore in Pender Harbour. The only bona fide Easthope expert still around was Gordie Goble, the ex-Easthope employee who ran a tiny machine shop on the site of the long-abandoned Easthope engine foundry in Coal Harbour, ministering to the dwindling population of Easthopes in the hands of oldtimers and collectors. I could phone him long distance, but Joe told me he'd been getting him up to go over the indestructible old motor every spring for years, and I had to assume everything was in perfect shape. I decided Elmer didn't know what he was talking about, and only wanted to tarnish my triumph. The reason the motor idled rough and stopped when I put it in reverse was no doubt just cobwebs. Joe hardly used it and it needed to be run-in for awhile. I cast a knowing grin in his direction as we pulled out. Small and mean, I thought. That's the Pottles all over.

It was 6 PM when we left and the *Beaver* only made seven knots

so we knew we couldn't get far, but we wanted to have our trip
begin. We suddenly couldn't bear to stay in the harbour another
night. We decided to tie up at my old stomping ground, Greene's
Bay. The main bay where my father's camp had been was seamless
forest down to the water, and you could barely even find where
our old log dump had been blasted into the sidehill. The only
obvious sign human foot had ever been set there before that
moment was the burnt-out hulk of Clarence Cook's west coast
troller, the *Morien II*, which had come to rest on the beach below
the falls in the years since we left. I shut off the engine and tried
to commune, but the place did nothing for me. I wondered if it
was me, the place, or the time of day. Maybe if we took our clothes
off and jumped in the water, or stayed until morning. Morning
was always best for feeling a place. But I didn't want to hang
around down here where I'd been before. I wanted to plunge
northward, to some of these places I'd heard of all my life but
never seen: Von Donop's Inlet, the Yacultas, Hole-in-the Wall,
Blind Channel, Loughborough Inlet, Forward Harbour, Topaz
Harbour, Knight Inlet. New and strange places were the surest
way to strip away the numb crust and bare the feeling stuff.

We had no actual plans. Joe had said, stop in and see Olaf
Hansen in Port Neville, why don't you? and that had established
an unconscious goal in my mind, but I wasn't getting too set on
it. In the geography of the world that existed inside my mind, Port
Neville was a long way away. It was "up north." Among the people
I worked with currently, more had been to Paris than to Port
Neville. But Joe seemed to think it was in our range. I had
mentioned Minstrel Island, and he didn't even seem to think that
was out of the question.

Since becoming a half-assed historian of the coast, Minstrel
Island had loomed ever larger in my mind. From the turn of the
century on it seemed to serve as a nerve-centre of the logger's
universe, the Dodge City of their wild west. For me it would be
like finally making it all the way to Mecca, but I would be satisfied
with less, if only I could recapture some of that shivery old feeling
about the mystery and wonder of the coast to recharge my mythic
batteries.

I couldn't even remember for sure where I'd first experienced
the feeling. Once my Dad had taken me somewhere up around
the Yaculta Rapids on the *Hi-Tide*, a little steel tug owned by

Gordie Cochrane, a friend of his. It might have been then. Another time I'd hitched a ride to Port Hardy with John Daly, a Pender Harbour fisherman. But that had been a pretty fast blast through, and John talked so relentlessly about the capitalist pig Yankees ruining Southeast Asia and the importance of eating bran and skiing Hollyburn in the early days and how drinking during pregnancy had begotten a generation of imbeciles and big corporations grabbing all the profits that it was hard for the coast to get through.

I was losing sight of when it was I'd received these spiritual messages, and I sometimes wondered if I had dreamed the whole thing up. But it had been firing my dreams ever since, a spark glowing inside my brain like a chip of plutonium. And when I fumbled to tell of it, people like Joe, and all the ten thousand readers of the magazine, lit up with recognition. Going out to look for tangible evidence seemed worth a try.

Puff-puffing our way toward the top end of Big Redonda, I veered in toward Redonda Bay. I had high hopes of finding something there that might stir a feeling or two. In the twenties Redonda Bay, then called Deceit Bay, had been big doin's, with a railroad camp, a shingle mill, a cannery, and a store that supplied a galaxy of little camps up Toba, Bute and Ramsay Arm. Jim Spilsbury, the Savary Island pioneer who travelled these waters over and over from the early twenties on, first as a radio repairman, then as owner of Queen Charlotte Airlines, told me Deceit Bay was a hive of activity going night and day when he and his pal Jimmy Anderson took a load of shinglebolts there in 1922. Fish packers unloaded under floodlights at the cannery and the shingle mill ran three shifts. Deceit Bay was full of wonders in those days. The logs were brought down the steep slope to the saltchuck by means of a funicular railroad, and the bay was dominated by a big paddlewheeler which was pulled up on shore between the various buildings. This was the SS *Transfer*, a 122-foot paddlewheel steamer originally built in 1893 for Captain Irving, who had it in service on the lower Fraser River for a good many years. In its final resting place its staterooms housed an army of Chinese workers while its boiler supplied steam to drive the mill and cannery. Electric lights blazed all through the night, a rare thing on the coast of those days.

In 1922 the Union Steamers called regularly at Deceit Bay and work boats from nearby logging camps thronged about the wharf to patronize the well-stocked store. When Spilsbury called in his radio boat ten years later the story was different. Competition had forced the cannery closed nine years since, falling prices closed the big railway logging camp, and fire got the mill. The cannery still stood, water running continually through its many wooden vats to keep them from drying out. The electric light fixtures were still in place, but never lit. The lonely storekeeper, Sid Vicary, used a kerosene lantern. Vicary felt at that time the cannery machinery was too obsolete to be run again, but in fact the canning operation was restarted and run a short time in the forties by the legendary canner Francis Millerd.

Legendary. There I am saying it again. Does Millerd deserve the title? He wasn't legendary like Billy the Kid, like D'sonoqua. But I want to call him that because on the coast, a lot of people spoke of him over a long period. He pulled a lot of stunts. His name lived on in people's talk.

I had built up quite a romantic idea of Deceit/Redonda Bay in my mind, and was very keen to stop the night to look for traces of past glory, but my hopes were soon dispelled. Rounding the point we were confronted by a large sign ordering us to turn back. Redonda Bay was now the site of a wilderness prison camp and strictly off limits to the law-abiding. But even from a distance I could see there was no trace of the old town remaining, only a white quadrangle of portable bunkhouses.

We stopped for the night a few miles further on at Church-house, the Indian village with the tall white Catholic church outstanding in the forest gloom and all the multi-hued houses. As of 1987, Churchouse was the coast's newest ghost town, the population having moved more or less en masse to Campbell River. In 1974 it was not known as a place especially friendly to outsiders, but there was a government dock there, and it was already crowded with yachts. We found room with the little local boats on the inside, which was less bouncy anyway. Churchouse is pretty exposed. The next morning we got up at seven, fuelled up at Stuart Island and blasted through the Yukes while they were dead slack at nine.

Cordero Channel leads the small boater north from the Yaculta rapids. On this day the water was very blue. On the near side, toward a row of bluffs I recognized from dreams, it got greener, then black. I wondered why they made such an impression. They weren't the highest I'd seen. But maybe the bluffest. They hung over the channel just north of Shoal Bay, dusted lime green and peach, and scarlet from lichen. I swung over so close you could reach out and touch the rock wall and catch hold of outleaning bushes. Mary was alarmed to be running at full speed so close to shore, and I laughed at her worry.

The Fraser River paddlewheeler SS Transfer *provided both steam and accommodation to the community of Deceit Bay (now Redonda Bay).* JIM SPILSBURY PHOTO.

Signs of abandoned logging caught my eye on both sides of the channel. On the far side where last time through I had seen an old ruined camp with its grey cookhouse collapsed at one end, still standing at the other, there was now a new camp with white mobiles and fresh brown logs. The steep sidehills were etched with the wavery lines of old cat roads, angling steeply toward the beach. I thought of the trip I'd taken around Nelson Island with my dad the year previous, looking up at wavery lines like these. Dad had said, "It hurts me to look at roads like that, clawed into the rock with little old cats, every half mile another one that some poor bloody fool put the best years of his life into."

His sympathy was stronger for having spent the best years of his life doing just that himself.

My ear was troubled again by the noise of the motor. Since our first run up Agamemnon Channel I had been being bothered by the sensation that the motor occasionally lost revs, the spaces between the POFF POFF POFF's becoming every so minutely longer.

Looking up Phillips Arm from Shoal Bay, 1940s. JIM SPILSBURY PHOTO.

Whenever I concentrated on it, I found I couldn't tell for sure whether it was really happening or I was imagining it. Then I would ask Mary if she noticed anything and she would say yeah, I think I did, but then she would cock her head to study it for a moment and say, "Oh, I don't know. Maybe not." But one time off Grief Point we kept debating it until the motor actually stopped. After a few moments it started up again and ran as normal, and it hadn't happened since, so I tried to put it out of my mind. It wasn't easy to do, and every time it seemed to slow, I would be seized with insecurity again. But I kept telling myself this was the motor that built the BC coast, maintained by a guy who assisted in its manufacture; nothing could be more deserving of unencumbered trust.

As we passed north of the rapids we began to notice a change in the type of boats we encountered. Closer to the populated centres they had been predominantly smaller pleasure craft, mostly Canadian, but now they were mostly American and large They would swerve off their courses and come close as they passed, admiring our authenticity as their wash made like to swamp us. We glowered and refused to return their friendly waves until the burden of so much disapproval began to weigh us down. We began waving back, but listlessly.

Coming up to Loughborough Inlet, I pointed out the Last Arbutus Tree to Mare. It hangs out over the water near the beach, and the oldtimers all swear it's the last one you see as you go north, although this has never been proven by accredited research. Until you go past that spot you never realize arbutus trees do end, that they're a fetish of south coast homebodies only.

We spent half an hour debating on whether we should turn up Loughborough to see the ruins of Roy. I was intrigued by Roy, although I knew practically nothing about it. The reason was, I'd seen a picture in the *Glory Days of Logging* of a toothless bush ape standing by a log dump, which the caption identified as Stewart Holbrook, at Roy. Holbrook was the author of *Holy Old Mackinaw*, a book which had attained the status of a sacred text among those of us who looked for redemption in coastal history, second only to Grainger's *Woodsmen of the West*. My whole desire to see Roy was based on that fifty-year old photo, which is why I distrusted it. Holbrook probably only spent a month there, and left no traces that could have been identified five days after, let alone fifty years. If it was like most old photos in books, it was probably mis-identified to begin with. Holbrook was probably standing beside a log dump at Royston. But I'd nurtured a desire to see Roy for years, and being within half an hour of the place, it seemed foolish to deny it. Finally we swerved up the inlet.

Roy began as a camp, grew to a steamer stop, and continued as the "capital of Loughborough Inlet" with its own post office into the forties after the logging finished. A man named George Byers found a use for the thousands of acres of fire weed growing on the slash of the ruined forest by putting in eighty hives of bees. In 1936 when Jim Spilsbury began stopping in his radio service boat the *Five BR*, Byers was still there running the post office, along with a colourful-sounding bunch of neighbours: Baldy Martell, Colonel Rolston, Guy Fox and Harry Blue. I don't know that this Guy Fox was connected to the one who tried to blow all the politicians off the planet but if he was, I'm sure he would have been very well received on the upper BC coast. Baldy Martell was still living somewhere up the inlet in 1974 and sent scrawly letters to *Raincoast Chronicles* expressing his appreciation of what we were doing and hinting we could do worse than devote some space to him. There was no sign of him around Roy when we got there. There was no sign of anything but a few rotting piles off the low, overgrown shore. We turned back to Chancellor Channel.

We had managed the Yaculta and Greene Point rapids without any trouble, but now we were coming up to rapids I didn't know anything about. They had a particularly hairy name: Whirlpool Rapids. We didn't have a tidebook for the northern waters and I had lost track of what the tide was doing. I didn't know if we would be stumbling into it full blast or dead slack. I found myself regarding these rapids as the most fearsome of all, partly because of their name and partly because they were farther north where everything was more mysterious and scary. I fretted about going through or bypassing them around the back side of Hardwicke Island.

It's not a good coast to not know where you're going. Every few miles another course opens, seeming to offer about the same attractions, and weighing the options every time can give you a nervous breakdown.

I watched a boat ahead of us that looked like a converted forestry launch. We'll go where it goes, I thought. It turned down Chancellor to go around Hardwicke. I didn't follow. Unreasonably, I decided to try the rapids anyway. The current would be coming against us, I rationalized, so we wouldn't be sucked into the whirlpools, we could always back out. The choice was not made on behalf of my nerves, but just making it unburdened me some.

The Chief, a mountain behind the Yacultas that looks like the profile of an Indian chief with headdress looking up at the sky, finally disappeared from sight after appearing, disappearing and reappearing most of the day. I felt abandoned in our moment of need. Half a mile downstream of the narrows the water was still quiet. On the right the shore rose into a steep burnt-off sidehill of bright reddish hue, almost a bluff, with all the trees gone to white sticks. It looked like stubble on a red-faced wino, and nearer shore where they had logged, rows and rows of bleached white stumps like tombstones. Coming into the narrows, there were still only a few feeble upwellings. There wasn't as much turbulence as there'd been in the Yaculta. Somehow we had hit it at dead slack. Later, John Skapski told me it didn't matter much anyway. He ran his thirty-eight-foot gillnetter through on any tide, without bothering to check. On the biggest tides it could get a little messy no doubt, but the scary name was a bit of a fraud.

Forward Harbour opened on the right, the mountain at the entrance a perfect greentreed cone. Next to it and wider, Jackson Bay. According to Spilsbury, both were peppered with settlers in the thirties, but now the fuzzy second growth lay a solid carpet of green. On the left, the shore of Wellbore Channel continued as it had been through the rapids—little knobby points joined by low necks covered with a frizzy growth of alder and maple, and pebbly beaches. Rounding the point into Sunderland Channel, we were surprised to discover big turquoise whitecaps marching down, row on row, before a brisk summer westerly. The seas didn't worry me terribly, because the sky was clear and the sun brilliant and it just didn't seem a time to worry about weather. A Pender Harbour boat, the *Dan Cameron*, passed and turned into the calm of Wellbore Channel, making us feel we were not entirely alone on the face of the earth.

Working our way up Sunderland into the main stream of Johnstone Strait, we found the seas increasing. If the *Beaver* V hadn't been so good in head seas I might have started to worry, and thought of heading back to Forward Harbour, or Topaz Harbour, where the Dougan Brothers camp would provide a friendly tie-up. But the *Beaver* was showing she was made for it and threw herself across each succeeding swell with a will, so I kept her heading into it.

It was the wrong thing to do. We didn't know it because we hadn't turned on the radio for two days, but there was a gale warning out. The *Dan Cameron* was the last boat we would see for hours. Everybody else on the coast was tied up waiting for it to blow through. By the time we were looking up the broad freeway of Johnstone Strait, the swells were as wide across their backs as the boat was long, and things were starting to crash around with the force that breaks. The water was black with wind, and standing at the wheel back of the wheelhouse the spray was whipping me in the face until I had given up feeling salty and rugged and started to admit to myself it was stinging about as bad as I could stand. But there was nowhere to get out of it on the *Beaver*.

There was a large bay on our right, Blenkinsop Bay, but on the chart it looked shallow and treacherous, seeming to me to offer doubtful shelter in a blow this big. Still I might have tried it if we hadn't been so close to Port Neville, only two or three miles further on. Nothing really bad had happened yet, I told myself.

The skiff was practically jumping out of the water and the shock on the tow rope had begun pulling the smaller boat's front deck loose from its hull. Each surge sprung a few more nails along the gunwale. In another minute it would be gone, and our margin of safety with it. I didn't want to take my hands off the wheel, but this was desperate. I called to Mare, who was below clutching the table with both hands, saying nothing. Reluctantly she took the wheel and held us into the wind while I hauled the skiff close, lept over the surging water between the two boats and tied the *Beaver*'s inch-thick stern rope securely around the skiff's front seat. My weight in the bow of the little boat caused it to dig in and lunge wildly from side to side like a lassoed calf. I hauled on the rope with all my might to get close to the big boat, but holding strain on the rope, I couldn't get free to jump across the gap. I knew then I had made an incredibly stupid mistake in leaving the big boat. One moment I was five feet above the big boat, the next five feet below. It made me dizzy. If I fell over, Mary would never be able to get back to me. I had never thought to tell her how to go in reverse, or even slow down. Now she couldn't hear me above the roar of the gale, and in any case was more than occupied with holding the course against the thundering seas. As strength began to drain out of my arms, I became aware of being very close to tragedy. I imagined her circling in gathering dusk, mountainous seas battering the boat, screaming with despair and fear . . . I put all the strength I had left into one hard pull and leaped.

I was luckier than I deserved to be, and landed with most of me aboard the big boat. The skiff shot backward and the rope snapped tight under my leg, throwing me to safety.

It still ranks as my closest call that was all my own fault.

The gusts were piling on wilder and wilder, the waves coming huger. White hills reared up before us, bearing down as I tried to steer the boat to its best advantage, only to plough into the next wave at its worst. My eyes were riveted on the little island a mile or so off that marked the entrance to Port Neville, but it didn't seem to get any closer. Every time the boat stuck her nose into a big one the Easthope would lug down and almost seem to falter, then pick up again as we came on top and slid down into the trough. What would I do if it stopped again? I went over the steps in my head. First, try to restart it, and if you succeed, run back into Blenkinsop Bay and jog behind the island until things calmed down. If can't restart, get in the skiff and start the outboard. But how to get a proper towline on? You could try towing with the one on now, by putting the outboard in reverse, but that would pull the skiff's stern down and swamp it for sure. The right thing to do of course, would have been to rig a proper towline first, then undo the first one, but I never would have figured it out in the state of mind I was in.

I kept on, searching every wave for a chunk that could put out our prop or a deadhead that would smash out the bottom before we could get into the skiff. There are just as many chunks in rough water as calm, I told myself, you just couldn't see them. The late sun turned the surface of the waves into glittering gold foil. Between blinding flashes my eyes would see green and black voids full of chimerical deadheads. I waited for every pulse of the engine with arrested heartbeat.

It took us three hours to make two miles. The motor never quite stopped, but sometimes it seemed so feeble I could hardly tell if it had or not. Within a few minutes of turning into Port Neville the water was calm as a millpond and full of American yachts, all amazed to see us materialize out of the storm. I admitted it was a touch lumpy out.

Port Neville had a government dock on pilings, with a most picturesque clump of ancient buildings on shore, all of weather-worn axe-hewn timbers like something out of the wild west. The building near the float had been the store, but now seemed dark and full of cobwebs and junk. A back room still displayed a red post office insignia, the only shiny new thing in town, and you could buy a stamp if you could find someone to unlock the door. Olaf Hansen let us into his house to talk, but had less to say about the history of the place than I expected. His father had started the business, logged the hills and built up the trading post during the glory years, when the inlet was full of homesteaders and the smaller fishboats and tugs had to come in to refuel, unlike the new ones, which ploughed through to Port Hardy nonstop. Ole had grown up there, and evinced a certain noble bearing befitting his family's position, but seemed a little downhearted about the way things had worked out.

The emotional terrors of the trip up had drained away our spiritual lethargy and left us ready to take satisfaction in being alive. After a good meal and a night's sleep we chugged down the inlet three miles to the narrows, where someone told us you could wade for abalone at low tide, but it wasn't low enough. We clambered ashore at the little headland on the north side of the narrows called Robber's Nob, which was the site of a famous petroglyph, the Deer's Head. We found it etched deeply into a flat slab of granite, a powerful, symmetrical design. Most rock carvings I'd seen showed no more sense of artistic form than a bunch of grafitti on a warehouse wall, obviously not done by the same hands that made the highly formalized designs on the house fronts and totem poles, but the Deer's Head was a master design executed by a real artist in hard granite. Robber's Nob was a delightful location, obviously one of the Indians' favourites to judge by the thick midden, and had a bright, inspirational air about it — a quality I have often encountered at petroglyph sites. In those days I imagined a spiritual connection, but now in my skeptical middle age I would probably attribute it to siting. Which may be talking about the same thing. In my skeptical middle age I don't presume to know.

Johnstone Strait was flat as glass when we got back out on it. The motor seemed to have recovered its health and popped us along the five miles to Havannah Channel and Minstrel Island country in forty-five minutes. Things were going so well I decided to stop and try jigging a cod off Broken Islands, still exposed to the moods of Johnstone Strait. I'd heard Ed Warnock say he loaded the *Henry Bay* with big ling there one time, and I was ready for a feast. Slowing down as we approached the reef, the motor turned cranky and stopped. It started again and stalled as I put it into gear. I decided to try where we were, and I no sooner threw the jig over than it was vibrating with life. I pulled up a tiny rock cod.

"Throw him back," Mary said.

"He'll tell the other guys," I said.

"Ah, he'd be more trouble to peel than he's worth."

I threw him back, and we fished for half an hour without another bite.

"That little blabbermouth," Mary said.

Meanwhile the wind had sprung up again, turning the water around the island black. The dark spirits of the place rose up, shaking the air and making us realize what a foolish thing it was to stop in this hell-hole of reefs and surf where most people held their breath and pressed the throttle until they reached the shelter of Havannah Channel. I started up, but as soon as I put it in gear, the engine died. I got it going again but it popped and missed and ran so weak it wouldn't go into gear without dying. Fear once again gripped my chest. Big rips and rollers now pounded the seaward side of the island, not a place to challenge with a motor that might stop. I got the boat in gear finally by burning the clutch and tried to go in behind the islands where out of the corner of my eye I thought I saw a seiner slip through, but halfway in we found ourselves surrounded by kelp.

"Did you get the impression that a seine boat went through here a few minutes back?" I asked Mare.

"Nope."

I turned around. The sea outside the island looked meaner than ever, but water is softer, I reasoned. I swung far to seaward, thinking to keep enough water between us and the shore that I could pull us clear with the outboard if we lost power, and we edged around pop . . . popop . . . pop as tense as a climber edging around a ledge on a mountaintop. It kept going, and by the time we were heading into the calm waters of Port Harvey, off the side of Havannah Channel, it was running regular and we were back to the guessing game of is it running full speed or no? We wanted to believe the trouble was gone, that it was dirty gas now cleared, but I couldn't stop it from undermining my faith in the boat, and I knew I was going to have to solve it properly before I could relax and get on with the trip.

When I'd come through with John Daly, we'd stopped in Port Harvey to see an old gyppo logger named Dick Donovan. His

camp was only half an hour away and I had it in mind to talk the
motor problem over with Dick, but before I could well see the
outline of his bunkhouse I could tell things had changed. There
was a huge tent of orange plastic hulking in the woods behind the
house, big enough to house a forty-foot sailboat, which I had no
doubt it actually did. When you see a shed like that on this coast,
it only means one thing.

Donovan's boat was still there, so I thought he might be too,
but no such luck. The camp had been taken over by a an American
family named McAllister, and the boat they were building was
amazing: a good forty feet, maybe more, with funny sharp points
at both ends, and welded up out of metal.

"Aluminum, eh?" I said. "That's a surprise."

"Nope," the gangly, drawly father said. "Steel."

It had such unusual lines I knew it must be modelled after some
kind of weird traditional fishboat from the Bay of Biscay or the
outer Hebrides, so I asked him what it was.

"Pinky."

"Is that a type, like?"

"Yep. Nova Scotia mackerel boat. It's a Colvin design, he made
'er over ta steel, like."

"It'll be the only one around here for sure."

"Yep, she's against all the goin' ways. She's steel, which ain't a
poploor material, she's double-ended, she's big and heavy so's it'll
take a storm to move 'er . . ."

Despite his hillbilly manner, he was obviously an exacting
craftsman. The work on the boat was immaculate. The welds were
flawless and every new seam was carefully sandblasted and painted. There was no heavy metal in it except the keel. The boat was
fine-boned like a bird, all lightweight, intricate webbing. It was
going to be junk-rigged. The kids were swarming over the hull like
ants scraping and painting and sand blasting and voiced disappointment when the dad called a coffee break. They were all
precocious as hell and spent five hours a day educating themselves
by correspondence, shunning the public school at Minstrel. Now
they skipped the coffee break, instead running down the path to
swim in the icy water. The wife was not as relaxed a person and
showed the nervous brittleness you often see in the faces of
women raising families in isolated parts of the coast.

I asked the man about Dick Donovan, and found he was logging down at Pitt Lake. McAllister was very interested in the motor problem, and offered to look at it, but I put him off.

"I doubt you'd know this motor, it's an Easthope," I said. I was pretty sure Easthopes had never made it to the Ozarks. He agreed a little reluctantly, but told me there was an oldtimer just a cattywampus crost' t' slough who would be able to fix me right up.

I asked them about the bay we were in, Port Harvey, and found they already knew a lot of its history. Until the First World War there had been a settlement there called Cracroft, with a beer parlour and store, and it had rivalled Minstrel Island like Cimarron rivalled Dodge City. In *Woodsman of the West*, M.A. Grainger's 1903 novel that was for me the Bible of the wild west coast, Cracroft was referred as Port Browning, and one afternoon the hero left the beer parlour at Minstrel Island, which he called Hanson Island, crossed the Blowhole in a rowboat and followed a path down Cracroft Inlet to the Cracroft beer parlour. Cracroft Inlet was one of the more pretentiously named sloughs on the coast, a narrow, mud-choked gut that divided West from East Cracroft Island, and it ran right past Donovan's property.

The old Cracroft beer parlour had been a large frame building built on a flat rock just above the saltchuck. Grainger passed a happy evening there listening to a fiddler accompanied by another man who tapped on the fiddle strings with chopsticks. The barroom was crowded full, with men sitting all around the walls on chairs and benches and standing at the bar two rows deep, and a few moments after his arrival there was an eruption of shouting voices, followed by a short, sharp fight and a long, slowly subsiding growl of argument. The noisiest man in the bar was a hulking young American hobo who did an unsteady clog-dance bawling, "I'm a bobcat with tousels in me ears." Some nights before, André the Frenchman had stomped on the hobo's face with his caulk boots, leaving it hideously disfigured. When Grainger asked some men why they didn't stop André, they shrugged and said, "Maybe André had something against him." Like most of the buildings in logger country, the floors of the Cracroft Hotel were pocked and splintered from the spikes in loggers' caulk boots. But the Cracroft Hotel, if you looked closely, also had boot-pocks in an unusual place: on the barroom wall. The story behind this unnatural wonder has been told so many times it has come to rank as one of the legends of the coast.

Port Harvey at that time was quite a handlogging centre, and when these solitary, independent men took a break from their brutal struggle with the sidehills, they tended to overcompensate. On this historic evening they had settled upon the pastime of dashing against the wall to see how high they could run up it in their caulk boots. The trick was to beat the last climber's height, but at all costs land on your feet when finished. If you fell, the next round was on you. The owner, Charlie Cavanaugh, measured the amount of beer he was selling against the damage to his wall, and decided to cut the boys off. They protested without effect, then huddled down at their rowboats, and came back with a dozen screw jacks, the main tool of the handlogger's trade, which they jammed under the uphill side of the building and began jacking. The pub creaked, seams popped, and it teetered precariously over the chuck. Cavanaugh rapidly re-calculated his position and opened the bar.

I'd heard this story from someone else, and told it to the McAllisters. They betrayed no sign they'd heard it until I was almost finished, then chimed in unison to beat me to the ending. I felt like a fool, naturally, but they didn't seem to mind. Usually when you stop at these little isolated places the people were so glad of fresh conversation they treated you like royalty, but here they seemed tense and impatient. The kids looked bored and wandered off. The wife seemed impatient as well, although the man tried to make up for the rest. He started telling us a story about the old Cracroft storekeeper, but she wasn't satisfied by the way he went about it and took over. This storekeeper was also the postmaster apparently, and whenever a local woman sent in a mail order to Woodward's, he would open the envelope and cross off any items which could be purchased from him. Mrs. McAllister said they'd learned all about the place from some former resident who had written them a long, fine-print letter. The idea of a good local history source excited me, so I asked for the name. They didn't have it. Mrs. McAllister had burned the letter. She wasn't sorry.

"She wanted to correspond but I didn't," she said, flatly. None of them seemed to care greatly about the history around them. I asked if there were many oldtimers I could interview still living in the area, and she started to shake her head, but he cut in and said,

"What aboot that oldtimer just a cattywampus crost over yonder? D'yew think he'd talk?"

"I doubt it, and if he did I doubt it would be of use." She spoke to him as if we weren't present, with a peremptory edge to her voice. He sighed and looked at her doubtfully.

"I don't know, he told me some things one time—if he gits warmed to it. What aboot old whatzis, down thattaway...?"

"Mackay," she said. "Well, they'd certainly have no trouble getting *him* to talk, if talk is what they want." They eyed each other, as if on the verge of a scrap. He turned away, and addressed himself to us.

"Shoore, I think you oughta stop and see old Mackay. He's a real oldtime handlogger. Bit of a character, but he's been around here fer a coon's age. You'll see him going inta Minstrel, on the side there. Bright orange boat."

"What about the other one?"

"He's the one you want to see abooot yeer motor anyways. Hat—Hadley. There's an old Mr. Hadley and a young. Yew want the old. Git out in the channel agin and it's jist a cattywampus crost th bay. You'll see it. A real fine old feller."

The head of Port Harvey was a drying sand flat, but they said there were few clams to be had. What there were instead were thousands of big moon snails crawling around. I remembered Dick Donovan referring to these slimy monsters as "escargot" and saying he had found a way to make a gourmet meal of them, but the McAllisters hadn't heard of that, and I couldn't enlighten them as to the recipe.

Before leaving I brought out a copy of Raincoast #2, which had the photo of the windjammer *Pamir* on the cover.

"I see a lot of square-riggers around here, this might be of interest," I said. He smiled.

"Yep, we've all got the fever," he said.

I was glad to get away. They seemed so sure of themselves, so disciplined and purposeful it gave me the shivers. I envied them greatly. They had figured out what to do in life and they were doing it. The rest of us were just wasting our time. But I ended by feeling sorry for them. When they finally got the boat under sail several years later, they discovered one of the younger children was prone to severe seasickness, and their dream fell apart. They cashed in their dream boat on a pocketful of filthy lucre and lucre and went separate ways. Still, the story they left behind at Port Harvey fits right in.

I was still hoping the Easthope would suddenly pick up and start running perfectly, not believing it could really have anything wrong with it. But it continued to cough and sputter, so I made up my mind to make the cattywampus our next stop. Havannah Channel was calm and warm-winded, with a yellow steel spar and grapple working above Boughey Bay, a little point called White Beach Point that gleams with clamshells in front of an abandoned Indian reserve called Matilpi.

We found the cattywampus place, which locals called Hadley Bay, just at the downstream end of Chatham Channel. It was quite a scene. There were two big old dormer-roofed houses hunching over this pocket-sized cove, and at the water's edge a couple of large sheds. Beside them was a heavy-duty marine ways, and on the ways two new fifty-foot seine boats. There was quite a system of floats, with a fancy floating motorhome tied up along with several speedboats, a couple of small tugs and boomboats, two new aluminum gillnetters and a small barge loaded with cedar shakes. There was a good deal of rusty equipment lying around, and a diesel lightplant was ratta-tat-tatting away somewhere out of sight. There were people moving around here and there. Young people. I'd never heard of this place before, but it was well and away the most alive and active spot we'd stopped at. Hadley Bay. It was named that after the Hadleys, two generations of them; Merle the father, and Bill the son. I flushed my memory trying to determine where I'd heard that name, and then remembered a story I'd read in the paper. An upcoast family had been visiting relatives a few miles away in a floatplane, and when they landed back home they discovered the relatives' dog crouching outside the plane on a float, having somehow clung there as the aircraft took off, flew over the mountains, and landed. Now it all came back. The visitors were these Hadleys, and the relatives were the Hansens of Port Neville. The plane had flown from Port Neville to Hadley Bay with Olaf Hansen's dog hitching the cold ride outside. Hadley Junior was married to Ole Hansen's daughter, I think.

Hadley Senior was responsible for the bargeload of shakes, which we tried to tie beside. A short guy with curly hair and the look of a radio evangelist came bouncing out of a little day-cruiser to warn us off, saying the freighter would be coming to unload the barge during the night. Otherwise he was friendly and helped us pull the boat to a safe spot. Days later the bargeload of shakes was still waiting.

The bouncy guy was an American from Oregon who spent his holidays in Hadley Bay hanging out. He was in love with the old cattywampus and followed him around helping split shakes. As he explained it, old Merle was "just a fine human being to be around." We established a wary relationship, both aware of being spectators and not quite legitimate participators in the scene. We stayed out of each other's way. Walking up the float I was stopped by a young guy in a T-shirt poking his head out of the floating mobile.

"There's nobody up there. They're in town."

"Oh. Well, I was just going to go ashore, look around," I said stupidly. I hadn't really thought much about what I was going to do.

"What?" he said.

"I was just going to poke around on shore a bit."

"Poke around." You'd think I said pillage and rape.

"Yeah, I mean unless you think I shouldn't . . ."

"Well, there's nobody there. Bill's in town and he won't be back for one maybe two days. Did you want something?"

"Well yeah. I've been having a little motor trouble."

"Like?"

"Ah . . . it stops."

"Stops." he said.

"Yeah, and it won't come up to revs. It misses a little and runs slow and doesn't have any torque."

"Sounds like fuel," he said. "I can probably fix you up. What did you say it was?"

"An Easthope." I'd been waiting for him to ask that.

"Oh. An Easthope." He said "Easthope" very quietly. "That's different. Bill's your man, then. He might be back tomorrow night."

It turned out this young fellow, Murray Johnson, was with a Pender Harbour girl I was almost related to in a roundabout way. Her father was Vic Gooldrup, the well-known boat builder and creator of the two ships up on the ways, which were here to be outfitted at the machine shop, which was run by Bill Hadley. Bill was the young Hadley, but Murray said he's the mechanic in the family. I wondered, because I was pretty sure McAllister told us to hook up with an old cattywampus. I asked about the old Hadley.

"Merle, you mean. Yeah, old Merle, he don't work on motors. He's pretty old and he just messes around cuttin' shakes. No, Bill's your man."

From what he said Bill Hadley definitely knew Easthopes and had everything in the machine shop to practically rebuild the thing. I decided we might as well stick around and get to the bottom of this motor worry, although I kept thinking it would turn out to be either nothing at all, or something I should have done myself, like clear the needle valve.

The next day we had time to kill so we got into the skiff and set out for Minstrel Island, five miles away. Chatham Channel looked like a horror on the chart, with rocks all over and a five-knot current, but it turned out to be simple if you used the range markers. A straight, narrow alleyway, hills shaven, the odd tall tree here and there, then more green fuzz like a bad crewcut. About halfway down I saw the orange boat that must have belonged to the other oldtimer McAllister told us about. It was tied up to a float shack on the north side. Opposite, on the south hillside, I saw signs of fairly recent disturbance, small alder and a gouge in the earth running up the vertical hillside to a standing wooden spar. It was the first wooden spar I'd seen since I was a kid. I was tickled. It even seemed to be rigged. On the beach below it was a tangle of logs and busted chunks, which I decided were the remains of a chute which slid down the hill because they were all grey with age. I was tempted to go over, but the object of our journey beckoned at the end of the channel.

Minstrel looked like it should, I thought. Stuck to the backside of a steep little island, small batch of buildings and floats, old. Musty, mildewy, in dank shade on a sunny afternoon, a long pier on pilings and a quadrangle of new government floats clustered with American yachts. The most active building was the store, built over the water on pilings like a cannery and, parallel to the pier, a rambling cluster of tin-roofed sheds with little window-panes the size of a quality paperback. Inside, the floor was eroded by caulk boots at all the busy intersections, most deeply dished in front of the cash register where generations of Swede fallers had stood shuffling their spiked feet as they bought their Copenhagen

snoose. Stock included nails, anchor chain, batteries, charts, gal-
vanized buckets, frozen herring, minibikes, pennants, hardhats,
plastic totem poles, Sportyaks, soup, nuts, bolts and groceries at
twice normal prices. The owner was a stiff, hard-mouthed man
very much not a part of the local scene who said ninety percent
of the trade was tourists, and was thinking of closing during the

Minstrel Island from the air, 1950s. JIM SPILSBURY PHOTO.

next winter except on mail days. His wife was fighting middle age
with eye shadow and a tight sweater, flirty at the cash register. He
said he didn't like loggers, and the way she was getting the hairy
eyeball it made sense.

It was a shallow bay with a sparse few houses to the left of the
wharf and a few to the right, hugging the tide line. Ashore there
were two large buildings, either of which might have been the
hotel. The one nearest the water was a bit smaller, a long narrow
public structure of some kind with rows of small windows on three
floors. There was something funny about it's being so close to the
beach, almost like somebody had started to drag it into the water

and quit halfway. I could see a pool table through a ground-floor window. The other building was bigger and stood on higher ground, a frame three-storey barn with a steep moss-laden roof, the sides a moth-eaten grey stained with green slime, almost invisible against the forest that reared up behind, dwarfing the settlement. Looking closely, I detected faded lettering, "HOTEL."

"We had some ray-er times..." Minstrel during the '50s boom years.

So this was the Minstrel Island Hotel, one of the holiest shrines of logging history. This was where Grainger stayed in 1907, paying for his patch of bare floor in the attic by sawing firewood for the kitchen stove. Every serious logger between 1900 and 1960 had a story to tell about the Minstrel beer parlour, but now I couldn't tell if it was even in use. It had a dead look. The grass was six inches high between the planks of the boardwalk. I dragged Mary up to the door and tried it. It opened.

The first thing that hit us, since the light was too dim to see anything, was the smell. It wasn't a bad smell, but a distinctive one. It was the smell of a logging camp bunkhouse. It's special, and you could guess some of the components: tobacco, laundry that's dirty with sawdust and pitch, grey army blankets, straw mattresses, spilled beer, drying boot-leather, unbathed bodies. You expect to find it in a bunkhouse and don't notice it. But finding it somewhere else, you have to pause and think what it is. The only non-bunkhouse I ever smelled it in was a little shack in Gibsons where a logger friend of ours lived between stints at camp, reproducing the bunkhouse lifestyle so precisely at home he was able to duplicate the scent that went along with it.

"Jesus, it smells exactly like Pete's," Mary said. It was hard to say why, based on the present occupants—a couple of uncomfortable tourists sitting by the window and a couple of young guys lounging at a table with their legs hooked over chairs and who looked too quick to be local but seemed to know everyone. No loggers in sight, but so many bedded down in this building over the years their scent must have permeated the timbers. I was as uncomfortable as the tourists. There was no sense of public about the room. It was like we walked into someone's private home. Since we came in, everybody had been sneaking looks at us over their beer but nobody made the faintest outward sign of wanting to serve us. There was a bar, but it had nothing on it, no taps, no fridge behind it, no sink. It didn't look like a beer had passed over it that year. The other tables had a few bottles though, and they got them somewhere. Maybe it's self-serve, I thought. Hell, maybe it's BYOB. A BYOB beer parlour—the world's only. Finally a very tired and bored-looking older woman dressed in a floppy, shapeless sweater appeared through a dark doorway, dragged herself to the bar and said, "Wanna ya want?"

"Beer," I said. "Two beer."

"Wut kine?"

"Blue," I said, on the basis that all beer is the same and that's the only one I could ever remember.

"Don' have that."

"Okay, what have you got?"

"Lucky."

"Whatever." She brought over two warm ones, and sure e-nough, it was Lucky Lager, the brand the boys used to sneak into the big bunkhouse in the fifties. As a kid I thought its name meant them: lucky loggers. But I hadn't seen it in years and didn't know it still existed.

A radiophone blurted into life in some back room, Campbell River calling Minstrel Island, Campbell River calling Minstrel Island, Campbell River calling Minstrel Island and she dragged herself away to answer: Yeah, Minstrel here. I took the opportunity to snoop around. Behind the bar was a little room littered with ripped-open beer cases in front of a bulky white household fridge. An adjoining room was empty of tables, the floor rain-warped and in the middle a battery on charge. For some reason I was sure this was the room in which Grainger saw all the passed-out drunks lying this way and that like frozen corpses at the Massacre of Wounded Knee.

Looking over the railing on the way down the dock, I noticed something funny about the mudflat underneath. It had a peculiar texture to it, as if it were pebbled with stones under the film of mud, but it wasn't stones, it was bottles. Hundreds, thousands of bottles, covering the entire acre or so beside the wharf. I had never seen so many bottles anywhere in my life. I went back to the shore end of the dock and walked down onto the mudflat. Barnacled, broken, weedy, the bottle shards outnumbered the stars in the sky, ones below filling the gaps between the ones above. They were all old. Tall beer bottles, Kik-Cola, the brown ringed ones with Orange Crush in an orange diamond, unheard of whisky brands and one rusty caulk boot.

My old friend Gwyn Gray Hill, who has been cruising up and down the coast keeping an eye on things since 1928, points out that the bottles at Minstrel are one of the mysteries of the coast. Why are they there? You don't see them in other harbours — Gibsons, Heriot Bay, Irvine's Landing... Perhaps because there is practically nowhere to stand on Minstrel except the dock, the heavy drinkers favoured it as a location for their work. Or perhaps it was the only place on the coast where there was a large population of bottle-tossing drinkers but no commensurate population of local kids to collect empties the morning after.

Pondering the matter in the murk under the pier, I realized that, for all I had heard about Minstrel, I knew virtually nothing about the place. Back at Hadley Bay that night the cattywampus oldtimer came home so I headed up the hill with my tape recorder. Merle Hadley was a very pleasant, soft-voiced man probably somewhere in his late sixties. He seemed at peace with life. His corner was in order. His house had an air of well-worn comfort, and he and his wife both spoke as though they just couldn't imagine being anywhere else than they were or anybody else than they were. A shy man, he was a bit taken aback at being interviewed, but he wasn't refusing. We sat at the kitchen table.

"Well let's see, my first trip up here was in 1925." He had a better drawl than McAllister. Nine-teen twen-ty *fiiirrrrre . . .* Everything

The world's biggest bottle collection, Minstrel Island 1974.

was in this slow drawly singsong. It was lovely. You just held your breath waiting to hear more.

"That I knew of. But I learned to walk up at the head of Knight Inlet. My mother came from Denman Island and her brothers had a little steamboat and my Dad was also up there so they met up there."

The former Cracroft hotel, now serving as a store.

"Up at the head of Knight?"

"Up at the head of Knight." He recited the line like poetry, in waltzing iambs.

They were close to Jim and Laurette Stanton, the Knight Inlet homesteaders who settled there in 1919 and were later made famous by the book *Grizzlies in Their Back Yard*. Hadley's parents were handlogging up there and didn't stay, but the Stantons did. Laurette Stanton had died years back, but in 1974 Hadley thought maybe old man Stanton was still going up in the summers. He'd sold the place and spent the winters in Victoria, but he had the right to go back as long as he lived, and he went regular.

There was a Japanese logger named Takahashi going great guns around Minstrel in 1925, and Hadley came in to run donkey for him. Takahashi had picked up seven steam donkeys cheap when the Hastings Mill Company sold out.

"I'm tryin to think of the price that he paid—just next to nothing, you know. And this *Haro* that you show in your book there, Hastings owned that and they towed a scow up with four of those 10-by-15 Tacomas on it."

Hadley stayed with Takahashi for twenty years, working timber claims here, there and everywhere. The Hadleys got married in 1935 when Taki was in Cracroft Lagoon and built in Hadley Bay some time after. Minstrel went up and down quite a few times over the years. Its first bloom was in the time of the big railroad camps, from the turn of the century through the twenties. Then things slacked off a bit until the age of the gyppo came along in the forties and fifties. All of a sudden every bay had a camp. It was a beehive. There were never many more buildings than what we saw then, except for the restaurant, down along the beach from the wharf. This building had been knocked down by the snow a few winters earlier, and was thought to be the original hotel. Hadley didn't know when it was a hotel, but everyone called it that. There was a green spot on the beach where it was. With some alarm, I considered the possibility the present hotel was not the one Grainger had patronized.

In Pender Harbour we tended to mark off the historical periods by the various storekeepers who held sway, like English kings. "That was when Royal Murdoch had the store, or was it Jim Pope...?" In Minstrel they tended to go by owners of the hotel.

"The one that owned it when I first came was Neil Hood.

Evidently he'd got it quite cheap, you know, and it was not payin', then he built it up." The big long building with the pool table, I now discovered, was the former Cracroft Hotel, which had been towed around from Port Harvey on floats.

"Neil Hood done that. B'cause he was afraid that it would get big again there was so many tugboats over there. Evidently, if they could get a liquor licence, well any place'll boom.

"Taki had two loggers movin' floats, and they put that buildin' on the two big floats and moved it around. Set it right along side of the wharf."

Hood's strategy worked a little too well. Soon he was making more money than he wanted.

"He didn't like payin' income tax. After five thousand you had to pay income tax, and after only about three months, he'd be up there. When he felt like it, he'd sell you a beer, but a lot of times he didn't feel like it. They'd come to the door – 'Could I have a –' Slam! That was that. He wouldn't even let 'em get the words out of their mouth."

I pressed him for more Minstrel history, but he couldn't think of anything much to say about the place. They had a murder there one time...

"Tell me about that," I said.

"Well, I don't even know the fellow's name that was murdered. A fisherman though. He had, they figure, about seven hundred dollars in his pocket, and he was flashin' it around, you know. The last he was seen, he went up and he'd got a case a beer. The next thing, they saw this blood at the corner of the little freight shed, and then the ramp comes down, and the blood started there and it come all the way down and it crossed two boats. The boat he was put on went.

"But the goll-darn body drifted right back t' Minstrel the next day. Right into the wharf. The Murphy kid, he had a little raft there with a little outboard on it and he run right into it.

"When would that be? Oh, let me see... There was quite a bit of activity at Minstrel then. Port MacNeill Loggin' was goin' full blast. Bill and Sid were goin' over there t' school. Early fifties, maybe? I can't say.

"Scope, the policeman, knew it was an Indian boat, the third one out. They found a piecea pipe they figured was what done the job. This boat went to Alert Bay directly from Minstrel and dumped the body offa Bones Bay. They went to Alert Bay and this woman said that somebody had drowned at Minstrel Island. But the body hadn't got back yet. Nobody else knew it. So it was a dead giveaway right there.

"But both those Indians committed suicide. The police was questioning 'em and they knew they was goina be caught. One a them just gassed himself. And the other one jumped overboard. One was Pugels. Hmmn...what the heck was the other one? I don't know. They were from Village Island.

"There was more murders, but I can't think of 'em. There was one fella, I guess he went out of his mind or somethin', and he went and jumped overboard. There was always a lot of 'em hangin' around the wharf, leanin' on the rail waitin' for the steamer and partyin' on boats and what not, well, they saw it an' they pulled 'im back out. He got madder'n Sam Hell, 'e didn't wanta live, and so 'e jumped overboard again.

"They left 'im.

"Rita Wilson was just a young girl then and she was walkin' up these floats and right in b'tween the two floats was one a these fellas y'know, his hair was all out like seaweed and she jis' screamed murder. I ferget if this was the same fella or another one. That Union boat, you know, when it went astern it sucked in anything that was out there and it used to run the bodies right up on the beach.

"Oh we had rare times, alright."

I wish I could write how he pronounced those words: ray-er ty-eems. In that waltzing way. Even his wife laughed.

"When Neil Hood sold out, things started to go ahead. Izzy the Jew got it and he was trying to sell all the beer he could. In fact it was rumoured that he sold more beer in that hotel than all the rest of BC put together."

"That's a lot of beer," I said.

"Oh, a lotta beer. There was so many big camps in here."

Mrs. Hadley took it upon herself to lean toward me and whisper, "He means it was the highest selling *beer parlour* in BC."

He wasn't sure of the hotel's line of succession after Izzy. I wanted to know Izzy's full name, but he didn't know it. He said nobody ever called him anything but Izzy the Jew.

"How many owners sence that—waall, it was changin' hands one night after another." The current owner was a man named

Perley Sherdahl, a logger from the area. Perley was a throwback, the last of the oldtime Knight Inlet gyppos. Everybody knew the story of how he came to own the pub. The owner previous to Perley was a man named Russ Boyd, but he was occupied running a little logging show on the back side of the island and hired a couple named Rod and Louise Pierce to manage the hotel in his absence. One historic day, the Pierces came to the conclusion that Perley's presence at the Minstrel Island Hotel was not consistent with the standards they were attempting to uphold and they refused to let him in. Perley responded by going straight to owner Boyd, making him an offer he couldn't refuse, returning as the hotel's new owner and firing the Pierces.

I've written elsewhere that the Pierces were moved to make their unhappy stand against Perley because he was drunk and busting things up, which is what I was told, but this caused some longtime Minstrelites to rise to Perley's defence.

Perley may well have been a drunk, they agree, but he knew how to hold his liquor and hardly ever got noisy or broke major items of furniture. The reason he was turned away from the hotel that fateful day was not that he was acting up, but that he was trying to rent a room with a woman who wasn't his wife. And lest anyone get the wrong idea, these upholders of the Sherdahl name are quick to point out that Perley wasn't really in the habit of doing this sort of thing. His wife had moved to the city to find good schools for their four daughters and Perley, finding time heavy on his hands, had taken the time-honored expedient of partnering up with his camp cook. His champions wished it noted that he wasted no time un-partnering again when the missus returned. It was her, in fact, who'd served us the warm Lucky Lagers.

Perley was Minstrel's favourite character. Even Hadley, who seemed pretty skeptical about many of the area's haywire characters, had nothing but affection for Perley.

"He's a great guy, you know. Around Minstrel when he's corned he always gets on this thing, he's goina 'clean this place up.' He'll pile all the beer cases in the middle of the wharf and set fire to 'em. Another trait of his, like, on the Union boat, he'd walk down the aisle, and they had a glass to drink water but of course bein' a steamboat the water was always hot. He'd smash the glass against the side of the wall and walk on with that dumb look on his face you know—'who done that?' Oh, he's hard on the crockery. If he was havin' dinner someplace and he was settin' near a window, he'd just finish his plate and throw it out in the chuck. One time there he went to some peoples' yacht for Christmas dinner, they weren't from around here and they were quite excited to get the owner of the hotel in to dinner, so Perley comes, and after they were all done this here lady starts pickin up the dishes.

"Perley jumps up, 'Let me do that,' he says. So he loads up every dish on the table in his arms, staggers over to a window—ker-splash. The whole works goes into the chuck. 'Now we can take er easy,' he says. But this lady, she isn't taking it easy at all and she says to Perley, 'that was all the dishes I had.' 'Don't worry about that,' he says. 'We'll get more in the morning.'"

"Oh, he's a wonderful guy alright. Once there he was holed up in the Vancouver Hotel just drinkin' and drinkin'—'course the beer cases had mounted up, dirty clothes and all, the chamber-maid refused to go near the place, so old Perley, he thought, well it's time somebody cleaned this place up. Somehow he got a tin heater in there, with a couple three lengths of stovepipe and an elbow. He opened the window, stuck the pipe out there, stuck the elbow on, and shovelled in these here beer cases and old socks and stuff. And lit 'er up. Jeez, black smoke was *pourin'* up the side of the Vancouver Hotel, fire engines were roarin, people runnin around down below, cops come to the door—

"'What in Sam Hill you doin?'

"'Oh, just cleanin the place up.'"

I wondered if we'd see Perley around the hotel, but they said he was out sitting his camp. I wondered if he had anything to do with the rigged spar I'd seen on the way to Minstrel.

"Oh no, that's old Mackay."

I tried to remember the name of the second oldtimer McAllister told us to look up. "Mackay, is he that old handlogger who works by himself..."

"He works there all by himself but it's not handloggin'—he's got a machine up the hill with a scab line runnin' down to the chuck—the mainline goes down the hill to a tailhold out in the chuck and the logs slide down hooked onto a runnin' block, like, then he's got the haulback to pull it back. He walks up, sets the choker, starts the donkey, jerks the log around 'til it gets down, shuts the donkey off, walks down the hill and unhooks the turn, all by himself—nobody will work with him, you know. That's over on the far side. Then across this side, he's got a mess of stuff on a float and a shack there he sleeps in."

"Mackay," I pondered. "I'm trying to think if that's a guy somebody told me about. What's his first name?" I didn't say I wanted to see him, because I could tell Hadley didn't like him.

"We just call him Scabby Mackay," Hadley laughed.

"Because he operates a scabline?"

"Well no, he scabbed durin' the loggin' strike. It's the only time he could get work, I guess. Ha ha."

I gathered from the quick way this came up that Mackay's sin must have been of recent origin, and it dampened my enthusiasm about the guy. It wasn't until later I found out the strike in question took place a full forty years earlier, before the woods was even organized.

The next day Bill Hadley came back. He was perhaps forty, a mild, friendly man with no sign of his father's drawl and full of quiet confidence in his own ability. The whole Hadley Bay setup rested on his shoulders, but he carried it lightly. He didn't let on whether or not he really knew anything about Easthopes, but came right over to take a look at our motor. He got me to fire it up, listened to it for a minute, and signaled to turn it off.

"Do think you could get the heads off it?" he said. I asked him if he knew what it was. He said no, he didn't, but he'd like to see the heads. I wondered what I was getting into.

"You don't think it could be fuel, eh?" I asked.

"Well, it could be I guess, but I'd like to see those heads. I can take 'em off myself, but I won't have time 'til next week," he said. "There's just four bolts on each one."

I said, sure, I could take the heads off, if he thought we had to. "Alright. Give me a shout when you're done. You'll have to tie the manifold back somehow."

I monkeywrenched all morning in the hot fish hold, covered with sweat, grease and blackflies. Every time I turned around I got a sharp corner or a bolt in my side. It wasn't much of a job, but everything was made ten times harder by the cramped quarters. Finally I hauled the heads out on the dock. There was lots of carbon buildup on both and I could see one exhaust valve was partly burned away. When I showed Bill he shook his head and said, "It's a wonder that motor would run."

"That's the trouble then, you figure?"

"Oh yeah." He whispered it, as if to himself.

I was very alarmed. The Easthope was an antique. Parts for it probably took weeks to get, if not months. They probably cost like a Rolls Royce. We couldn't hang around here waiting for weeks. How would we get home? What would happen to the boat? Who would pay? We didn't have any money. Was this something I did? Surely it couldn't have been like this the last time Gordie Goble looked at it. I asked Bill if he thought it had just happened coming up, or it was a long time thing.

"Oh no, you couldn't have fried that valve like that just coming up here. It's probably been going like this for five, ten years, for all the running that motor does."

I asked him how we would go about getting a valve.

"The valve is no problem. It's just a Ford valve. The head is the problem."

"The head?"

"Yeah, if it's cracked. I can't see anything, but it's a pretty good chance there'll be a crack where that burn is. But you might be lucky."

He took the heads up to the shop. I was beginning to feel very lost. The trip was turning into a disaster. I looked out at a pair of crisp white yachts turning into Chatham Channel at ten knots, their bow waves grinning white. Those kind of people went through life without knowing the kind of trouble I seemed to make for myself day in and day out. What a fool I'd been out there in that storm, telling myself I had the most reliable power on the coast under me. Now, I could see clearly, it was a miracle the thing hadn't snuffed out during the blow and got us killed.

There was nothing useful I could do the rest of the day, so we decided to take the skiff and fire over to check out the other oldtimer. I was dubious about the scab stuff but tickled at the prospect of seeing a wooden spar in use, although I couldn't figure out why the wood I'd seen at the bottom of the hill looked so old if it was fresh cut.

When I got there I still couldn't figure it. There was a slight bay with the hill rising steeply behind it. The track up the hill was grown up in alder eight feet high, but there was a line snaking out of the bush to a stiffleg in the water. The dirt around the line looked as if it had been scuffed around recently, but not much. There was a string of grey old logs forming a semicircle with the beach, and floating inside it such a worthless-looking bunch of old broken slabs, skinny saplings and punky-looking chunks I couldn't imagine the purpose for which they had been collected. We tied to a makeshift raft with a couple of stubby pikepoles, a Gilchrist jack and a couple of boomchains on it, with a banged-up skiff tied alongside, and I got out and stood on the boom.

I'd heard a faint hooting noise up the hill, and now I heard it again. I looked up. There was something jostling the bushes a ways up the skidway. I caught glimpses of an aluminum hardhat. In a few minutes a tall, stooped figure was on the beach waving the hat and making an odd hooting noise like an owl. We untied and idled over. The figure was dressed in ragged wool pants with suspenders over a grey Stanfield top. Grizzled would be the word for his overall look. Grizzled from head to heel. And big. Jim Mackay was one of these lanky, rawboned old loggers well over two hundred pounds with a flat belly. By now, between seventy and eighty years old, he was permanently stooped, but he must have been a good six-four or six-five in his prime. His face was broad with sad big eyes, a much-bent nose, high cheeks and a wide, expressive mouth that had evidently swallowed a few choker knobs in its time. It was a scarred, lined face, tanned, almost mummified by weather, and it looked like trouble.

"Well, well, well, well..." he spoke in a little girlish voice, grinning a mysterious grin. He seemed to have been expecting us. Later I found out he'd been watching us come across the channel from up the hill, and started down to meet us.

"I hope we're not interrupting your work," I said.

"Ha! That's a laugh, that is," he hollered. His normal voice was a rapid-fire, aggressive half-shout.

"My work's been interrupted for years. My whole life is one big interruption."

I told him we were in the area collecting logging history and were thrilled to find a wooden spar in operation. I wondered if we could go up and take a look. He was amused by this.

"Logging history," he said. "Well, you come to the right place. There's more history than there is logging in this goddamn outfit."

"What are you doing here?" I said, nodding toward the collection of broken chunks.

"That's a good question, that is," he said. "Here, put yer bow in here and we'll go have a coffee at my shack."

Normally nothing will stop a logger from getting out logs in the middle of the day but he obviously wasn't as dedicated to production as he could be. I stuck the nose of the skiff into the rocks and he pushed it out carefully to where it would clear the rocks when his weight pushed it down, and jumped in. I couldn't get over the feeling he was completely ready for us. He didn't even bother to tell me where his shack was, but of course I knew it was across the other side, tucked into a little bay for protection.

Mackay's one-man float camp was bigger than it looked from mid-channel, sprawled across a big cedar float. The float logs were sinking, eaten away to a weedy mess of anemones and mussels below the waterline. The parts that were still above the water were weathered grey and speckled with years of caulk boot prints, a thin cap of dry wood with frayed green edges. Here and there some boards were laid down and piled with junk. Oil drums stood about cocked at angles, one covered with a scrap of plywood held down by a rusty shackle. Kinky cable was sticking up everywhere.

We tied behind his fishboat, a clumsy-looking little troller with a bright orange hull. "That's the *Orange Crate*," he said with a grin.

I went over to look at a cluster of little fruit trees potted in grease pails. "Now, don't you laugh at my garden," he said. His plan was to establish a floating orchard, but it wasn't doing very well.

There were three shacks, a doorless toolshed dipping into the water at an angle, his bunkhouse, shingled and slightly more weatherproof-looking, sitting level on skids, and beside it one just like it except new. He'd meant to move into the new one he said, but didn't because he was too busy. He went to the middle one and pushed open the door.

"This is the Black Hole of Calcutta," he announced. The end of one skid stuck out just under the door sill, making a handy step. It was half slivered away from boot caulks. The air inside was heavy with stove oil, the room dirty but not filthy. There were piles of clothes and magazines in every corner, but none that looked more than a few months old. There was nothing rotting. A smoke-blackened Coleman camp stove sat on top of his grease-streaked oil range. A huge fridge stood beside it. It didn't work, but he still kept food in it. An iron cot sagged in one corner, and in the middle of the tiny room a table and a chair with a cushion crushed black and hard. The wall beside the door was festooned with fishing lures, souvenirs of a summer spent trolling in the *Orange Crate*.

I asked him if there were any good fishing holes around.

"Hell yes."

"I'd sure like to catch a fish," I said.

In the centre of the room were two cardboard barrels loaded to the brim with dry food. He picked out a handful of soup mixes as he went by.

"You guys want something to eat?" he said.

He pulled out a flat tin.

"Now look at that," he says. "How can they put that up? Sixty-eight cents." The label promised beefsteak pie.

"I bet you didn't buy *that* at Minstrel," Mary said.

"All this came from Kelowna," he said. "I got some sisters in Kelowna and they're retired. They worry about me. 'How do you live? What do you eat? How do you get to the doctor?' Then last winter, all of a sudden they start to take a notion, 'we know you're batching and you say prices are high in the store—I hope you won't get mad if we send you a—' and I get a great big goddamn box of groceries. So now every month a goddamn box of groceries comes. I just dump it in these here barls. You want any? Take anything you want. I'm going to have to dump it in the chuck pretty soon."

He paid the sisters back by canning up a few cases of salmon, but he was outraged at the price of the blank cans.

"Feel the weight of them goddamn things," Mackay said. Mary took one of the cases of empty cans and bobbed it, a perplexed look on her face.

"There's no weight to them," Mackay ranted on at the top of his lungs. "Three of those—nine dollars and some christly cents. But they got a monopoly, you see. American Can. That's the only way you can do business in this country—get a monopoly. Get in with the Liberal Party and get a monopoly."

His plan was to get Mary to cook something up, but she wasn't going for it. He had been very attentive and gallant on the way over, taking her hand when she didn't need it and insisting she lay his grimy jacket over her knees and apologizing every time he swore, which happened twice in every sentence and slowed him down considerably. Mare, being a modern woman, was theoretically opposed to being treated like a lady, but she wasn't assertive enough to make an issue of it. She just looked sour. But when he showed the other side of his oldtime chivalry and started beckoning her toward the stove, she was having none of it. I leaped into the breach and made coffee myself.

"I want to know about Minstrel." I said.

"Ha! Minstrel, eh? You don't have enough time."

"How long have you been around Minstrel?"

"Oh, Jesus, I've been here this last time around here — musta bin handloggin 'n horsin' around here twenty years."

"But you were around here before that?"

"Oh, I was in and out of here. Travellin' back and forth since, oh Christ, I don't know when."

"Were you here for any of these murders?"

"Hah! The only one I know of was when the Indians murdered old Spitz."

"Spitz — was that his name?"

"Yeah, Spitz. Siwash snuffed him comin' down the dock and took his roll. But I never heard tell of any more than that. Course there might have been, years ago."

"Merle Hadley mentioned some others, but he couldn't remember details." Mackay's ears perked up at the mention of Hadley's name.

"So you were talkin' to old Hadley were ya? I guess he give ya a real earful about what a rotten bastard I was, eh?"

"What's he got against you, anyway?" I was worried about the scabbing business.

"Oh, I'm ostracized around here. They figure I owe 'em money for work they did on my boat, but I ain't payin' it. I don't mind payin' a *thousand dollars* for something as long as I get my money's worth. But when they try to turn around and harpoon me, well bullshit on 'em. Now, to straighten the shaft in that boat . . . put a bearing in . . . do a little caulking — NINE HUNDRED AND SOME GOD-DAMN DOLLARS!" He roared the words. His voice continually leaped to a roar and fell to a squeak, and twisted and writhed like a cat. He had all the moves of a practiced bullshitter, gained on the floors of the Dominion and Grand and Minstrel Island beer parlours.

"Two years ago last April. Oh, they're mad. They're tellin' everybody about me."

I told him we had to get some work done on the motor.

"Oh, you poor guys."

I had a sinking feeling in my stomach. "What do you mean? Bill there seemed to know what he was doing."

"Yeah, and he knows how to charge, too." Wonderful, I thought.

A cat materialized from under the cot and rubbed against my legs. "See that cat? She's about fifteen years old," he said. "I can't get her fat. Do you know she won't drink milk? Once in a blue moon, that's all." The cat yowled, and Mackay bent down and yowled back, sounding more like the cat than it did itself. "No, I know a spot down here that's good fishing," he said, straightening up. "Dandy. Just down here by Turnour Island. Last time I was fishing — about this time of year — do you know a fella by the name of Don from Sechelt? Mechanic?"

"Maybe."

"Ennaway, I caught a great big forty-nine-pounder. And the kid from Minstrel that was workin' in the store there, his dad used to have a herring pond down there, they came by with Don just as I hooked this fish. It was a big one. I brought him alongside and I gaffed him. But I didn't clobber him right. I missed. And he twisted the goddamn gaff outta my hand. I brought him in again. I said bullshit on you this time, and I grabbed an eight-pound sledgehammer I had there. Well, he came over onto the deck and he fought, and he kicked — and I landed on top of him, full spread like this so the sonuvabitch didn't get away — excuse my French — and I got my hands up into his gills, all the time trying to brain him with this eight-pound hammer, you know, bouncing off the deck and off my foot — well, Don was watching and he said he laughed himself bloodywell stupid. I was fish, slime and scale inside and out like I fell in a tub of glue. I was spitting out scales for a week. I caught fourteen good ones in that spot."

"Great," I said. But before I could propose a trip down there, he was onto something else. He had taken off his caulk boots. His socks were bright purple. "Look at the dye outta them goddamn shoes!" he said. "It's poisoned me twice already. It's in the leather. Can you believe you live in a country where it's legal to put out a shoe like that? I've had these things over a year now and look at it!" I remembered men from my deep past calling caulk boots caulk "shoes." He was the real Mackay alright.

"What's the story on this Perley?" I said.

"Do you know where the Dominion Hotel is in Vancouver? You look at that sometime and you'll see that's the Sherdahl Building."

"You mean there's a connection?"

"His grandfather built that. Perley inherited it. He was the fair-haired boy."

"What happened? Lose it in a poker game?"

"Hell no, he's still got it. He gits six dollars a day from the estate. He calls that his beer money. Then there's Sherdahl and Kimball. Everett Kimball was his stepfather and he had a pretty good camp. Perley got that too."

"So he's pretty well fixed?"

"Well, he got stuck when he bought that beer parlour. I don't know what he paid for it but I heard ninety thousand. Now Manning offered him forty and he wouldn't take it. But he won't fix nothin'. He hasn't put a goodamn cent into it in the fourteen years he's had it. That's why he's got every goddamn nickel he ever made. Tight? When he gets drunk he makes a big sunuvabitch of a noise, you'd think he was a millionaire, the way he talks.

"Oh Jesus, Jean gives 'im shit! Suffering Christ, she locks 'im out of the beer parlour. Drinkin' up the profits. She hit 'im over the head with a case of eggs one time. Laugh! I never laughed so much in my goddamn life.

"There was a bunch of us around there drunk. Perley and I were partners then and we're supposed to be out loggin', but we decided to play poker. Me and Campbell and a bunch of 'em, we went over to Joseph's floathouse. I didn't know, but before he came over Perley went and took a hundred dollars out of the safe. Jesus, did she light inta him! I was upstairs. Frank Howard was an old fella that was around here and he come up to my room. 'Jesus Christ, you gotta stop 'em. He's going to kill her.'

"'If he's going to kill her, he's going to kill her,' I said. 'I can't stop him.'

"I finally moseyed down the stairs and they were barkin' at each other 'til she took a box of eggs and bust it right over his head. I started to laugh. She looked at me and she couldn't help herself, she started to laugh too. Oh, she lays the law down to him, but he just laughs.

"Pat Carney give Perley quite a write-up when she was up here looking for the best logger that time," he said. The Pacific National Exhibition was putting up a trophy for their logger sports competition and wanted to name it after the best logger of all time, so they sent Carney on a search up the coast. This was when she was a columnist on the *Vancouver Sun*.

"For some goddamn reason I'll never understand they ended up picking Panicky Bell, but she come up to Minstrel lookin' for talent and Perley give her the full load. In her writeup she went on and on about Perley. She said, 'Every boss logger should have his own beer parlour.'"

I asked him what it was about men like Panicky Bell and Roughhouse Pete that made them stand out, when there were thousands of others who worked alongside them, like Mackay himself, that you never heard about.

"Well Panicky, the goddamn clown, it was self-advertising. Jesus Christ! You know what he did at Silver Skagit, the goddamn crazy asshole? Y'see, the Americans had the Silver Skagit. And we, as Canucks, did the logging. It was an international project and Panicky was running it.

"Well, they were havin' this dress-up dinner for all the brass, and Panicky came around and invited a bunch of us to come — Roy MacDonald, Herman Smith was there, and Big Bill Byers. A lot of the oldtime rangitangs, and all of them my size or bigger. Panicky was sittin' at the fifty-dollar end of the table with Knudson and all the goddamn bigshots, and he had us set up at the other end. So then he'd say to these Yanks, 'Hey, you wanta see some real big Canadian bush apes? Take a look at those beauties down there at the end.' Dirty bastard, he just invited us to put on a freak show for these nobs.

"I knew Roughhouse Pete, too, the goddamn prick — excuse my French. Just a real alky. You'd just see him down on Powell Street, by the Union wharf there. He had a big gut on 'im like a laundry bag at the last. He always had black eyes. Everytime he got down on the skid road there he'd get em. He was just a booze kitten. He'd sneak a bunch into camp and peddle it. Oh, the lies that the bugger could tell! Just bullshit. The last time him and I were in the same camp was at Reed Bay for McCoy and Wilson. Before he went to the Rock. Then he was at Shenanigan Lake when I was there. I guess he died in the thirties."

"Oh, when you were a riggin' tramp like me you got to know all those old bastards — Dog-Face Joe, Ten Spot, Bullshit Bill, Black Angus Macdonald, Spooky Charlie Lundman, Pegleg Whitey

Hoolan—if you didn't see 'em in camp you'd see 'em in town. In them days we all holed up somewhere's down in the east end of Vancouver for the winter shutdown. What they call Gastown now, that was a city within a city, it was our place. The hotels there all catered to loggers, everything catered to loggers. The Grand Hotel. That was the famous one.

"In my time the Grand was run by Ernie Clarke, 'The Logger's Friend.' He'd kind of play den mother—keep a guy's roll, make sure he got bailed out if he landed in the slammer, make sure he got the boat out in the spring in case he was too snaky to crawl down to the dock on his own. Guys that went broke, he'd give 'em a few bucks for sweeping up and maybe put their room on the tab if he figured they were good fer it. Sometimes he'd line a guy up for a job, especially if that guy owed him for a winter's room. He wasn't the only one like that, but he got most credit for it.

"It's hard to explain what it was like then. A guy felt more like he had a place in the damn scheme of things. When the camps got going you'd drag your ass down to the Union Steamships dock, get on the *Cassiar*, get your stateroom and all, snoop around and see if there was any babes on board, maybe get together in somebody's room for a hair of the dog, trade gossip about which guys were going to which camp up the line. Well, before you know it, the boat's comin', let's say into Lasqueti Island. You'd all go out and hang over the rail, everybody on the island'd be there on the dock, there'd always be somebody you'd know. Charlie Klein'd be tryin to talk you into gettin' off to help him for a couple of weeks, women'd be screamin' scandal back and forth, some gyppo maybe would be there catchin' freight and guys up on the boat would be after him about work, he'd be sayin', well, have you ever run a Skagit, yup, well—last-minute negotiations, the skipper'd be listening from the bridge to see which way it went, maybe hold the boat a bit, people'd be stumbling along still yappin' as the boat eased back, shouting and waving—and this would go on all the way up the line to Rivers Inlet, at every stop. That kinda kept things together, you see. The coast in them days was like a buncha people along a street seeing each other all the time on the way by. It got to be kind of a family affair. It all seemed a lot closer together than it does now."

When we said we'd been down for a look at Minstrel, he right away wanted to know who was there? Who was there? Just tourists, I said. Yeah, he says. There's never anybody there anymore. Then Mary remembered the two young guys who'd didn't look like locals but seemed to be staying there, and Mackay deduced they must be the two stakers up staking the knob. "There's all kinds of copper up thoro, right thoro," ho oaid, pointing at a rocky pinnacle with a Cherokee cut across the channel. "I know, Perley and me logged it one time. Jim Dewdney, he staked it last year and these companies, they read about it in the *Gazette* so they sent out these punks to stake all around him in case e's got something. They wanted me to go up and show 'em, but shit I wouldn't have anything to do with the young bastards. If they was for themselves, okay, but not for some yank arsehole cumpny — excuse my terminology."

We'd stayed longer than we'd planned and I'd get up to go but he'd start another story, and I'd be sitting down again. He kept bringing up the fact he was in a hurry to finish up his claim and I was worried about the prime working time he was losing on our account. Finally we got out the door, expecting he would want a ride back to finish the day's work. It was only 3 PM.

"Ah, to hell with 'er. It's too hot to climb that hill now. I'll go over when she cools down. I gotta watch my ticker." But I could tell just by the way he said it he was finished for the day.

We buzzed back to Hadley's but nobody was in the shop. I found Bill inside a seiner but he hadn't had time to flux the heads. He'd do it in the morning. He was talking now as if it was a foregone conclusion the head would be cracked, and sure enough, by the time I got around the next day he was able to tell me it was, in two places. My heart sank. What now?

"Well," Bill said, "you might just be lucky. I might know where you could get a head for that."

"Where?"

"Oh, I've got a couple over in the cove. There's two complete motors. They were good, but I don't know what kind of shape they're in now. Nobody's been over to look at 'em for awhile." Again, he was too busy to do anything for a few days, but I persuaded him to let me go remove a head myself. Leaving Mary to read her novel on the *Beaver*, I zapped back out Havannah Channel a couple of miles and turned right into Burial Cove, a pleasant sheltered little bay, totally abandoned except for a ruined cabin and several big cherry trees. I had expected to find boats up on skids, or at least dragged up the beach. Instead all I could see was what looked like a deadhead sticking up, but when I got closer turned out to be the mast of an old Fraser River gillnetter submerged well below the tideline. I went exploring for a few hours and came back at low tide when the boat lay exposed in the mud, with another one alongside. One looked to have been floating until fairly recently but the other was black and falling apart. I couldn't believe these two wrecks were what Bill had sent me for, but there was nothing else in sight, and they both had rusty, ruined Easthope motors in them.

I checked the newer one first, but its engine was a three-cylinder model of much later vintage than ours, and had obviously different heads. The motor in the second boat was a two-banger like ours, but it had been under water so long it was just a brown mound of rust. I was very disappointed but decided to strip down the good motor anyway, since I was there and had the chance. Something would be saved. Maybe a head from it could be traded for one that would fit ours or something. Maybe Bill would be disposed to give me break from the astronomical charges Mackay had been warning us about. This motor had a few barnacles on it, but came apart with ease. I took off the manifolds and heads and clutch and found them in surprisingly good shape. I was so encouraged I decided to have a try at the older motor too. It had been in the salt water quite a few years. All that was left was a furry mound of red rust bestrewn with seaweed and studded with barnacles. The nuts holding the head on had lost their shape and become soft lumps of rust. I couldn't get a wrench on them, so I hit one with a cold chisel. To my amazement, the brown crust broke away and the black nub moved. I hit it a few more times, and it became so loose I could unscrew it the rest of the way with my fingers. The threads had been coated with graphite and were still sharp. The other three nuts were similarly good and within a few minutes I was breaking the head loose. It popped off. On the outside it was mushy and shapeless with corrosion, but inside it was still oily and dry. I stripped both motors of anything I could get loose, thinking this would be the last chance for them to make a contribution to the dwindling community of Easthope users. The skiff was so loaded I was worried it would swamp as it ploughed through the water.

I rushed up the dock with the rusty head and showed Bill. He turned it over in his hands, looking at the rust-eaten outside and the dry inside. "Jesus, that's lucky," he said.

"Can we use it?" I said.

"Should do. We'll clean 'er up and stick some valves in and it should work."

I reminded him we were in a big hurry to get on with our trip. He grinned. He was working around the clock on two hundred-thousand-dollar seiners that were supposed to be ready for that summer's fishing, and the season was almost over. I felt his grin on my back as I walked down to the boat. I wondered if we'd ever escape Hadley Bay. But I felt good about the work I'd done stripping those motors.

The next morning we went down the Channel for another try at seeing Mackay's wooden spartree in operation. It was around 11 AM but he wasn't up the hill yet. I looked over at his shack and saw him just starting over in his skiff. In a few minutes he was beside us.

"I was just comin' when I saw you," he said. We started following his cable up the hill. The logs had gouged a deep ditch in the clay of the hillside, the sides slimy wet and textured with the winding pattern of the mainline. Someplaces it was two feet deep with mudwater and so steep you had to grab huckleberry bushes with both hands while your feet flew out below. He had a route worked out all the way up and kept shooing us this way and that. He had been up and down so many times stepping in the same place every time there were footholds worn into the clay like an endless boot-pocked stairway.

"See that hemlog right there?" he said between gasps. "That's the one I was tellin' you about I chased them bears up, all three of 'em went up there like a streak of greased loonshit — pardon my Sanskrit — I carry the axe and shovel and bang 'em y'see, to warn 'em off. I don't want to surprise that big old sow."

He showed us another garden, a little patch of roots and rocks about two yards square that he'd dug-up and planted with six-year-old seeds, but none of them sprouted. He laughed a laugh that sounded more like a whimper and shook his head in wonder at his own foolishness. The climb made me puff but both Mary and I managed to keep ahead of him. He kept finding excuses to stop and talk about his bears and the song sparrows the crows chased away and the edible elderberries. He'd had a heart attack a few years back and he had to watch he didn't overdo it but he still climbed up and down that hill to unhook his logs and wrassle hangups and right now had the hangup of them all, halfway down the hill.

"Holy Mexican Jesus, will you look at that mess," he yowled,

Minstrel Island, 1974. The peaked roof at centre is the old store, since burned.

waving his dented hard hat at the tangle of logs and stumps and cables. The tree stood on a bit of a flat with quite a pile of barkless busted chunks pulled up around it. Any working spartree I'd ever seen was bright, with red bark and sticky sap, but this one had been up so long it was black and weathered. Like the muddy chunks below in his boom, the wood in his cold-deck pile looked worthless to me, but the price of timber was at an all-time high and apparently he got something for them, either as pulp or fuel. It was what they call a salvage claim. The standing timber was logged eight or ten years before by a Crown Zellerbach contractor, but they left a lot of the small and broken wood and he was cleaning up under a permit from the BC Forest Service. But with his heart, his hangups, his bears, his song sparrows, gardening etc., it'd been slow work. He had been forced to go back seven times to beg for extensions to the permit, each time more desperately.

The forestry was getting anxious to burn the slash and get the ground back into production, so the ranger swore the current extension was absolutely the last. There were now only seven days left on it. There were a hundred or so chunks in his pile and he only got two down the hill on a good day. Meanwhile everything

Jim Mackay at his one-man floatcamp, 1974.

was hung up. Mackay got quite sweaty and wild-eyed when he thought about it, so he tried to keep bullshitting and not think about it.

I stood under the tree trying to follow his explanation of how he swung his blocks without climbing the tree, using an open-face hook on the passline. After three tries I still couldn't get it. His donkey was an old 10-12 Lawrence, and I was anxious to see it run, but it was out of gas. A little sheepishly he told us he was waiting for his pension cheque to come so he could take a barl down to Minstrel and get some. I thought we were coming up to log, but it turned out he was just showing us around. Until the money came through he was going to spend his time getting his boom in shape. We straggled back down the hill. As we passed the hangup he snatched his hardhat off, slammed it down on the butt and roared with sudden fury, "Look at that hoozified buckskin sonuvabitch — my only good choker down six feet in loonshit, you filthy-livin' cakzicker!" He was so mad he forgot to apologize.

I helped him stow a few logs in the pocket and suddenly he was propositioning me to go to work for him. "If I'm not cleaned up by the third of next month I'll lose my deposit," he told us. I said we were on holidays, and we had to get home soon to get out number four. "How much would you want? C'mon." He kept at it. "I'll take both of you. Greeneyes here can cook for us. The two of you for two weeks. Name your price."

Mare was getting a little tired of standing around watching us, so after an hour or so I decided to go, saying I have to get back to work on my motor. Mackay threw down his pike pole and said, "Ah hell, let's go over and bullshit some more." I threw a glance at Mare, she shrugged, so few minutes later we were back at his cabin. I noticed a couple of absolutely the most haywire crab traps I had ever seen lying out on the float. They were homemade out of plastic hose and fishnet.

"Are there crabs around here?" I asked. We had a good trap on the *Beaver* and I'm thinking how nice it would be to have a feed.

"Oh hell yes, up Cutter Creek. Lots of 'em." He pushed one of the traps with his toe. "You gotta pull these up fast because the crabs can get out." He looked around at his floating junkyard self-consciously. "Everything I got is haywire but I can't fix it because I'm too busy doin' nothing," he said.

Inside, I got him back on the subject of Minstrel.

"You know, old Oscar Soderman was one of the first guys in Minstrel. He handlogged there before there was anything. It was just him. That must have been before 1900."

Oscar Soderman's name was known to me mostly because of his wife, Sidney, a notorious ex-madam who took over as his camp manager and came to be feared by two-hundred-pound choker-men from one end of the coast range to the other. They had operated a good-sized float camp in Soderman Cove, near Port Harvey, up into the forties.

"Harbledown was the first place settled in this part of the coast. And you know who was the first settler? A Kanaka, Sonny Kamano. He came straight from Hawaii and jumped ship, Christ, it must've been in the 1880s. Kamano married an Indian and raised a family, then Jim Joliffe come in, he was from Nova Scotia, and married one of Kamano's daughters. He run camps all over, Jackson Bay . . . he had his own steam tug and towed his own logs."

As Mackay described him, Jim Joliffe seemed a possible original of the Carter for whom Grainger toiled in *Woodsmen of the West*, since both were Nova Scotia–born loggers who owned their own steamboats and worked around Knight Inlet just after the turn of the century. Mackay didn't have an opinion on that, but he had some more scrambled notions of early Minstrel.

"Soderman had a handloggin' licence — they had handloggin' licences then you see. Old Bendickson down Hardwicke Island he had one — I don't think they're any of them left. Christ, you could go here and there you know, you could stop anywhere you liked as long as it wasn't a timber limit. Well Soderman, he sold his to this old King. And then somebody else got hold of it. Then Neil Hood wound up with it. I'm not sure when Neil got the hotel. I know he had it in 1919, but how long before that, I don't know. Prohibition came on, the 1914–1918 war, you see. And the place evidently stood open. There was nobody there, no licence or sales or ennathing. Now, after the war, prohibition was repealed and Neil Hood got 'er up and runnin' again. That place that's behind, with the poolroom and that, that was the hotel at Port Harvey. Neil, to stop the licence from comin' in there when they were comin' back, he bought that. Moved it to Minstrel so they couldn't get opposition down there. Towed it around on floats. He put it to good use later. There was times he had every room in it full and every room in his own hotel full, and still was turning guys away."

Things were starting to fall together a little bit, at least concerning Minstrel's earlier history. I knew the hotel was built sometime in the first five years of the century, when the Knight Inlet area was in the midst of the boom Grainger described in 1908:

A year ago I came to Port Browning [Port Harvey] and found a district of islands and inlets firmly occupied, in appearance, by man: camps scattered through it; steamers running directly to it; machinery at work; hotels and stores at business — everything old established. An old-timer told me he could remember when the first men came to hand-log . . . And that dim past was *only seven years ago*.

This period of growth was then cut off by the outbreak of World

War I and the Minstrel Hotel, the bar dry, lay empty until Neil
Hood resurrected it shortly following the war's end. He kept it well
after Hadley first came in 1925. Isador Herawitz, the man locals
remembered only as "Izzy the Jew" had it during the peak years
of the forties before selling out to Buck Munn and his wife Grace.
These were the important names connected with Minstrel until
Perley Sherdahl bought the hotel from Russ Boyd in 1960.

Izzy presided over the period of greatest activity. Mackay said
sometimes on a Saturday night there, every seat would be taken
and guys'd be lined up all around the walls, three hundred at a
whack. So many boats at the dock it looked like mussels on a flat
rock. Nowadays, he said, they didn't even bother heating the
building in the winter, and if you wanted a drink you took it in
Perley and Jean's living room. But in busy times every room was
packed. In the winter the heat was always bad and the plumbing
froze so the guys just pissed out the windows.

"Now, I'm not kiddin' you, you'd take a careful long look before
you walked past that place. And stink? Omigod! In the spring,
with all those drunks rainin' 'er down all winter, holy snuff-col-
oured Christ — excuse my Latin — you could smell the place goin'
by on the other side of the channel."

Izzy was the opposite of Neil Hood, scrabbling after every
penny he saw — literally. The guys would throw pennies in the
urinal, then watch Izzy come out of the can holding something
in his hand and go in the living quarters. They'd signal the whole
pub to be quiet, listening for the sound of the water running in
the sink, then they'd roar with laughter.

The next morning early we woke up to find Bill Hadley aboard
installing the heads. The rusty blob I'd salvaged was now sandblasted down to fresh metal, looking like a new casting. He'd done
both sets of valves. Within an hour he had everything buckled up.
I started the engine. I didn't recognize the sound, it was so
different. Instead of going chuff chuff chuff it went bark bark bark.
It was harder, like a hammer pounding cement instead of like a
broom beating a rug. I took it out for a run and it went half again
as fast as we'd been used to, although it really seemed like five
times as fast. Blinding speed. I was overjoyed. This was the real
reason coast people loved the Easthope, not because it never

broke down, but because when it did you could patch it up with stuff that was laying around on the beach.

My only remaining concern, a serious one, was what the charge would be, but when I asked, Bill said, "I won't charge you for the parts because of all that work you done strippin' those motors. So three hours at $14 and we'll call it square."

"Fair enough," I said. I felt like kissing him, but my Scotch grandmother had conditioned me never to let on when I thought I was getting a bargain.

"A head costs $130," he said, "so you made yourself $130 over there."

I wrote him a cheque and pulled out feeling very proud of myself. A lot of guys in my place would have been completely stumped. Maybe I wasn't quite the useless tit some of my detractors back in the Harbour might think. But as soon as I thought of the Harbour I thought of old Old Elmer Pottle warning me about the way the engine sounded back before we started. He had been right all along.

We had only three days left before we said we'd be back, so we had to head straight south, but we thought we better go have one last goodbye at Mackay. Heading into rock-studded Chatham Channel with the *Beaver*, I realized how much we'd come to feel at home there. Before, I wouldn't have taken the big boat into a place like that without stopping to fret over the rash of crosses on the chart, but now I wheeled through with hardly thought. Thanks to our engine trouble, we had really become a part of this place.

Mackay was working over at his claim for once, beating on his jackpot with a cracked peavey, and as usual it didn't take much argument to get him to stop for a coffee, this time on our boat. I thought he would be interested in admiring the *Beaver* V, but he hardly noticed it.

"Where's the motor, oh, I see, back in the fish hold. She's bin made into a *yacht*, then." That was the end of his interest.

To my dismay, he was still on his kick about having us work for him. I was afraid if he kept at it I would have to say something that would hurt him, and I wanted to part with good feelings. Looking back after all the hundreds of days and weeks I've frittered away since, I can ask myself why I didn't give him a few days, if just for the sake of being able to say we'd helped the last of the oldtime bush apes clean up his last claim. I suppose I thought his little salvage operation was pointless anyway, something he did only for a reason not to join his sisters in Kelowna, and to keep faith with his old lost world of Johnny-on-the-Spot and Step-and-a-Half Phelps and Eight-Day Wilson and Ed Dahlby and Harold Brownson. I wouldn't have been surprised to find he actually had no sale for the wood at all, and just let his chunk boom drift away in the end. Also, I hadn't seen him do anything to lessen my general impression that he was probably a thoroughgoing old reprobate you'd like less as you got to know more.

I met a young fellow later who'd lived around Minstrel, and he had Mackay down as real trouble. "He tried to steal my wife!" the guy said, with such indignation in his voice I could only conclude old Mackay must have made a pretty good stab at it. Still, I felt I was kind of cheating Mackay, because he'd given me what I'd come looking for.

Our last conversation with him was given mostly to his favourite preoccupation — cataloguing the stupidity of the damn fools who ran the show. As far as he was concerned, the country was now so buggered up there was no place left for an independent working man who wanted to put in an honest day's work without kissing anybody's ass. "The scissorbills run everything now," Mackay sighed. "They've about run all the good men off the claim. The timekeepers have taken over."

He looked suspiciously at us. We were obviously on the scissorbill side in his eyes, and here we were blowing our last chance to get right. "If I lose this claim I don't know what the hell I'll do," he moaned. There was nowhere left for him to go. In the old days, when you got feeling like this you caught the *Cassiar* down to Vancouver and hit the skid road. But you couldn't go down to the skid road anymore because the fast buck artists had tricked it out as a tourist trap. The last time he'd been down there he couldn't find any of his old watering holes because they all had new names. He got so turned around he ended up putting the hustle on a lady cop. "Can you believe a man'd be as stupid as that?" he said, shaking his head. Minstrel was all he had left. He went down in the daytime for grub and freight, but he hadn't been there at night for two years or more. There was no point. There was nobody there but Perley and his warm beer. I asked him if he thought the place would liven up if they opened the woods up to small operators again.

"Sure it would, but what's the use of talkin about it? The big cumpnys have all the timber and they aren't ever going to give it up.

"We *know* the big cumpnys run the show. We *know* that. The big cumpnys put us independents out of the way because we showed 'em up too bad. What I can't swallow is the way these guys loggin' around here now play along, cuttin' the big cumpny's timber for a percentage. They're not loggers, they're sharecroppers!"

"What about your boat?" I said. The *Orange Crate* had an "A" licence for salmon fishing, which was worth its weight in gold at that particular time, due to the licence freeze recently brought in by the federal minister of fisheries, Jack Davis. If he couldn't fish it he could sell it for enough to live in comfort for all the years he had left.

"Ah, the goddamn fishing industry is buggered up worse than logging," Mackay ranted. "Davis, that goddamn scissorbill, he's right in with the cumpnys, you know. Jimmy Sinclair, he owns BC Packers and Trudeau both. What a goddamn scandal that is. That boat there, I bought it five years ago for twenty-seven hundred. Now I could sell it for twenty-seven thousand. Well, them big cumpnys own hundreds of boats. Thousands. Big, big seiners and packers. Christ, yes. Well, can you think how much that cumpny stock went up on account of this Davis Plan?

"People are so stupid. Us Canadians must be the stupidest people on earth."

We left him standing in the door of his black little shack, making a shy little baby-wave and putting on a stagey hurt look. I kept up with Minstrel news when I could after that. Bill Hadley died tragically in an accident at his shop. Perley's boat was found drifting with no one aboard one day and he was never seen again. People said he did it on purpose because for his type of guy it was all over. The store burned down and some bright-eyed developer demolished the hotel and all its ghosts, but thankfully went broke before he could carry out his plan of replacing it with tourist cabins. When I was last up in the summer of 1989 the only building left was the old Cracroft Hotel, which was being recycled as a store.

Mackay hung on for years, until they finally dragged him off to a home in Campbell River, too miserable to die. But every time I pick up a newspaper and read about Jack Davis getting re-elected in spite of his fraud conviction, or about the Tories signing away Canadian natural resources under free trade, old Mackay's voice comes back to me, echoing across the water: "Us Canadians must be the stupidest people on earth."

HAS ANYONE SEEN THE
WORKING CLASS?

For Tom Wayman

A young American woman with a PhD has written me
saying she wants to devote her life to the working class
and can't decide if it should be in some third-world country
or Canada. I haven't been able to reply for over a year
although I feel an uncertain responsibility
to speak up for our bunch

A friend I owe much to has put her up to this
after reading some things I wrote about driving cat
and I struggle to be worthy
of their confidence: *the working class*
the *Canadian* working class — oh thou elusive wraith,
long have I avoided this moment of truth

I think of my brother who still gets dirty for money
— but pulls down more in a year than the local doctor

I think of the Communist Party and its confident talk
of a Canadian proletariat — but then at election time
polling fewer votes than the Rhinocerous Party

I think of the time that student marxist group at UBC
got all charged up with its own propaganda
and marched down to free the embattled workers at Canron

and the Canron bosses had to call the riot squad in
to stop the men from leaving their work
to pound the piss out of these damnfool students

I think of all those loggers I grew up with
how they would turn away from any attempt
to class them together, especially
as any sort of underprivileged species
—the funny look that would pass between them
when some hapless tourist came to camp
and made the mistake of saying "you fellows. . ."
in that special class self-conscious way. . .

I think of how the young guys wanted so much to be rich,
to go to Hawaii and drive a new Cadillac
instead of a ten-year-old one
as long as this wouldn't make them into shits

I think of how some did get rich
and liked it fine
although they didn't do so good
at not becoming shits

I think of how the the gillnet fishermen
used to mock their ever-so-serious union rep
and how they didn't care to hear
that what they thought was a proud career
was just some smarter men making monkeys of them
I think of how the one word I never heard
in the workingclass town where I grew up
was the word workingclass

The more I think about it the more the Canadian working class
takes on the shape of some impossible fiction

until this one Saturday in January Sticks Andersen
a salt-soaked old troller who's been around forever
is in my kitchen bitching about the price of live-landed lingcod
and another neighbour, a nice-enough guy from the city
who has never worked with his hands and has a bigger house

for weekends than we do for all year round
comes tapping at the door to see if we can help him
start this little bitty powersaw he got for Christmas.
He's got the operator's manual memorized
but cranks it like a baby —
one good snap is all it takes
and he's tickled as hell — "I was afraid I had a lemon," he says

We can see he'll never get the load of firewood
he wants for his new French parlour heater
he'll saw both feet off first
but Sticks doesn't want to make him feel bad
so he says, "By God, I could use some wood . . ."
and we lead the guy back in the bush with our own battered Stihls

"What size wood does that there new boiler of yours take?"
Sticks asks and we rip through a bunch of nice downed fir
as our friend frets and fusses with his saw
measuring off each cut with a steel tape —

"We musn't mix up our pieces," he cautions us with irritation
tugging his few hard-clawed chunks away from the growing pile

"Well, you know, this is comin pretty easy here," Sticks says,
"Why don't you just pull your bus up here and we'll throw on a
    load."
"But most of this is *yours,* . . ." the guy stammers,
realizing for the first time we've cut every piece to his size,
"I couldn't let you . . . you must take some for yourselves . . ."
"Ah, me 'n Flash here can get wood any time,"
Sticks replies. "We'll come back tomorrow."
"This is worth money . . ." the other mumbles,
digging out keys to his new Cherokee Chief and breaking into a
    trot

leaving Sticks and I standing there confronted
once again
by all the difference that is class

THE CADBOROSAURUS
MEETS HUBERT EVANS

I don't believe in flying saucers. I don't believe in ghosts. I don't
believe the eighteenth-century concept of free enterprise can be
revived by wishful thinking to cure all the complex ills of our time.
I never did believe in Pierre Trudeau's charisma. I'm skeptical.
Believe me.

But I do believe in the Cadborosaurus.

No, I've never seen one. I've got something better than that.

Hubert Evans saw one.

I knew Hubert a long time before he revealed this to me, a few
years before he died at age ninety-four in the spring of 1986. Some
people, if they saw a sea serpent, would try to make a career out
of it. With Hubert, I don't think I ever would have found out if I
hadn't been sitting in his front room in Roberts Creek that day,
looking out across the glassy calm Gulf towards Nanaimo, when
a new report of the Loch Ness monster happened to come on the
radio.

"What do you think of that?" Hubert asked, very evenly.

Hubert, as anyone who has spent even ten minutes in the
healing balm of his presence will aver, was one of the most
admirable beings ever to dwell amongst us. You can tell just by
looking at the picture on the back of his novel O *Time in Your
Flight*, published when he was eighty-seven, recounting with
scientific precision what life was like back in 1899 when he was
eight — surely one of the greatest feats of pure memory in litera-

164

ture. Hubert had a gorgeous mane of fine white hair and a visage reminiscent of Mark Twain's except with compassion in place of Twain's conceit, and whereas Mark Twain became bitter after he got to be about fifty and wrote nothing more of consequence, when Hubert turned ninety in 1983 — sixteen years older than

Mark Twain ever got to be — he had just finished publishing another fine, optimistic book about his wide-awake life in the twentieth century. By that time his body was truly the proverbial tattered coat upon a stick, but his mind was still better than yours or mine ever was.

"Bunch of malarkey," I said, going back to my first impulse after some thought. It was unusual for him to make mention of anything so frivolous.

"We had one here, you know."

"One what?"

"A sea serpent. Or some sort of sea creature quite similar to the way they describe that one over there."

"No!"

"Well, I've never told many people, but it's a fact," he said. "It

was in 1932, right out there where you're looking. I was up on the
back lot with Dick Reeve, our neighbour, working on the road—
that same one you drove in on to get here. Bob Stephens, the old
Scot from down the beach—he's dead these many years—came
puffing up the hill and said, 'By God now, you've got to come down
and see what you make of this. We've had the glass on it for half
an hour. It's the damndest thing.'

"It was late afternoon with the water dead calm just as it is now,
and the sun was low so the water was just a sheet of gold. And
here, out just beyond that deadhead, was a series of bumps
breaking the water, all in dark silhouette, and circled with ripples.'Sea lions,' I said. 'They run in a line like that sometimes.' 'Just
you keep watching,' old Scotty said. And just a minute or so later,
along at the end of this series of bumps, up out of the water comes
a shaft—this was all in silhouette, so we couldn't see detail,
although the outlines were very clear—up, up, up until it must
have been six or eight feet out of the water. There was a spar buoy
out on the reef then, which was about twelve inches through, and
I could see this thing was about the same thickness—certainly no
smaller. 'You know, it could be a log,' I said. I'd seen a crooked log
sometimes catch in the current and roll, so a limb comes up like
that—when you see something you don't know what to make of,
you keep trying to explain it by the things you know.

"But right there as we stood watching, none of us breathing a
word, the top end of this shaft began to elongate horizontally,
until we were presented with the profile of a head, very much like
a horse's in general shape, with eye bumps, nostrils and something
in the way of ears or horns. The neighbour down the way said it
had stuff hanging down like hair but I didn't see that. I tell you, it
was a feeling, watching that head come round as if to look at us.
It just put the hair up on the back of your neck."

When Hubert finished telling me this I was just as speechless
as he must have been at the original event. Knowing him as I did,
it was not possible to disbelieve. Apart from the fact he is a very
reliable observer of west coast nature, I don't think I have ever
encountered a person more careful of his reputation for getting
things right.

I had to accept the facts as given. The problem was a matter of
re-ordering the suddenly fractured cosmos around them. How
could such a thing occur and not be known? How could any

person, even one of Hubert's character, look upon such a thing and not have it mark him in some way for the rest of his days? Had he ever tried to write about it?

No, he made a point of not doing so, although he told the kids at the time, 'If you can find a camera and get a picture of this, it might be the biggest thing that ever happens to you.' So they went rummaging all over Roberts Creek and found a camera, but no film. After a few minutes Hubert went back up to work on his road but his daughter Elizabeth, who was about eleven then, had come home from school and watched it for half an hour more as it worked its way down the beach towards the mouth of Roberts Creek. When Hubert's neighbour Dick Reeve came up from taking a look, Hubert said, 'Well, what did you see?'

'I know what I saw but I'm not telling anybody,' Reeve said.

"There were reports after," Hubert continued. "The police boat saw it and got a good description, accurate measurements and all. There were many sightings. You could look it up."

I'd heard of the Cadborosaurus before, but I'd always dismissed it as an attempt by the Victoria Chamber of Commerce to borrow yet another of the beloved mother country's tourist attractions. As I now learned from a search of the newspaper file at the Provincial Archives, the legend rested on reasonably impressive factual ground. The first records, if they can be accepted as such, are prehistoric. Salish Indian mythology is rife with appearances by a friendly Caddy-like creature called by the Sechelt *T'chain-ko*, and there are a number of very ancient petroglyphs at Petroglyph Park in Nanaimo and at other sites around the Gulf of Georgia recording shapes remarkably like the one described by Hubert. At the other end of the time scale there have been scattered sightings as recently as the late seventies. But Caddy's credibility rests mainly on a flurry of sightings which took place on the lower BC coast between August 1932 and 1934.

The first reported sighting in this series, and the one which gave the creature its most enduring name, was made October 8, 1933 off Victoria's Cadboro Bay by Major W.H. Langley, a prominent barrister who was then clerk of the legislature.

Sailing past Chatham Island one Sunday in October 1933 with Mrs. Langley in their sloop *Dorothy* at about 1:30 in the afternoon, the couple got a close view of the monster's back, which was "nearly eighty feet long and as wide as the average automobile."

It was greenish-brown, serrated and "every bit as big as a whale but entirely different from a whale in many respects," according to Major Langley, who added that he had spent time on a whaling ship and knew his whales.

His report in the *Victoria Times* elicited another from Mr. F.W. Kemp, an employee of the Provincial Archives, who had seen the monster in the same location the previous August but had kept quiet about it, fearing ridicule. Mrs. Kemp had been sitting on the beach when she saw "a commotion in the water which threw a wash against the rocks similar to that caused by a motorboat."

Mr. Kemp was summoned, and as the party watched from a distance of three or four hundred yards, the beast "slid about ten feet of its head and body onto the rock and commenced to rub itself against the rough surface." They could plainly see its serrated back, which near the tail "resembled the cutting edge of a saw" and the sun, glistening on its body, clearly showed its colour to be greenish-brown. After two or three minutes the animal slid off the rock and went on its way down the channel, "thrashing the water into a lather with its tail."

In the following two years there were dozens of Cadborosaurus reports from Cowichan Bay, Nanaimo, Pender Island, the north arm of the Fraser, Sooke, Campbell River, Alberni Inlet and the Queen Charlotte Islands—by fishermen, steamer captains, quarry owners, an excited new photographer who ran after it without taking his camera, the assistant accountant of the CPR's coastal operations and a wealthy businessman with a steam yacht full of distinguished guests.

All of the sightings reported a long looped body with a cow-like or camel-like head mounted on a long, slender neck. One of the most convincing later reports was made in February 1950 by Chief Justice James T. Brown of Saskatchewan's King's Bench.

Impressive evidence, but in all these great questions like the existence of God or the Sasquatch, the crucial thing is not the mass of evidence that almost convinces you, it's the sliver of doubt that remains, holding the verdict forever open. To remove that final obstacle to conviction takes something special, and that's why I feel compelled to spill Hubert's special secret after all these years. After hearing him I know sea monsters exist. This in itself is a sufficiently important fact that it needs to be said; it changes a lot of things. But I am equally excited by the realization that I may have stumbled upon the ultimate description of Hubert: he was the sort of person who, if he told you the Cadborosaurus exists, you suddenly discovered you believed in Cadborosauruses. I would be hard put to say which is more remarkable.

BILL SINCLAIR AT 90

GARDEN BAY BC JANUARY 9, 1971: Bill Sinclair turned ninety on Saturday. Ninety, that's old.

That means he was twenty when it was still the 1800s, and say thirty before he saw a car.

A grown man when some clanky old thing with candles for headlights and a top speed of seventeen miles per hour was considered a mind-boggling technological triumph, and still around to see the world grow complacent about flying to the moon.

He ogled both minis and hoop skirts, and saw the world change its thinking accordingly.

Events our history books fumble with were personal memories to him.

How could one head hold it all? And what questions could you ask such a man, with a puny twenty years' perspective, that wouldn't make him laugh out loud, especially a man who had spent that time as an author and reputed savant.

I began to worry a little as John Daly's truck bumped down past Ted Girard's and Ivy Potts' to the old man's place on Sinclair Bay.

I was hoping to come away with the all-time New Years Centennial Champion feature story for my little homegrown newspaper, the *Peninsula Voice*.

If John was guessing right, I might not have to ask anything.

He kept patting a flask in his pocket and saying, "This will get him talking."

I had seen Bill Sinclair only once before, gassing up the *Hoo Hoo* at Lloyd's about ten years ago, but I recognized him instantly. His face was very distinctive: very long and thin, with a high nose,

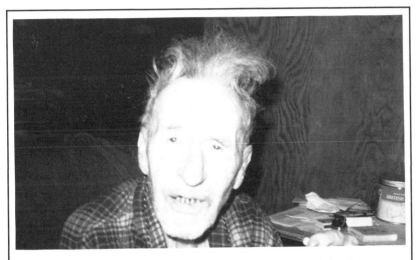

Bill Sinclair making the supreme effort on his ninetieth birthday.

close, small eyes, its length accentuated by a tuft of thick white hair on top of his head.

There was something distinctively Scottish about his face, as there is about John Kenneth Galbraith's, a cragginess.

He wasn't exactly jumping for joy to see us. "Who the hell..." I heard him mutter to his wife Ora, and then louder, "Oh, Daly." He was propped up in front of the kitchen stove with a well-used electric blanket up to his chin, facing in the direction of a TV which was on a Bugs Bunny cartoon.

He noticed me and held out a crabbed, cool hand, but kept his eyes on the TV. I tried to remember who told me he was blind. He had been able to tell I was a stranger easily enough. Most of the time he paid no attention when spoken to, but sometimes he replied brightly and clearly. I was perplexed. Nothing is harder than to speak when you're unsure of a person's senses.

John was busy clanking glasses at the sink.

Finally I ventured something about the weather, which was quite mild.

"Pretty good for March alright," he said, then, noticing my abrupt silence, "No. What is it — April?"

"It's your birthday."

"My birthday is in January."

John thrust a glass of rye in front of him. "Many happy returns, Bill!"

Bill pinched the glass in his stiff fingers like a crab and stared intensely into it. "I hope to hell not," he muttered. He sniffed the drink and looked up at the bottle. "Good God, Daly, do you carry a bottle with you everywhere?" He took a tiny sip and set it down.

Curses, foiled, I thought.

"You know it's hard for me," I began rather shakily, seizing an interval, "to think one man's mind could stand the change there's been..."

I was cut off by a groan.

"Oh Ora, why didn't you let me stay in bed?" He sat up. "I'm going back to bed."

Ora sat him down. "The Dalys have made a nice dinner and invited lots of people."

I started to wonder how possible it would be to get Judge Mittelstead's interview done an issue ahead of time.

John and Ora decided to get the show on the road before Bill crashed, so soon we were struggling up the path, John and I on each side of Bill, and Ora following.

Before long the path turned bumpy and one-lane, and Bill quit trying, sending his mind back to the bed perhaps, and leaving us to do as we wished with his husk. From a pure engineering standpoint the solution would have been a piggyback but since we were dealing with an honorary fellow of both the Canadian Authors' Association and the Fishermens' Union, we continued three abreast, trying to give steady support as we clambered over logs and ripped our feet through salal.

"Living to ninety years of age is absurd," Bill grumbled. "An old man is nothing but a curse to himself and a burden to the people around him."

I dug around in my mind for a fatuous counter but his logic had wiped them away.

"I ought to die but I can't."

"That's 'cause you always get the middle," I said, whacking my shin on a windfall and stretching his arm. He kept wanting to know where we were.

"If I pass out just bundle up and pack me," he said.

At the car I opened the door and stood waiting, though John had gone around the other side and it was obvious Bill couldn't make the step himself.

"Here, pile me in there," he said impatiently, as though we were dealing with a sack of spuds.

He was light as a feather. For some reason I expected him to be quite leaden.

On the way over I tried luring him into conversation again, this time about his writing. I mentioned *Gunpowder Lightning,* one of his more obscure books, thinking he would be tired of hearing about *Poor Man's Rock.*

"*Gunpowder Lightning,* eh," he said, grinning. "Ha ha. *Gunpowder Lightning.* Yes, sir."

"That was your last one, wasn't it?"

"I don't know. *Poor Man's Rock,* that's the best one."

We hauled him up Daly's steps and plopped him in a chair by the oil range. The room was filled with people—Jimmy and Eleanor Reid, Ivy Potts and Tony, Sinclair's daughter Cherry Whittaker—a vivacious, impressive woman—and her two grown children Geoff and Janie.

The table was set for fourteen and the sink was a forest of bottles and the scent of baking salmon filled the room.

John's ex-wife Pixie was bustling around sloshing out drinks. Bill, slumped in his corner, took no notice of the excited laughter and proved insensible to attempts to get him involved. Finally he had to be hauled off to the bedroom, where he fell on the bed like an exhausted child and pulled the covers over his head.

Not to be deterred by the failure of the feature personality, the group quickly leapt into loud, vigorous political arguments—an inevitable feature of Daly gatherings—and I managed to get the topic around to my newspaper often enough to bag three half-year subscriptions. Finally we got going on the subject of Bertrand William Sinclair.

Bill was born in Edinburgh on January 9, 1881. He came to Canada with his mother at eight, stopping at Regina. His mother married a man he didn't take to so at age fourteen he left for points west, demonstrating the pluck that was to so distinguish him throughout life.

By nineteen, Bill was cutting enough of a figure in cow country to inspire author B.M. Bower to write a book about him. *Chip of*

Bertrand W. Sinclair around the time B.M. Bower used him as the model for her famous book Chip of the Flying U.

Pioneer American western writer B.M. Bower, the first Mrs. Sinclair.

the Flying U sold in the hundreds of thousands and made her famous. It is recognized today as an early classic in the realistic western mode. He also attracted the admiration and lifelong friendship of the fabled cowboy painter Charles Russell.

A few years later Bill and Miss Bower, in private life now Mrs. B.W. Sinclair, made for California. Here Bill spent two years as an unregistered student at Stanford University, sampling a prodigious variety of studies and adjusting his head to the intellectual temper of the times, which was in the flush of its first romance with Karl Marx.

He and Betty Bower came to a sudden though amicable parting

of the ways and by age twenty-five Bill had married again and taken up residence in Vancouver.

His encounter with Miss Bower and the art set had left Sinclair, the rough-hewn Montana cow man, with the bug to make it as a man of letters. As early as 1908 he had published a light adventure story *Raw Gold*, and in his new home near Kitsilano he set to work on *North of 53*, a wild, Londonesque novel of the Arctic.

Cherry was born in that house and has vivid memories of her father at work. "He had incredible powers of concentration. I remember him standing in front of the fireplace, thinking. Mother would call him to supper and he would say yes, dear. An hour later Mother would call him again and say supper was ruined. He would say migod, why didn't you call me?"

The manuscript was accepted by Little, Brown & Company and published in 1914.

It was quite a mixture, with blizzards, fisticuffs, grizzlies, Victorian sex queens and lots of Montana cowmen, but it drew a reasonable press and sold well enough to make Little, Brown & Company interested in a contract for more of the same.

The New York *Sun* called it "a readable, well written book showing much observation and good sense." Another reviewer said, "It is rich in strong situation, romance, and heart-stirring scenes."

The biggest noise in town those days was being made by the loggers, so Bill started a book about loggers. *Big Timber*, finished in 1916, was another puppy's breakfast of murders, love affairs, sordid villains and stout heroes — now against a background of forest fires instead of blizzards, but it also found eager readers on the eastern market and Sinclair's writing career picked up further momentum.

From the time he arrived on the coast Bill had spent much time cruising the Gulf of Georgia, drinking in its green beauty and getting to know the men who fished it for their living.

One place which caught his fancy particularly was Squitty Bay on the south end of Lasqueti Island, ten miles southwest of Pender Harbour. In the mouth of the bay was a good trolling reef which every spring during the blueback run attracted a motley collection of broken old handliners in rowboats.

Here he set his next book, the one for which he is best known, *Poor Man's Rock*. In it he tells the story of a stout-hearted Scot, Donald McRae, who is driven to Poor Man's Rock by a ruthless cannery owner, Horace Gower, who is in turn reduced to fishing the rock by McRae's even stouter-hearted son Jack.

There is no use trying to sell the modern reader on *Poor Man's Rock*, or any of Sinclair's Canadian novels for that matter, though some of his westerns were reprinted in England as late as 1958. He wrote for the popular taste of his time, and nothing is as unforgiving as the popular taste when it changes.

Poor Man's Rock deserves at least kind remembrance however, on several counts. One is the sincerity of its devotion to the coast and the men who came here in the early days to make it their home. The author's own yearning shows through when he writes, "Here a man still had a chance. He could not pick apples off the fir trees. He must use his brains as well as his hands. . .a reasonable measure of security was within a man's grasp."

Another redeeming factor is the incisiveness with which Sinclair lays open the perfidious canning monopoly which has held the fishing industry in its palm from that day to this. His observations on it are perhaps more relevant today than when he made them.

It was to be Sinclair's most popular book, nudging a hundred thousand copies before sales dropped off. This places it among the best selling Canadian novels of all time.

His admiration of the fishing way of life was no passing artistic fancy, and after publishing *The Inverted Pyramid*, another look at logging, in 1924, he rigged the *Hoo Hoo* with poles and began to spend increasing amounts of time living the life he wrote about in his books. With the publication of *Burned Bridges* in 1932 Sinclair ceased to call himself a writer and turned to working the *Hoo Hoo* full time, though he found time on the side to produce another light adventure, *Down the Dark Alley*, in 1936.

As a troller, he was known as shrewd and fearless, but restless, spending an uncommon lot of time gadding from ground to ground.

In 1920 Sinclair established his first home in Pender Harbour, but he did not begin living there full time until several years later.

He had done well from his writing and had a big house built in Sinclair Bay, keeping lots of lively company and a Chinese man-servant who perpetually warned him, "these people just eatin' up your money, Mr. Sinclair." He built his present house on the point when the original burnt down in the thirties.

The servant's money fears were not borne out until 1961, when a collision between the *Hoo Hoo* and a gillnetter off Lloyd's point left Sinclair staring at several thousand dollars of debt.

His pluck nothing weakened over the years, he mortgaged the house, hit the grounds early the next spring and "ploughed hell's half acre" for all he was worth all summer. By fall he was two

Sinclair aboard his faithful troller the Hoo Hoo *in the '30s.*

thousand dollars to the clear—not bad for a man of eighty-one.

He kept fishing for three more seasons. In 1964 he fell ill for the first time in his life, and two years later he was forced to end his forty-seven-year partnership with the beloved *Hoo Hoo*.

After supper had disappeared and conversation had started to slacken, it was decided to have another attempt at rousing our guest of honour. Ivy Potts had brought along a little cake, which was lit up and set out, surrounded by enough bottle-shaped presents to float the poor man through the rest of his drinking days.

Bill shuffled out blinking on Cherry's arm, amid cheers and a rousing chorus of Happy Birthday Mr. Sinbillgrandadfather.

He grinned for the first time all evening and started to apologize, "Damn, I wish I could be worthy of this gathering, but I just feel too..."

But the group was in no mood for contrite apologies.

"Blow it out!"

"Open the presents!"

"Speech!"

Bill sat down and looked around, a bit of a twinkle creeping into his eye. He blew the candles out and started peeling open the bottles. Janie bent close to him and he caught a handful of her long, coppery hair, fondling it rapturously.

"In our family we've always had beautiful women," he said. "I'm glad to see this isn't changing."

People swarmed around him reading out greeting cards. "To a man who is old enough to know where it's at and still young enough to get it."

"That one's a bit late."

One lady crowding a bit close let out a shriek as a bony hand snapped out and clamped onto her bottom, less delicately than is generally thought proper.

"Bill! You maniac! Get away from my bum!"

"How am I supposed to know it was your bum?" His voice was now clear and strong. "I'm not familiar with it, am I?"

Calls resumed for a speech and he wavered to his feet, one hand on the chair and another on a glass of sherry.

"The troller's song!"

"The one about the prune!"

"A few words for the press..."

He chose the one about the prune.

> Every prune is just the same,
> Each young one like its dad,
> Except not wrinkled quite so bad..."

Then he raised his glass, tilted his head back and swallowed until it was empty.

But that was it.

He turned and made for the bedroom, holding his head.

FOR THE BIRDS

I want everything *ordinary*.
I don't want any big excitements
that might lead to trouble.
I forget how I got this way now
but I know I had my reasons.
I think it was all my friends
disappearing into black holes.
But it's tough, the way things are these days.
Dropping in on Pat and Lorna
for a few days, he sees the apocalypse
in every line, in every sip of wine
so I go with her to the store
thinking the brown grass and hard
clench of prairie fall might
spell relief but within a block
we're in trouble up to our necks.
A fat little bird of some prairie kind
is flopping around on a frozen field
having hit a wire and snapped its wing.
Instinctively I look away and keep walking
but no such luck: Lorna gasps, stops,
looks imploringly at me.
She is not used to walking with men
who shy away from challenges.

Her poems, too, are full of
extreme words and spiritual breakthroughs.
Can't we do something? she says.
If Pat were here he'd step on its head
(though not without suffering horribly himself) I say,
making no move to step on its head.
After about half an hour of soul-searching
we walk away leaving the pathetic fluff-ball
reeling in the wintry dusk,
feeling morally squalid.

You can't escape it, it seems.
Years later I am in Vancouver
hurtling from door to door on business
desperate to get home that night
and I run up Werty's stairs hoping we can
get through his drawings in ten minutes —
right away I can see I'm in trouble:
Werty has this preoccupied look —
We're in a bit of a crisis here, he says.
And it's the helpless bird thing again:
a baby robin has fallen down and crawled
into their yard just ahead of an army
of alley cats. Werty has put it up on the roof
but it can't fly and the parents don't show,
while cat eyes glint from every shadow.
I hope for a quick move by one of them,
but with the caution of the predator, they wait.
I decide to help find the nest,
somewhere in the neighbouring trees
thinking only of getting Werty free for myself
but am mistaken for a back alley prowler
and end up fearing for my life.
I am too exasperated for amusement,
but Werty is in beyond my reach,
sensing the bird's peril like his own
me thinking maybe this is why he draws so well
so I suggest phoning the SPCA
but the tired voice just says the city
is crawling with fallen robins

and advises us to give it to our cat.
I end up driving Werty and bird to some sanctuary
far on the other side of the city
where it is assigned a case number
and we are advised on visiting hours.
I hope you didn't mind, he says
and even though it's too late for anything
I actually feel sort of *good,*
it was such a spunky little bird
when you got to know it

Which is the whole argument for the other way
what you get when you get involved
you get some nice little birds in your life
make connections with what counts
when I get back to where I'm staying
tell Bryan how I lost my day
he says, *hey, I've got something to show you...*
hands me a new anthology
Haven't read it but I noticed your name here...
It's a poem by long-forgotten Lorna
about that other bird

dedicated to me

SMALL VICTORIES

People come to see us sometimes
we put them out in the back
Mare keeping them occupied
while I sneak out and hide
armfuls of papers in drawers
push things into piles
hoping they'll speak to us
in the morning   all that clutter
gotta trash it out some time

Steve comes in says he was up
til 3 AM looking over my books.
Says his neck is still sore
from reading sideways.
What an amazing bunch of books
you have he says what a library

I just stick stuff out there
it's not a planned event,
I say. It couldn't be he says
it's remarkable. He is perhaps
the best-read of our acquaintances.

I've never given a thought

to my books that way, what figure
I, in my idle acquisitiveness,
may have described.
I find myself basking in this
previously unsuspected
description of myself

It was like the time in highschool
the principal said I stood
above all others *for poise*
something I had no use for
but seized upon with secret glee.

Sometimes you receive these little
unsought victories which are
no less delightful for

being worthless

How It Was with Trucks

From the time I was a big-eared boy eavesdropping on bunkhouse BS in my father's logging camp I have been captivated by the power of common speech. Later when I studied formal literature I often had pause to reflect that the memorable lines held up as examples of timeless genius were not that different from some of the good zingers I used to hear back in the bunkhouse. The more I explored the idea the more convinced I became that the speech of ordinary people concealed a world of linguistic accomplishment parallel to that of our written literature, a conviction which dovetailed with my belief that genius lurks unseen within much ordinary life, like the fire opal that hides inside a dull stone. This is the notion that led to the writing of many articles and three full-length books — A *Hard Man To Beat*, *Spilsbury's Coast*, and *The Accidental Airline*, all using the vernacular technique which has since come to be known as oral history.

My first successful foray into the genre was this account my father and I wrote for *Raincoast Chronicles* #3 about his experiences in the early days of trucklogging. It came about somewhat by accident owing to the fact that I, like most sons, didn't give the old man much credit for knowing anything special and went to him intending only to ask if he had any ideas where I might start researching the story of how trucks took over from railroads as the principle method of hauling logs during the 1940s. He was even less prone than me to set himself up as an expert, so the approach

184

suited him, and he soon found himself musing about what he took to be his own unremarkable experiences in the trucklogging world. It was only after I had gone back to him for the third or forth session it dawned on me that I had stumbled onto a better eyewitness to trucking history than I could have hoped for, but I was afraid he would clam up if I let on so I kept pretending I was only collecting incidental background material. I limited my note-taking to the odd name and date and I didn't even consider using a tape recorder, recreating his words from memory afterward. He didn't twig what was up until ten thousand copies of the magazine were spread out all over the BC coast. I don't think he ever quite recovered from the shock.

There's a lot of jaws been broken over the question of where and when trucks first got into the woods — hell, they can't even settle on where the first railroad was, and trucks are a lot harder to keep track of than trains.

They can't say who made the first horseless carriage as far as that goes, but they can tell you who put the country on wheels — that's clear, Henry Ford. And as far as I'm concerned the man who got the BC logging industry into trucks was Bill Schnare (pronounced *snar*).

There were trucks in the woods before Schnare, lots of them, but they weren't getting all that far. Trucks were taking over every other hauling job there was by the mid-twenties so it didn't take any brains to try them on logs. Tretheweys had an old White around their mill, must have been 1922, out at Abbotsford, and you'd see it struggling by once in a while with some old stump-rancher's logs chained on, but that was kind of a joke, like putting boxing gloves on a kangaroo.

Trucks couldn't be used the way they were operating in the woods those days, they were too rough. Those old bush apes were used to clubbing ox teams on the skidroad and crashing around in the woods with heavy steam equipment. They just didn't have the touch, their touch was too heavy — they'd wreck a truck just loading it.

Everything in the woods those days was made to be thumped around. If they hit a flat car with a log, the worst that would happen would be it would jump off the track, and if that happened they'd just hook on a tong and yank it back.

I remember seeing them flip a truck loading with a duplex at Haney once. They set it back up real quick and kept on loading like Charlie Chaplin, just like it didn't happen. The truck drove away too, but as she took the turn out of the landing you could see the old wooden cab slouch off to one side like a stack of loose pancakes.

To those oldtime loggers trucks were just too frail and fussy. It threw them off to have one on the claim, like it did having a woman around. Gas engines made their heads spin. They could get along without 'em. It was the age of steam.

They were still logging the valleys, rolling out big trainloads of number one fir all day. When going got scratchy, they just pulled stakes for the next valley. Lay rails into the middle, set up the skidder and the skyline, and haul wood for all she's worth.

In '58 I was driving for Blondie Swanson up Theodosia Inlet and you could look down and see where Merrill, Ring and Moore logged in the thirties. There were big spoked wheels, a mile across, side by side the length of the valley. It was all back in second growth by this time and you didn't notice it at first but once you did you couldn't miss it, the old yarding patterns in the shading of the new growth. We were up thirty-two hundred feet in the last bit of timber on the mountain, which is the real change in logging from their time to ours. While the going was that good, it's no wonder they laughed at trucks.

Just the same there were some pretty fair trucks on the road by 1930. Federal, Fagel, Reo, Godfordson, Day-Elder, Fisher-Hayes, White, Leyland, Thornycroft, Diamond T, Packard. There were so many makes it was rare to pass two the same or even know of two exactly the same at first, like boats. A lot were built in machine shops on special order, and there was no standard rating.

There isn't much to making a truck, at least not the way they did it. Just brace up two pieces of eight-inch channel for a frame, Timken axle, Gryco transmission, Hercules motor. Any blacksmith could make the springs and driveshaft out of stock, and the radiator just hung in a cast iron frame. The radiator frame and the cab were about the only places they had any chance to use their imagination, and half of them just bolted an open seat across the frame.

Actually they were good trucks. You could throw a hell of a load on one of those old crocodiles. Just make sure you're on good ground. A touch of downhill helped too. Too much and they'd be scraping you up though. The goddamn brakes on those things weren't meant to be taken seriously.

Frank White with a 3-log load, Vedder Crossing, BC.

You did have the emergency brake. Great big squeeze-handle emergency brake on the side of the cab. That was the true measure of the truck, the emergency brake. The bigger the truck, the bigger the handle. Some came right up to your chin.

I remember when the Detroit trucks first came out, they had a little handbrake inside with the button on top same as now, and the guys'd be peering in the cab and saying what the hell kind of truck is this?

Those old emergency brakes would work alright, but one good stop was about all they had in 'em, and you damnwell saved it for an emergency.

Some had the gearshift on your left too, but mostly it was where it is now, on the right. All the selector part of the gearbox was open — big sliding cast bars always full of mud and sticks. It'd take a twenty-pound pull to shift. Took just about the full reach of your arm. With sixty-five horsepower to work with you did a lot of reaching.

But those old Hercs, they had damn near a six-inch stroke and you could lug 'em down to where you could count the revs like cows going over the mountain. You'd wait till one wasn't going to make it, then pull 'er out and stomp the gas down for about half a minute to get the revs up to where you could get into the next gear.

The only way they could even those old four-bangers out was to hang huge cast iron flywheels on 'em, absolute top they could stand would be maybe two thousand revs. Any more'n the fly-wheel would come right through the floorboards at you. More'n one man was killed that way, going down a hill with too big a load, the fly wheel flew apart.

The steering wheels were great big wooden things about three feet across and flat. Had to be, because they had about as much reduction in the linkage as a bicycle, you were hangin' on for all you were worth all day long. That was the main battle, to keep the front wheels going where you wanted to go and not where they wanted. You studied the road a long ways ahead. Under normal conditions you had the edge in brute force, but a rock or a rut could tie you in a knot. The spokes would blur just like an airplane propeller, Jesus, if anything was in the way, you could write it off for about three months. Next time you see an oldtimer driving, take a look how he holds his thumbs. Outside the wheel. It'll take three generations to wipe out the habit. Once the flying saucers cleared out of your head, chances are you had a broken front wheel to deal with too — wooden spokes couldn't stand the least amount of sideways pressure. They were a real headache, wooden spoke wheels. In dry weather they spokes'd get loose in the felloe and clatter. If you didn't fix them quick the wheel'd collapse like an old wooden chair. They had special little half-round wedges and you'd see guys stopped on the side of the road banging them in.

Driving truck in the very early days was one of the real bullwork jobs, besides all the problems of being something new. Those first truckers, the men who brought trucking in, were a special breed. Half Edison and half Sasquatch.

They say the first truck show on the coast was Forbes Bay, just by the mouth of Toba Inlet, in 1926, and that may just have been the first big one. I never saw it myself, but I heard tell of some outfit where they used a truck to drag logs over a skidroad around 1920.

There was another outfit that tried to use trucks on pole rails with concave wheels. You can see how they were thinking — they were thinking here's a horse that doesn't get tired, here's a loco-motive that only costs eight hundred dollars. They treated it like a locie too, they built a raised track out of timbers, fore and aft it was called because the timbers were laid fore and aft instead of crossways like a punching road. It was two tracks, with squared saplings for guard rails, and open in the centre. At first they used sixteen-inch tracks, then the Compensation Board made them come up to thirty-two. Built on a gentle slope just like a railroad because of the no brakes, and no sharp turns because they couldn't figure how to make a truck so it would turn with a load of logs on it.

Come to any gully not real easy to fill and they built a timber trestle. Now let me tell you, coming down a plank road in one of them old hard-wheeled bastards, sittin' out in the open on a board seat, a couple three thousand-foot logs jiggling around up behind your head, no bulkhead for protection, that steering wheel kicking like a bull in your hands and mechanical brakes — you were earn-ing your two dollars and eighty cents a day. Trestles rattling and jumping around, mud squeezing up between the planks? With mud or a touch of frost you could no more hold that thing on the track than you can hold a greased pig with one hand. You sure tried, because to go off meant you went over, and not too many guys survived that. They nailed down everything they could find for rip-rap, to give the planks some grip — branches, canvas, wrin-kled tin. The best I guess was old stranded cable. It got better as it got whiskerier. But still they killed men like flies.

I can remember Dutch Parbury talking about driving up at Brown Bay — that was what Brown and Kirkland called one of their early truck camps — said you'd be looking through your floorboards going over a trestle and seeing straight down through seventy feet of clear open space. Boards broke and jillpoked all the time — God! When he started out they asked him if he thought he could handle the "chute" and he'd said, oh yeah. One trip and that was it. He told the push, "I can see how you get a man to do that once, but I don't know how you get 'em to do it twice." In the Depression, with families starving, it wasn't so hard.

It was a ridiculous thing to do with a loaded truck if you think about it, try and support it for miles on a wooden platform, but coming to it after years of skidroads and railroads, it must have looked like the only thing to do.

It took a fortune's worth of timber, and you couldn't use it again like rails, so it was something only the big camps could afford. On top of that they couldn't keep the trucks running. I remember hearing that truck logging had failed, something in the same way you hear helicopter logging has failed.

But some outfits kept trying and got it working pretty slick. Jeremiason had a pretty good show up Vancouver Bay, and there was a bunch of Whites working at Holberg. The most famous I guess was Pioneer Timber at Beaver Cove. The setup at Pioneer was the work of the mechanic, Archie McCone. There was a real gyppo Edison, Archie McCone. Every camp he was at was full of gadgets and cute ways of doing things he invented. There were a lot of Gyro Gearloose types in the woods one time, I guess the problem attracted them: get those logs in the water without working so hard. I remember this Swede handlogger up Frederic's Arm who worked an elaborate system of canals that somehow used the tide and moved logs for miles. The main improvement at Pioneer was the McCone pre-loader, which eliminated the delay and banging around of loading. The trucks had detachable bunks, and they'd build the load on spare bunks while the trucks were away, then when one came back he'd just drop the bunks he had and back under the loaded ones. It was used for a long time. Everyone copied it.

McCone had a pretty slick way of turning trucks around at the dump too. At Beaver Cove it was a special problem because the bay is shallow and the road went away out on piles. They could have backed up, but McCone built this turntable at the end so that when you drove onto it you hooked a cable, and the cable pulled on a drum that turned the whole thing around as the truck moved ahead, and by the time you got to the end you were back where you started, pointing the other way.

They made the fore and aft system work, but look at the trouble and expense to build something like that. They still couldn't go up hills, and the timbered road was very inflexible. You left it where it was and brought logs to it same as a railroad. So it didn't cause any real major change. You still stuck to the valleys and used huge yarders to reach way far out for logs.

McCone was a master craftsman and famous in the woods. He built trucks himself, from scratch. It's funny, thinking about it, because Schnare wasn't anywhere near the man, he was just a little wizened-up old deaf mechanic from Abbotsford, and he never invented a damn thing, he didn't even bring anything into the woods, anything that other guys here and there hadn't tried already.

Schnare wasn't even a logger, he'd never been near the woods. But he was the guy, from his dirty little garage in Abbotsford, who saw where logging was heading before anybody else. He had something, but I still don't know what it was, to be truthful. It's not as if I haven't spent enough time thinking about it. It must have been some kind of insight that was so close to obvious common sense that you never saw it. The only real clue I have is that he died a millionaire and I'll die broke, and we were both doing the same thing.

It really starts with the three-ton truck. Detroit started making three-tons I guess in 1932. They'd made some bigger trucks before that, and they'd made lots in the one-ton range but these were the first what you'd call modern trucks.

There hadn't been any really organized trucking around the Fraser Valley up until that time, but in 1927 the Cariboo Highway went in and when the three-tons came out a few years later, there were hauling outfits everywhere. Les McGarva and Irv Parbury started two rival milk-hauling outfits in Abbotsford and ran them out of the beer parlour. They had tables in opposite corners and trucks would be pulling up and leaving outside all day. McGarva had four '34 Chevs and I started driving for him. Schnare did a lot of our repairs and he used to make Les mad as hell.

"You guys don't know how to use trucks," Schnare would say. "I could put twenty tons on those trucks." We'd go as high as eight tons on them sometimes, and they'd just be dragging their belly pans down the road. Schnare figured he knew everything because he'd run steam thrashing machines, and we thought the old coot was just talking silly. I know what he was thinking now, he was thinking he'd make 'em into six-wheelers—put tandem axles on the back—like he did on all his trucks. It wouldn't have worked for us though, we had to zip into town and back, we had to move hauling milk in cans.

Schnare's place was a kind of hangout. He was a pretty snarly old bugger, but there was always something going on. Things were always happening to him and he was always telling about it, like the time he was in the York Hotel and the window stuck. Somehow the damn thing fell down on his arms and he had to shout down onto the street for someone to go in and tell the desk. He was close to sixty, I guess.

I was there when he got his first truck. He had a Ford dealership and he sold these two guys a 1934 three-ton truck for hauling into a tie-mill. They didn't make any payments and finally Schnare went out looking for 'em.

"Cakzickers took off on me but I got the goddam truck," he says. It was all battered and rigged up in some haywire way for hauling poles and he didn't know quite what to do with it.

"Mack, you tek that goddam truck," he says to Rendel Mackinnon. "You could mek money hauling logs."

We all figured he was trying to suck somebody in, and he was I guess but what happened was his son Stan, I guess Stan was seventeen or eighteen then, he was listening to it all and afterwards he persuaded the old man to let him quit school and go hauling logs with this truck.

Well, by god if Stan didn't do alright, and the old man started to get interested. The next thing you know old Schnare was going around saying, "They don't know how to use trucks in the woods. I can haul ten times what they're hauling with the same trucks."

Still, nobody took him very seriously because all he ever had to do with trucks was working on 'em in the garage, he had never run 'em before.

Schnare, he had quite a few other trucks he'd sold to other guys, and everybody was behind on 'em, it was the Depression and there was no money anywhere, so whenever he wanted one he just had to go out and get it.

So he took back two more trucks and sent 'em out hauling logs. Somewhere he found bogeys and made 'em into six-wheelers. They were the first six-wheelers in the woods that I know of and it was true it made them a far better machine, especially on the rough dirt roads.

Then he got the contract up on Vedder Mountain and he rigged up three more old Fords. That's when I went to work for him.

They were logging up behind Cultus Lake in a patch of timber right up on the mountain. B & K had logged out the whole valley all up around the mountain, but this patch had been left because it was too steep to get the railroad into it.

You couldn't see the fir in that forest. It as all cedar and maple, thick — you couldn't see the sky anywhere, and every once in a while there'd be a big black fir stump going up into the maple leaves. You honestly couldn't see any more than that, it was so thick in there. They smashed it all down, it was a different world. But God it was lovely wood. I've never seen fir like that again. They had to chop notches to get the tongs on the logs. For a month I averaged just over three logs to the load, and there were lots of one-log loads. The biggest I think was 8,700 feet. And it was a buckskin — and only thirty-two feet long. Nine feet I think, nine feet at the butt, and straight. It sat in the landing for a long time and we kept wondering which one of us was going to get it. Finally they gave it to Les Bates on Number Three with the reason that he was the oldest. Also didn't have a family.

Top heavy! If that log rolled six inches to one side the truck would go down the bank like a dog wrestling with a bear. Those one-log loads were cinched to the frame, that's what I hated — they would take you with 'em.

I had a hard time at first. I couldn't get used to Schnare's crazy way of doing things. Working with McGarva we'd had new trucks and we were pretty good to them. I couldn't believe the hammering they were giving these poor old Fords.

They were loading with a Skagit on a crotch line and you never knew what was going to happen next. A Skagit was a little donkey made out of a Fordson tractor, and it could barely lift some of these logs. They went up very slow and came down very hard. Logs were dropping and banging around, and the tongs dancing and snapping every time you looked around. A crotch line can only pick a log straight up, they can't swing it, so you had to move the truck to get it placed right on the load. The loads they were packing on those trucks, you had to have it in perfect balance or you couldn't drive. But Roy, the guy who was head loading, he'd let you spot the truck, then hop out before they picked up the log. You couldn't stay in, the way they'd knock the truck around, it would buck you out, or else spear you on the gearshift. The goddamn old cab would crash and flap, I thought it would fly right off. Not that it would have been any loss — it didn't have any windows or doors as it was.

The goddamn things were so overloaded you could pop the rear end just starting out in the landing. You could twist off an axle any time you wanted. Hitting a pothole you didn't even see, the truck would heave like a schooner in a gale and creak and squawk. It was bloody frightening with all that hill in front of you. And there was a lot I didn't know about driving with a trailer. If you hit the truck brakes before the trailer brakes and the cinches had worked a little loose, the logs would slip ahead and jam against the bulkhead. Then you couldn't steer, the front wheels would just skid across the corner into the bank. There was no way to move the logs and no powersaws, so you got out the axe and chopped the ends of the logs back a foot or so. After I chopped twice through one six-foot butt I started catching on pretty fast.

They had planks laid down over the old railway grade and coming back from my first load a plank flipped up and jillpoked the trailer off into the ditch. Then coming down the second time I got too close to the edge to let some French fallers pass and the goddamn old single-axle trailer pushed the shoulder out. I lost the load and they had to bring the cat nine miles to pull me out.

I was thinking good God, how do these guys do it, because I'd been driving for a while on the highway and I figured I knew how to handle a truck. But I just wasn't getting anywhere, and I was wondering if I should go quit or let Schnare fire me.

So when he came to see the truck he grabs me by the shoulder and says, "Don't you worry, Bud, I'm gonna get you a new trailer and you'll be hauling more logs than anybody here."

He could be good, but he was so miserable most of the time you don't remember. Your time was always short, and any bill he ever paid he'd scribble "S & S Trucking, 1% off" and shave a couple bucks off. That was just the price of dealing with Bill Schnare. But men paid it, that was the thing about logging. Men would do things for a guy like Schnare they would never do for Macmillan or the companies because he was a character, a person. You could talk to him. You might be making the tight old bastard rich, but that gave you a feeling of satisfaction in itself.

Well, after I got the new trailer I was away. That's another thing.

I didn't know the reason I couldn't stay on the road was because of the goddamn haywire single-axle trailer I had. I thought it was something wrong with me, and so did the other guys. Schnare could see it was the trailer, but that was so obvious as soon as I made one trip, it was hard to even give him much credit for knowing it.

Those trucks of his looked so goddamn awful you were afraid to get in 'em, in case they would fall down and you'd be trapped in the wreckage. They had no brakes at all worth talking about on the trucks, you were always fighting that. One time I got so tired of struggling and sweating I said enough of this damn nonsense and worked all weekend on my own time bushing up the linkage and putting in new linings. The first time I hit the brakes Monday the back wheels stopped so hard the whole goddamn truck stretched, and then I couldn't get the brakes off. The linkage was pulled so tight I couldn't even get a pin out to unhook it. Finally I chopped the rod with a chisel and just left it hanging. There was no way of keeping those mechanical brakes working.

Just a little while after that I was on my way up for a load and I met Les coming down in a long straight stretch. It wasn't steep, but his brakes were all used up from the hill and I didn't dare stop because I'd roll back all the way to Sardis, so we just sat there creeping towards each other with funny looks on our faces. We smashed together, steam was flying, Jesus we laughed.

The reason Schnare could get by was, on the trailers which is what really counts, he had real good brakes — five-inch drums and vacuum power, which was new then. Still, that wouldn't have been enough to hold those loads back without burning up, but he'd rigged up little water tanks on 'em, and you'd just stop at the top and open the taps. That was a hell of an improvement. With that, Schnare's trucks could handle the hills, and with the extra axles and big tires he could handle heavy loads on dirt roads.

Like I say, none of this was new or even new to the woods, except maybe the tandem idea. All these things were sitting around waiting for someone to put them all together on one truck. It was like coming up to a chess game, and suddenly realizing one side has his pieces set up so he can clean the board in three moves, but they don't see it because they're thinking some other plan. That was the way Bill saw logging in 1934. It had to be, or how else could some deaf old farmer with a dirty little garage out in Abbotsford walk in and take over like he did?

After I got the new trailer I had no more trouble staying on the road, but I still wasn't getting the loads. I couldn't get the goddamn old truck into high gear down on the flat. "I'll fix that," Bill says, "I got sumpnin will get thet truck moving." So one day he flags me down and he's got a supercharger. Well it was a little better, but I still couldn't get up there, she wouldn't hold on in high. So Bill says, "Here, I'm going to come with you. I know that goddamn truck'll go faster'n thet." It frosted you a little, because old Bill couldn't even drive himself.

So I get rolling and get into second and just about ready to go into third, and he shouts, "No, no, no!" He's signalling faster. So I keep my foot down on the gas and the poor little V/8 is hammering and screaming, I wouldn't have thought it could stand it. "Okay!" he says, and I drop it into third. Going into fourth I wait till my foot won't stay down any more, it's just shaking, but when I reach for the knob I can see him waving — it's so loud you can't hear — "No, no!" and I keep pressing until there's waves of heat pouring back over us and I'm watching for the pistons to fly up through the hood — "Now!" he says. Taking that extra bit all the way up, you could just get 'er to stick it in high if you kept 'er pinned right wide open, and that's how you'd go from Sardis right to the river, clear across the Fraser Valley.

I went through a motor every three months but that's what Schnare liked. He had a whole yard full of new blocks, and we'd change 'em in two hours on a Sunday. He spent half his time scrounging old parts, and whenever anything bust, he'd be right there and shove in a new one. Breakdowns didn't scare him — he was a mechanic. That's where he had it over the loggers, they were afraid of things going wrong because they didn't know what they'd do if they did.

I remember one time we were putting a new rear end in and there was no gasket. "Use string," he says. We didn't know what he was talking about, so he gets down and sets this string in grease so it'll stay put, winds it all around the bolts "Now slap it on," he says. "We'll fix 'er better when we got time." It worked, just like everything else, and the truck got another load before quitting time.

We were getting paid five dollars a day and two dollars if we got over four loads, and one week in August I was top driver with sixty-five dollars. I figured there was nothing but money working in the woods.

Goddammit, I liked it. It was a big job and I was good at it. We had those haywire old trucks working so you couldn't imagine how it could be done better. You got so you could hear the truck, you got tuned to its noises and the feel of it, so much you could tell how it was working, you'd had the whole thing together and apart so many times you were conscious of every goddamn bearing and how it was turning. You'd see a new grease spot on the ground in the morning and think that goddamn packing's getting loose again, and if you didn't fix it at least you'd make sure the thing didn't run short of oil. If anything started to go on the brakes you'd catch the slight change in the pedal or notice a wet spot on the wheel. When you get that sharp you get to the point nothing's an accident, it's always you missed something or ignored something, nothing really serious happens so long as you're on the job.

And if you did get into something, you knew how to get out of it. Say you lost your brakes — the water got plugged and the brakes started to burn up. A green driver wouldn't know what was happening until suddenly he was freewheeling down the hill, and there's nothing to do but jump and let the truck go. A guy who was on the bit would have seen the steam getting thin in the mirror five, ten minutes before. Even if the green guy did catch that he would have probably dynamited right there and pushed the drums all out of shape or he would have headed straight for the ditch and put the logs through the cab. The guy who knew what he was doing would wait for a good spot to go off, an in-curve where he could get the trailer hung up first, before the truck.

You got so slick at everything you'd start taking shortcuts, like using the brakes to help get around a corner — if you touch the truck brakes you turn sharper, if you touch the trailer brakes you straighten out. Even a little thing like a mud puddle. A driver who knows his brakes are hot would go half off the road to get around a little puddle, but another guy will plough right through it and the cold splash would crack the drums. Then the truck would run away and they'd tell his widow, "the brakes failed."

There's a million things, but you get so goddamn smart after a while you get thinking nothing can happen to you. It was an art, it's gotta be.

I'm sure if a historian were to write a book about truck logging he would start with some old farmer with a Model T and never mention Bill Schnare, except maybe in a list. But I remember people talking after that show on Vedder Mountain. There were claims like that all over the country, that the big association camps had left because they were considered inaccessible. Now Schnare and this little gyppo had gone in with an old 75 cat and a haywire little donkey, punched in a dirt road, laid planks in the soft spots, kept moving the road close to the timber so there was no yarding, and they made real money.

There were remnant patches all up and down the coast, every logger knew of a few, and all of a sudden here was a way they could be logged. Old trucks were suddenly at a premium, and anybody who could get together a Skagit and a truck were going logging on their own.

Schnare was picking up more old trucks wherever he could get them and taking jobs all over. He'd hear about some operator starting up or thinking of starting up. Then he'd go talk to 'em and the first thing he'd have them sign one of his "contracts." They were the damndest things — he'd write 'em in pencil in a battered old notebook he had, with all his own wording and they probably weren't legal or anything else but he figured it was the ark of the covenant. When we were finishing up at Vedder I remember he got all excited about measuring the distance we'd been hauling because he had it in the contract that if the haul got over twenty miles the price would go up. "I know it's over twenty miles goddammit, we gotta figger some way of measuring that road." What he finally did was, he painted a white spot on one of my back tires at the dump, then followed me all the way up in his car, counting the turns of the wheel. "Drive slow," he says. The way he figured it all out it came to just over twenty miles, and he made the logger pay a couple thousand bucks extra.

I moved with six trucks to Nanoose Bay where B & K was cleaning off a mountain patch much like the one on Vedder. The road wound back and forth up the hill, but coming down Schnare had them put a run straight down the face of this hogback ridge. When you were coming up to the edge all you could see was the blue sky and the fishboats out on the gulf. Then you dove. One time I ran out of water near the bottom and the brake drums melted and welded right onto the linings. Had to cut it all up with torch. Guys' tires were catching on fire all the time. You had your hand on the door handle a lot on that hill.

There was always a big argument about whether your brakes got hotter coming down slow or fast. Some guys claimed it was better to go fast because it meant the brakes were on for a shorter period of time. Other guys said the wheel still went around the same number of times but it was going around faster so that made it get hotter. The fast guys argued back that it got hotter going around slow because you were pressing harder and there was more friction. The way I figured it, you have to think of your brakes as a heat pump. Their job is to drain off the potential energy of the truck at the top of the hill by converting it into heat energy on the way down. The longer you give them to pump off that energy, the cooler they end up, but I could never make guys see that.

It was at Nanoose; there was this little guy head loading, Corky his name was. Bouncy kind of a guy, quick you know. Natural clown. Whatever he was doing, it looked funny.

He was up on the load swinging a log as it came down. I think what happened was, there was a cat working there, and they snagged the line or something. Anyway, the log suddenly swung up and he jumped straight backwards for the browskid, the big log alongside the truck.

I was standing about fifty feet away watching. There was a piece of bark stuck in his corks, and he slipped right down on his ass onto the ground, his head went "crack" on the log. I remember somebody saying jeez, you can hear the echo. He just sat there against the log, and we thought he was clowning. Then somebody says hey, you alright?

He was dead. Little knot size of a two-inch nail went right through his skull. Damnedest thing you ever saw. We couldn't believe it.

Quite a few other hauling contractors got going right after Schnare and by the late thirties there was a real boom in small-time operations going on all up the coast. Places like Texada Island and Jervis Inlet or up Johnstone Straits where the timber hadn't been extensive enough to interest the steam loggers or else had gotten too steep for railroads, men were swarming in with gas yarders and trucks. They'd yard a load into the tree, then to load they'd take a line rigged up with tongs, lead it through a block up the tree, and pinch the end of it in the windings of the mainline drum. The tree was rigged with a lean so the tongs hung out over the truck. They called it a pinchline and it was just one of the ways of getting by with one machine. Stuff like that really got going in 1940 when Archie McCone and Jimmy Lawrence brought out a cheap, light gas yarder called the 10-10 Lawrence. You could get 'em for twelve hundred dollars minus the sleigh. It looked like the boom could go forever.

Just about the time everyone was starting to talk about what a wizard Schnare was with cheap old trucks he turned around and bought four brand new fifteen-ton Macks. They were the first trucks Mack sold in BC, and Charlie Philp originally got set up as a distributor to deliver them. They had twelve-foot bunks and three-foot stakes and they cost twenty thousand each. It was the most anyone had ever thought of spending on logging trucks and a lot of people thought the old man had made an awful mistake. People said they were too big for logging, too heavy for the roads and the small operations would never pay for them.

They went hauling at Port Douglas up Harrison Lake and nobody'd ever seen anything like it. They had 502-cubic-inch motors and air brakes and they would go up twice the hill and haul three times the logs of anything else around. You couldn't stop 'em. That was 1938. After they had been hauling two years truck logging wasn't a small-time method any more. It was the modern way to move logs. People had been saying trucks would never touch railroads in railroad country, but after 1941 nobody was putting any new money into railroads, they were punching in road. Northwest Bay was one of the first big camps to go all trucks, and in 1946 Schnare took sixteen new Macks into Franklin River for Macmillan.

They had mobile loaders to scoot from setting to setting and the trucks were radio dispatched and they never stopped. They had Swedish steel for drilling rock to ballast the roads, they had shovels to load it, trucks to haul it and cats to spread it and they've been building road at the rate of thirty miles a year ever since. Must be up over five hundred miles now. The main spur is like the Trans-Canada Highway. Franklin River was designed around a new concept of logging, where you have small mobile yarding equipment and you keep adding onto your road so you're always close to the timber. After that locies started disappearing fast.

Schnare sold out in the fifties. I don't know how much he was worth but when Matsqui District put out a bond issue for their sewers Schnare bought the whole goddamn thing. I remember the first time I ever saw Schnare I was a kid selling raffle tickets and he grumbled and gave me a hard time, then bought the whole book of tickets. He died sometime in the early sixties.

After Nanoose Bay I quit Schnare and bought my own truck, a heavy-duty Dodge, a beautiful truck. I don't think there were more than three ever brought to Canada. I figured that what an ignorant old man like Schnare could do a smart young guy like me could do twice as good.

At first I was hauling at Palmer Bay over the old railroad grade, which was supposed to have been the first railroad on the coast, then I moved to Garibaldi for North Shore Timber.

That was quite a show. It was owned by a little Hungarian Jew who'd been chased out by Hitler, and he'd scared up the most godawful ragtag bunch of alcoholics and old wrecks for a crew you ever saw. The war was on and men were scarce. The super was some toothless old coyote who'd been in the woods since they were using stone chisels, but he was so rummy half the time he didn't know where he was.

The first thing I saw him do when I got there, Les, the Hungarian, had some beautiful handknitted wool socks drying in the office and Zeke stole 'em. Naturally Les saw him wearing them, they had fancy zig-zags, and he just couldn't believe it, that his superintendent would steal his socks.

Another time we went in for breakfast in the morning and the cook was passed out on the floor with lemon extract all over his face. Zeke had it in for the cook anyway because he'd caught him sneaking a sandwich after hours and threatened him with a cleaver, so Zeke was grumbling to Les and I how you couldn't dare leave shoe polish or shaving lotion sitting around or the cook would drink it on you. The camp boat had a big alcohol compass in it and I said how it was funny nobody'd got that yet. Les said after he left, "You shouldn't have said that in front of Zeke, he's worse than the cook." Sure enough, next day I checked and the compass was bone dry.

One day old Zeke was standing on a stump out in front of the tree, so bleary and shaky he didn't see that he was in the bight of the haulback and all that was holding it was a little sapling. The sapling sawed through, and the line picked ol' Zeke up right by the ass like a hundred-yard bowstring and flung him seventy feet. Joe Beef, who was another relic from Cordova Street — I never did know his right name — he was pulling rigging and Zeke came down right beside him. His ribs were sticking out and he was bleeding and screaming, and Joe Beef says, "Ah, shuddup y'ol sonvubitch, that's just the shoe polish coming out." They got him plugged up and shipped out to Squamish.

That night in camp Joe Beef was telling us, "You know, ol' Zeke looked just like a leaf floatin' down through those trees." He survived, and came back as bullcook, sweeping out the bunkhouses. Same camp where he'd been super.

This Les Kurze, it all must have been quite a shock for him because he was an aristocrat in Budapest, his wife was in the opera and all that, but the funny thing was he seemed to really enjoy these guys. Not enjoy them, he admired them, he used to say there was no other men like them in the world. Everybody liked him too, he was a damn fine man. He had no business to be running a camp though, the only reason he ever got any logs in the water was we put them in for him. That camp just ran itself, these old bastards were pretty slow until the sun got up, but nobody ever had to tell 'em what to do. It was the only camp I ever saw where they didn't give signals. They'd just glance at each other.

I was getting paid by the log, so every time I got over twelve logs I would pass out a pack of cigarettes for everybody on the loading crew. It didn't take them long to get saving all the small logs for me, and leaving all the big ones for the company truck. The only guy who didn't fit in was this little pissant named George on the company truck, and it didn't make a damn bit of difference to him but he was always meowing, "Look at all the money you're making." He's still up there, driving a schoolbus.

I got them to put Bob Hallgren head loading, he was just a kid then, I said you put the kid on loading and we'll take care of it for you. We did too, I even kept their old truck going for them. It was a good place and I was making money so I didn't mind. Later I moved the wife up and my eldest daughter was about three feet high then, I'd send her under the trucks to grease the throwout bearings. She could do it standing up and she loved it, but she had snow-white hair and it would be black, jeez the wife would scream.

One day she tripped on a cut-open barrel and put about a three-inch gash in her leg. It didn't bleed, but this white baby-fat just bushed out like popcorn, like it was under pressure. I damn near fainted, but the doctor just shoved it back in and slapped on a bandage.

A friend of mine, Harry Bannerman, got to be super for Macmillan over at NorWest Bay and set me up with a contract for three trucks. I didn't like to leave Garibaldi, but it looked like a real step up so I sold the Dodge and got three used trucks from Philp, the same Macks Schnare had first brought in.

I figured I damn near had 'er in the bag. It was a good haul and I was getting the wood but the big company situation was an altogether different world from what I'd been used to. You never knew what was going on. One day they would say, go to the west side, haul three loads. Then at noon they'd say, go to the east side and haul a load. The only people who had an idea what was happening were the bosses, and they just said, "We'll let you know in plenty of time what you're supposed to do." It was like being in school. Nobody was trusted to have any brains.

But at least Harry was in charge so I could feel safe. Then he got transferred. Turned out he'd been wrangling with the old guard group from Nanaimo, and they were too much for him.

As soon as Harry left they started putting the screws to me. There was a side that was so muddy my trucks were the only ones that could get into it and they told me if I would handle it they'd see I got looked after. I was losing an axle or rear end every day, and I would be up all night working. I'd have breakfast in camp and go back to work without seeing the wife for two or three days at a time. One time the cat had to push me and wrecked my trailer. "Use one of ours," they told me, "Go ahead, take it." Come the end of the summer my scale was so low I couldn't cover my parts bill. Not only was there no compensation for the rough going, I got a bill for twelve hundred dollars for trailer rental. Anywhere there was bad going that's where I'd be sent. I didn't have radios, and the dispatcher would talk to the company trucks, then they would stop my trucks. George Robinson told me, "You can't stand this. You come back here and I'll have some good loads for you." He'd lay aside a few good loads, then one of my drivers would flag me down and say, "They want us over at the other side."

After a while they brought in a young kid with a haywire old

Ford. He was from Nanaimo, and around Nanaimo they'd hated contractors from the mainland ever since Schnare came over. Besides that they were all Masons together. This kid couldn't do anything wrong. He was getting as much wood as all three of my trucks.

I can see now, I was trying to tell myself it wasn't happening. I'd seen men screwing each other around like that when I was a kid working for Safeway, but the whole reason I liked the woods was nothing on the job was more important than how you treated the other guy. It just gave me a sick feeling to think it was changing.

I bitched to the dispatcher, but that was bitching to the drill sergeant. "You're getting the same as everybody else. Just go where we tell you and you'll do alright." Other places you'd make a guy like that come clean quick enough, but there they've got you by the short ones, they make sure of that. With me it was my contract, with the men it's seniority and the blacklist. The whole thing with the old style logger was, he was a journeyman, he was a pro for hire, and if he didn't like the way you said good morning he took out his time and caught the boat.

The story is told of Pete Ohlson, the Roughhouse Pete of the Swanson poem, how one day they passed this new rule that anyone quitting had to turn his tools into the office before he got his time. Pete figured when they started playin' around like that it was time to find another camp, but he didn't say anything and the next day he went out with his crew to move a side. They took down all the rigging and piled it up on the machine and then moved the machine over all the logs and stumps out to the track and loaded it on a car, which was about three days' work ordinarily. Then after supper he goes into the office and asks for his time. "You can't have your time till you've turned in your tools," the timekeeper says.

So Pete goes to the bunkhouse and rounds up his crew and rounds up a locie and goes up and hooks onto the donkey and hauls it down to the shop, hooks a stump, skids this enormous machine with all its shackles and lines and blocks over in front of the office steps. "Okay," he says to the timekeeper, "Here's my tools y'little sonvubitch, now give me my time."

In the end I was ground right down to a frazzle and I had no choice but to break the contract and pull out. That's when I began to see it was all over. When Schnare started, trucks were new and risky and the companies were willing to pay someone else to work out the wrinkles. Now trucks were proven and the companies were all getting their own. They'd put in a new tax law so trucks could be depreciated thirty percent a year and it worked like a tax dodge. Instead of declaring income as dividends they were piling it into big diesel fleets with fourteen-foot bunks, radio control and all the rest.

Now I could see why old Schnare had been in such a rush. He

saw the door open, and he'd been around long enough to know how long it would get left that way. I turned my trucks back to Philp and went logging on my own.

There were still a few doors open in gyppo logging. Just before I turned in the trucks I did some hauling for two brothers in Parksville who had a little 10-10 Lawrence. Between them they were putting out four loads a day worth five hundred dollars a load. It was just a matter of doing the right thing in the right place, that was the theme of the gyppos, but I was still looking when the last of the timber got tied up by the companies and the door was closed on that too.

So now you work for the companies. If some little thing goes out you park and radio for the mechanic. He spends half his time driving and you spend half your time sleeping. Doesn't matter much because the machinery's gotten so good and the job's been laid out so simple everybody can do the work half asleep.

You never think of your brakes, the drums are nine inches wide and it's all made out of miracle alloys that work white hot, half the guys don't even know what the pedal's hooked up to. There's just one guy to load you and it don't matter how he throws the logs on because you hardly notice they're there, they're all pecker poles we would have left in the bush anyway. The trucks never stop but the driving's so sloppy you don't get any more logs than we did before. It's like everything else. They've done away with the work but not the worker.

THE MEN THERE WERE THEN

It sounds like something that's been
said before too many times
but I want you to know
I mean it, now, when I say
there are no men around today
like the men there were then.
You see those enormous tree stumps
with the notches in, and you don't think.
Those were big trees.
There are no trees like that today.
We think today what we do with machines
is hard work, but our trees are tiny
and they did it all by hand.
They did it all standing on springy, narrow
boards, stuck twelve feet up above the ground
sometimes canyons below them
swinging their axes into that big wood.
To move along they'd give a hop with one toe
held under the springboard, to swing it.
Then they'd stick the axe in the wood
and stoop to reach their saws, I never
heard of one who fell.
But one time one man when he
turned to reach for his saw,

he brushed that razor sharp axe
and it slit his middle
right along the belt line for about eight inches.
It didn't bleed so much but
his intestines came looping down like bunting.
When we came with the stretcher this man
was under the cut crouched on his knees
delicately holding up these gut loops
one by one splashing sawdust off 'em
with water from his waterbag.
There are no men like that
around today.

THE THIRD STIFF

Far as getting busted up goes it's safer on a boat
than most shore jobs   safest job there is
if you don't count drowning
Gillnetters especially
out on deck for a beer piss
boat leans one way
you lean the other—
kersplash.
Or reaching out over the rollers
to shake a log out of the web.
They find your boat idling up against a bluff
the next day, tow it into the float
nobody will tie up next to it.
One year up in Rivers Inlet
three guys went over in one week.

What happens then, they turn up a few days later
in other guys' nets. Guy'd see this lump coming up
and think it was a seal till it falls on deck
and an arm flops out to signal
shit-your-drawers time.
Two of these corpses showed up on schedule
but the third one kept us guessing for a while.
Fishermen are a spooky lot to begin with

and you have to have done it to know just how eerie
it gets out there in the middle of the night
all by yourself leaning over the stern
wondering just what sort of a ghastly item
the murk is going to puke up at you next
everybody in the inlet was just quaking in their gumboots
every time they saw something that wasn't a fish
come into the light figuring for sure
they'd snagged the third stiff

Sonny Iverson said this night he got so bad
he had to go knock back half a twenty-sixer
before he could get the rest of his net in
leaning over the stern to pull kelp out of the rudderpost
thinking what a damn fool he was to get so spooked
the whisky took his balance and plop
he's in the soup   his faithful boat
gliding serenely away into the night
and all he can think about is that damn stiff—
"now I'm in here with that sonofabitch!"
he's afraid to paddle, certain when he reaches out
he'll touch it and once when he brushes a chunk
he finds himself screaming like he's being murdered.
Then he hears something.
A kind of a faint swishing noise.
Swish, swish, swish—
He listens real careful and reaches around a bit.

There, right under his nose, is a moving line of corks.
Somebody is picking their net past him and all he has to do
is grab on and wait to be saved.
This works fine until he comes up to the other boat
and finds he's all tangled up in the net
and before he can say anything he's up over the rollers
crashes head first on the deck and knocks himself silly.
Of course the other fisherman just cuts loose
swearing and cursing all the foul luck in the world
figuring it's the missing stiff he's hooked onto
until Sonny starts coming to and moaning a bit
then the poor guy runs howling the length of the boat

bars himself into the house
cursing God and praying to be saved at the same time
it takes Sonny fifteen minutes to calm him down enough
to go get his boat.

THOSE BLOODY
FISHERMEN

Those bloody fishermen you know
they're not even human
not during fishing season
you know old Scotch John
take a look at
that man's hands if you ever
get the chance
left or right I forget,
one of 'em's got a hole
right through it
'e was running 'is lines out one time
feeling the fathom markers
with the flat of 'is hand, it was
the old bronze type of line, and a loose strand speared 'im
clean through the fingers
threaded 'em tight together
yanked 'im overboard
but 'e hit the gurdy clutch
goin' by   climbed back in
one-handed   cut the fingers apart
with sidecutters
each one separately
went on fishing
holes started stinkin' n goin' green

so he soaked 'em in the bleach bucket
he had there for his spoons
poked out the gunk with a broomstraw, holes got so big
'e could see through 'em
white furry stuff lining 'em
still he couldn't miss any fishing
holes closed up eventually
went bluish black   saw a doctor
end of the season, said
didn't that hurt?
Hurt? he sez, yeah by God it hurt
like a son of a bitch
passed out right there
in the doctor's chair
said later that was the
first time 'e stopped to think about it
and it hit 'im all at once

WHAT A WAY TO GO

He was haywire, terrible haywire,
old Farraro.
And that was what did him in.
They were tearing down a house.
Some free deal old Farraro'd got in on,
halfway up Black Mountain
and as usual they had a
terrible old truck that just barely ran.
They got this truck up there,
and I suppose they put a huge load on
which was bad enough right there,
but the worst thing was,
they had no ropes to tie the load down.
They would never think of a thing like that
beforehand, and apparently there was
none around, up on this mountain.
So the old man he took one boy
and sat out back, boy on the lumber
to weigh it down, and him up
on a big stack of naily plywood.
Well the brakes of course went,
and halfway down away they go.
Gino was the one at the wheel,
and by jesus now if he didn't

hold 'er on the road all the way down —
it musta gone a hundred miles an hour.
The kid and all the shiplap,
which was on the tail,
went off at the first bump, and after
they got all the rusty nails out of 'im
he was okay. But the old man,
he hung on. You can just see 'im
sittin' up there like a cowboy on a brahma bull
trying to save his plywood pile.
Still, there wasn't much else to do.
The kid saw it all, said he was
doing okay till just about the bottom of the hill, when
    finally
the wind got under the edge and up he went
like a sultan on a magic carpet
soaring on this naily sheet of plywood
hundrit miles an hour,
right out over the rockslide.
He went down a thousand feet.
But just think of it eh, sittin' there
both eyes open watchin'
the end of 'er fly up in your face
couldn't even get a hand free
to cross himself —

I KILL MYSELF AND MAIM MYSELF

As often as I think to, as many ways
as I can arrange. I never miss
a chance, on top of a boom
to miss a handhold and plunge
five storeys onto blasted rock.
Beneath a building going up
I always cause a rigging wrench
or a piece of just-cut plate
to plunge jagged and sizzling
into my skull. Under trucks
draining hot oil I let them
roll over me harmlessly except for
one low-hanging bolt which catches
my shoulder and rolls me into a
dusty oily boneless ball.
I never see a set of rollers but
I offer my hand, my wrist, my
crunching elbow, shoulder jams
skin burns and pulls loose
horrible snapping as of bridge timbers
breaking and the arm is gone.
The moment I arrive in the presence
of a new machine, I surrender myself.
I watch its bearings strain and

break as the soles of my shoes
disappear and I come out below,
gear tracks in pink froth, foreman
cursing my stupidity, men wondering
who'll get number seven now.
Tail-swings have scissored my head off
so many times. And snapping cables
like bullwhips after my balls.
I torment myself alive.
I kill and maim myself and daily pray
to confine disaster to the mind.

My Experience with Greatness

When I was a kid I wanted to be great. A great man. Didn't matter at what, my ideas changed daily on that score, but I just had this very sure feeling I'd be great at it, whatever it was.

As it turned out, I was right. I did get to be great at a number of things, or at least pretty great. But there are a lot of problems with greatness I never suspected as a kid, and the main one grew out of that fuzziness about the chosen field, or perhaps more accurately unchosen field, you get to play your greatness out in.

I guess the lesson greatness has taught me can be summed up in two simple points, two things they don't tell you about greatness in school that when you found out about them tend to turn the whole thing into a kind of hollow victory. Number one is that greatness is a lot more common than they would have you think. Number two is, the process of selecting outstanding people for public celebration is rigged against the vast majority of people who do truly brilliant, herculean, heroic things. There are all sorts of people locked in obscure struggle whose ultimate triumph we will never read about, who but for fate, might have demonstrated the same mettle on the world stage amid international acclaim.

Take me.

I'm a really unfortunate case, in that even my peers ignore my accomplishments because they're in fields where I'm the only guy there. For instance I am the undisputed world champion at catching the Langdale ferry from Pender Harbour in forty-seven minutes in a 1973 Volvo with no brakes and eight cases of books in the back. I proved this last Thursday.

The distance from Pender Harbour to Langdale is forty-eight miles so I must have averaged a touch under sixty, which isn't a qualifying speed at the Indy, but I'd give a lot to see A.J. Foyt try and duplicate my feat. For one thing, the stretch from Pender to Halfmoon Bay follows an old logging road. I know the guy who pushed it in, Art Shaw. He had one of these weird cats with the controls up ahead of the engine and a blade that lifted right up over the cab, and old Art was kind of a passive resister when it came to obstacles like rock knobs, skunk cabbage patches or big stumps — his strategy was to go around. A lot of the skunk cabbage patches have dried up and a lot of the stumps have since rotted down, but Art's loops are still there, immortalized in six inches of cracking asphalt. They have loops at Indy too, but I doubt they have reverse banks, changes of radius midway through and six-inch breaks in the pavement like the Sunshine Coast Highway does north of Halfmoon Bay. Most Pender Harbourites give themselves an hour-and-a-quarter to an hour-and-a-half for the Langdale run, and the all-time record, as far as I know, is forty-one minutes. But that was set in a new Porsche.

The thing about a 1973 Volvo is, this story takes place in 1984. Volvos are good cars. I've had two of them now. One '62 fastback that I bought off Walter Ibey for four hundred dollars in 1971, and this 1973 wagon I bought off Edith Daly two years ago. But there's one thing you have to keep in mind about a Volvo, and that is they're only built to last eleven years. The ads all say get a Volvo and it'll last eleven years, and that's true. But what the ads don't tell you is that immediately on its eleventh birthday a Volvo gives up like the one-hoss shay and becomes a deadly risk to anyone attempting to run a further mile.

I'd had a driveshaft out of this Volvo once and I'd replaced the clutch once and put a new set of used rotors and calipers on the front axle, but apart from some rattles and clatters and flaking-away fenders, it kept going pretty steady. But last January it had its eleventh birthday. The first clue was it abruptly started using a quart of oil a day. I noticed a black puddle underneath it the size of a medium pizza and traced the trouble to a loose tappet cover. I buttoned that up and it stopped using oil for about three days, when I found a puddle under it the size of an extra-large pizza.

This time it was a front main bearing seal. Still not realizing what the car was trying to tell me, I spent a very unhappy day and a half installing a new seal. A few fill-ups went by without my needing to add oil, then I brought it home with the tappets clacking like the Four Horsemen of the Apocalypse and found the oil level right off the stick. I looked underneath, but there was no puddle.

Actually the first thing that should have tipped me off was the rear wiper conking out. The older Volvo wagons were famous for that deliciously luxurious rear window wiper—it had a lot to do with my buying one—and I had always been impressed at the way this frivolous extra kept stiffly wiping, long after other unessentials like the radio, heater, trunk latch and emergency brake had corroded into oblivion. Blind Bob Wolpert, who runs an illegal junk yard up by the Spinnaker Road subdivision and is something of a purveyor of the new urban mythology, told me a Volvo is no good once that wiper stops and should be immediately abandoned on the roadside, but I have never been able to admit the supernatural into my real life decision-making process.

Anyway, one day after the extra-large oil puddle I got tired of driving without rear vision and remembered to turn the hose on the now completely socked-in rear window. The water from the hose didn't have the slightest effect on it. I took a close look and discovered the entire back end of the car was coated with a tarry amalgam of black crankcase oil and dust about three-eighths of an inch thick. I had to use a paint scraper and gasoline to cut a peephole. The next time I took it out, with clear vision of the road behind me for the first time in a month, it all came home to me. The road behind me appeared clouded in a bluish mist, where the road ahead was bright and clear. It was hard on the twists and dips around Pender to see more than a car-length behind, but going up the mile-long straight stretch outside Halfmoon Bay, the bluish mist became an inky smog completely obscuring the Peninsula Transport semi I'd passed seconds earlier. Thwarted from leaking her vital fluids away onto the ground, the old girl was now spewing it out of the exhaust with the emphasis of a sick whale spouting blood. I knew it was over then.

Having realized this, I also realized it would be a waste of time to fix any of the innumerable things that started now going wrong at the rate of one or two a trip—a strange lumpiness in the rear brakes, a half-turn or so of slack somewhere in the drive chain so it jolted like a coal train every time you touched the gas, a buck in the motor that would express itself going up hills and act on the drive chain lurch in a most alarming way—I knew I was going to have to get it up to the car dump while it would still make the trip under its own power, but I kept waiting for something good in the eight-hundred-dollar range to show up in the *Coast News* want ads, and kept thinking I could get one more little trip out of the Volvo.

This was how matters stood at 9:30 the morning of March 11, 1984, when Jake Willett woke me up with a phone call wanting to know how come I wasn't in Horseshoe Bay to meet him for our work poetry reading tour of Vancouver Island pulp mills. I had been supposed to take the 8:30 ferry from Langdale, meet him in Horseshoe Bay at 9:15, then take the 11:30 ferry from Horseshoe Bay to Vancouver Island and drive up to start our tour in Gold River that evening.

"Jake, you wouldn't believe this, but I just slept through the alarm." This was a fair enough lie considering it was the first thing I said that day, but it wasn't so good considering we have kids who wake up at 7 and go to school at 8:30, which Jake knew. The truth was I'd forgotten about our rendezvous, and about the entire four-day reading tour, and had been sleeping in quite determinedly with a pillow over my head.

"There's another ferry at 10:30. Can you make that?"

Jake is perhaps the most organized and reliable person on the Pacific Slope of Western America, at least among the work poets. He would be constitutionally incapable of missing a ferry. My only hope was that, as a labour writer of middle-class origin, he would understand what a working-class thing this was I'd done.

"Sure Jake. No prob," I said. "See you at . . ." I made my voice sound convincingly alert, I thought, but it was still too early in the day to add 10:30 and 1.

"11:30," he said firmly. "Don't forget the books."

"Right."

In a way it was lucky I didn't have any time to think, or speak to my wife. It probably would have ended in bloodshed. This wasn't the first time I'd done something like this, just perhaps the worst time. I stuffed a spare shirt and toothbrush into my briefcase and bolted for the door patting down my hair. Mary stopped

me with my wallet and watch, and a look made up of equal parts
of pity and fury, not safe to kiss.

On the front porch I halted with a realization that this rather
typical screwup had just taken on a truly horrifying dimension.
There before me in the yard hunched my blighted Volvo. The
night chilled me. A poem I planned to read later that day, about
the death of a logger, came into my mind:

> events
> in themselves ordinary,
> in combination deadly . . .

Not only was I about to attempt the twisty morning run to
Langdale in a completely unrealistic time, I was going to try it in
a disintegrating eleven-year-old Volvo that was unsafe to sit in let
alone drive, and not only was I going to ask God to forgive me this
temptation to fate, I was going to load the car up with eight heavy
cases of books. I couldn't take my wife's good little Toyota, because
I had to leave it parked four days at the Langdale terminal and
her constitution couldn't support life for over thirty minutes
without her Toyota.

The logical solution was to have her drive me and I could sense
she was just waiting for me to fall to my knees and ask, but
somehow the trial presented by the Volvo, with its risk of almost
certain death, seemed easier to face.

Going over the first hill I discovered the lumpy rear wheel
brakes had now totally given up, leaving me with brakes only on
one front wheel, which not only failed to much alter the car's
forward momentum, but almost ripped the steering wheel out of
my hands and pitched me into a granite bluff. So now in addition
to making the hour-long Langdale run in an unsafe wreck overloaded with books, I was going to do it with only one locking front
wheel for brakes.

I recognized that this was going to be one of the greatest tests
I'd ever faced, one that demanded every ounce of concentration,
of heroic nerve, that a person could ever be expected to muster.
I snuck up carefully on the big hills, coasting over their crests at
a near stall, nursing my shred of braking capacity along as far as I
dared test that shrieking, shuddering left front wheel, then letting
the old beast fly sixty, seventy, eighty miles an hour, making up

the time I lost bucking up the grades at the head of my ever-thickening black storm cloud of oil smoke.

I stopped religiously every ten miles to throw another quart or two of oil into the smoking hot motor, no doubt setting the world speed record for pouring two quarts of oil too, and kept my ear so attuned to every new rattle and throb I was able to just keep the motor on the edge where I was getting everything it had left without giving it the excuse it desperately wanted to pack up totally. Talk about living on the edge, no Edmund Hillary inching along a Himalayan ice shelf was ever so exposed and vulnerable as I was streaking through the intersection at the bottom of the Norwest Bay hill in that smoking pounding missile of rust, grease and steam. And yet I was on top of the problem. Nothing caught me by surprise. When an elderly woman in a fifteen-miles-an-hour Pinto pulled out in front of me on a corner with a car in the oncoming lane, I just cranked it for the shoulder and streaked past, skidding in the gravel. If I had given in to the instinct to even touch the brake, that left wheel would have jerked me into the oncoming car so fast no one would ever have known what hap-

pened. There were a hundred factors, all matters of life and death, which I had to keep juggling in my mind, never missing a one. I even remembered to slow down at the speed trap outside Sechelt, letting the Pinto overtake me and get nailed. Does an astronaut at his bank of blinking controls have so much to keep track of? No, all his equipment is forgiving and reliable and all his decisions neat and simple. Gus Grissom would never have made it past the hairpin at Silver Sands. But I made it to the ferry with thirty seconds to spare.

As it happened, there was a two-sailing wait and cars were lined up for a mile, but after what I'd been through nothing the BC Ferry Corp could throw at me could give me even a moment's pause. I just pulled into the oncoming lane, leaned on the horn and streaked through the lineup, yelling at the fluorescent-gloved attendant, "Emergency work—poetry mercy run! Gangway!", drove up in front of the baggage van and had six boxes moved before the fat lady from the toll booth had time to come puffing down.

"What do you think you're doing! You get back to the end of the line!" she barked. I smiled sweetly.

"Just loading baggage, ma'am."

Her buggy eyes followed the boxes from the drooping, dripping, hissing Volvo to the otherwise completely empty baggage van.

"That's not baggage! That van is reserved for hand baggage!"

"Are you telling me there's no room, ma'am?" I was done anyway. Her bosom was heaving under the blue Ferry Corp blazer as she struggled to contain her outrage, and before she could think up another institutional imperative to fling at me, I was into the car and gone back up the road. I just ran the old heap into the brush outside the compound and left the keys in it. Then I made for the ferry at a dead run.

It wasn't until I was leaning over the rail as the boat pulled away, watching the toll booth lady still waving her arms and regaling the man with orange gloves, that I let go. Waves of relief washed over me. I beamed at the luminous prop wash, the pale blue terminal buildings, the left-behind lines of cars, the dark slopes of Mount Elphinstone behind. And I just felt — great.

CODFISH AND CAPPUCCINO

For a guy who doesn't travel much, April was a busy month. On the fifth I humped my little red Mazda pickup down to the Vancouver Airport and caught a flight to Bologna, Italy. I got back from there on the thirteenth and staggered around home for a week trying to stop my head from spinning, then on the twentieth I parked my red wagon at the airport's new economy lot and took off again, this time for St. John's, Newfoundland. Do you know what the time difference is from here to there? Five-and-a-half hours. The hockey game comes on TV after the pubs close. The Newfies are closer to Bologna time than to ours by two hours.

That's one thing you come back from Europe with. What a jeezly huge thing is this blob we call Canada. Here we sit taking up half the northern hemisphere, and what do we do with it? My flight from London to Milan took about the same time as my flight from Vancouver to Calgary. On one I could look out the window and see all the great cities of Europe; on the other, two hours of logging slash and coal holes.

I have never wanted to go anywhere but the Queen Charlotte Islands. Call me a xenophobe, call me the typically smug westcoaster, I just never had the desire to travel, even in the sixties when all my college friends were taking to the big shining highway with *Europe on $5 a Day* stowed in their Trapper Nelsons. (Today's youth will need $50 a day. I wonder if they have it?) As a writer I always figured I had a lifetime supply of things that desperately needed writing about here at home, and I didn't want to cloud my vision with foreign landscapes. I thought, rightly or wrongly, that it was dreaming of the old world that had stopped earlier writers from being able to see the new one clearly.

But it was writing that eventually took me away anyway. In order to write about the coast I first had to become my own publisher, and after fifteen years of doing that I finally ran out of excuses and had to drag out my wedding suit and take my turn as president of the publishers' association. This carries with it certain obligations, one of them being to tramp around all over the place showing the flag.

Thus Newfoundland and Bologna in one month. What a mixture. Kippers and cappuccino in one swallow. But you know, in a funny way, it worked. Both made me think the same thing about BC. (Didn't somebody say the real value of travel isn't seeing foreign lands, but coming home with new eyes? If they didn't, they should have.)

Newfoundland must be one of the bleaker places human beings have chosen to stand against the elements. St. John's is two whole degrees of latitude south of us here on the Sunshine Coast — about level with Seattle — but it was snowing like crazy when I left on Tuesday. ("Aye, we see lots 'o this, By. It's when the sleet storms pull down the powerpoles into the roads I don't like it...") St. John's calls itself the oldest city in North America, but after four hundred years it still feels precarious, a flycamp at the edge of the world. Vegetation on The Rock is about the same as I remember it around Dawson City. From the air the towns look like lichen clinging to the crevices of a huge windswept boulder. Closer up, the houses look like oversized packing crates perched on the rocks and painted more shades of turquoise and lemon yellow than you see driving through the Sliammon reserve. But inside, the people are singing their heads off. Every damn time I turned around someone was grabbing a squeeze box and saying "D'ye know *I'se the By*, By?" I didn't, but that didn't stop them for a minute. They're used to having mainlanders stand around like portly statues, full of amazement and envy at their sinuous dance with life.

In Bologna, which is only two-and-a-half degrees south of St. John's, the temperature was in the mid-twenties and the weather

like early July back on the BC coast. Bologna's surroundings are
lush and inspiring. The hills are bright with manicured fields, the
highest, Monte della Guardia, topped with the imposing dome of
the Santuario della Madonna di San Luca. Picturesque brick and
stone archways cover the broad sidewalks, outdoor cafés and
shops. What North Americans are pleased to think of as the
"modern" covered shopping mall has been flourishing here since
the sixteenth century at least. You can walk almost anywhere in
the downtown under cover of these pleasant arcades, and if you
get tired, you never seem to be more than a few minutes from a
big piazza full of marble statuary, fountains and benches throng-
ing with laughing, wine-sipping students. If you must get on, well,
the buses in this very civilized city are free through morning and
evening rush hours.

On the second night I was there—a Friday—they shut the
streets down to traffic. They didn't block them, everybody just
knew to leave their cars at home. The downtown flooded with
people. Old people, young people, babies, dogs—coming up Via
Independenza toward my hotel, I had to detour around the
intersections because the crowds were so thick. As far as I could
see they were just wandering around showing off their good
clothes and visiting—at the top of their lungs. You'd think it was
VE day or something by British Columbia standards, but this was
just what they do there on Friday night. All the sidewalk cafes
were backed up three deep, the ubiquitous peddlers' wagons were
out in force selling Frank Sinatra tapes and sunglasses and what
looked like American hotdogs until you bit into one and realized
it was one of those delectable smoked sausages which have made
Bologna a household word around the world. Even the fast food
there is gourmet fare by our standards. The plastic-cup wine you
couldn't match in a Vancouver restaurant for twenty dollars a
bottle.

As in Newfoundland, I did a lot of standing around feeling like
a lump of something inert. The ordinary Bolognese-on-the-street
is so quick to laugh, to cry, to sense another person's mood, sing
a song or cite a noble thought. Pointing and mumbling, I felt
keenly the cultural disadvantages of having grown up in a
society where the only regular provision for civic gathering was
this thing called a beer parlour where the women were separated
by a wall from the men and you always had to watch what you

said if you wanted to avoid having your teeth rammed down your throat.

After the book fair closed Sunday, I climbed the four kilometres of stairs to the basilica of San Luca to admire its gorgeous view of the city in the setting sun, and there they were again; the long portico winding up the hill was swarming from top to bottom with kids and dogs and grannies and youths in flashy dress out enjoying their city as they had been doing for a hundred generations. On Monday I had a free day and went to Florence, the city of Michelangelo and the Medici, expecting to find it a kind of ghostly outdoor museum like the ruins of Skedans. I found it instead a vibrant, youthful city full of children and students and peddlers selling stylish leather clothing and irresistible food. It was the colour and verve of the place that caught my eye, not the fact all this life was swarming about the Medici Palace and tangling around the feet of Michelangelo's *David*. Someone told me four-fifths of the people in Florence at any given time are tourists, but if that is true, they are largely Italian tourists. At every museum and public garden I went to in Italy I found the Italians themselves to be their own most numerous admirers. They lounge on the statues as they eat lunch and make use of Lorenzo's once palatial Boboli Gardens to read their paperbacks, taking public advantage of the magnificence the Medici created all those centuries ago for their private glory.

It may be that there is no connection between the glorious cultural artifacts the Italians have so carefully preserved from their past, the high place given education of the young, and the stylish, literate, confident society of northern Italy today. But I saw it as all one rich mixture. Like a lot of Canadians, I've always regarded modern Italy as a bit of joke with its forty-eight governments in forty-five years, but by the time I left I felt like some underprivileged refugee from the third world, and not only because of the obvious fact they get so much more out of life. Italy today has it both ways. Unemployment is still twelve percent in the south, but in the north industry is booming. Their currency is soaring against ours. Their labour output is higher by twenty percent. Their life expectancy is three years higher than ours, their birth rate lower by thirty percent (so much for the Pope). Educationally they suffer an embarrassment of riches, with more diplomas than they can use.

All this and Tomaso Bamba, too! If that's what minority government can do, bring on the election.

When I transferred to the Vancouver-bound plane in Amster-
dam I was handed a local paper, the first I'd seen in over a week.
I avoided looking at it until we were over Iceland. I knew what I
would find and I wasn't ready to kill the warm Italian glow that
still lingered. Finally I got up my nerve and opened it up — not an
easy thing to do in the crowded sub-economy section at the back
of a DC-10. Following my usual priorities, I turned to the sports
first. All the underdogs were winning the Stanley Cup playoffs,
Wipeout City for my hockey pool, but I was glad to see it anyway.
Turning to cultural news next, there was yet another study revealing BC support for the arts to be lower than in any province except
Nova Scotia. Newfoundland was well up the list. On the education front, several policy makers in Victoria were voicing the
opinion that, after starving the public schools and universities for
ten years, the best way to deal with our plunging high school
graduation rate was not to restore the education budget, but to
make the examinations easier. The front page was all about
Vander Zalm cutting off welfare for single mothers — a virtual
xerox of a *Daily Mirror* story I'd been reading about British welfare
cuts in the airport before boarding. I wondered, is it possible
Thatcher's imitators follow her example that closely?

What nobody seems ready to acknowledge is the Italian example, where much more impressive success has been achieved
without penalizing the ordinary people, under the gentler leadership of Socialist Bettino Craxi and a left-dominated parliament.
It seems important to know that Italy recently passed Britain in
total GNP to become the fifth-ranked industrialized nation in the
world, but how often do we hear about it? This latest Italian
renaissance has been solidly led by home-owned small business,
succeeding despite a complete lack of natural resources in trans-
forming a have-not nation into a kind of Mediterranean Japan.

For the first time in my life I felt really depressed about my
home province and its people. When would they ever stop sub-
mitting to shallow, self-serving leaders like Vander Zalm and find
some richer, maturer vision of what the west could be? It was
never clearer to me that in order to have a vigorous economy you
must first have a vigorous, informed people motivated by a posi-
tive vision of life that is worth pulling together for. In modern Italy

they have it, here we seem to have lost it. I could feel the gloom of the place taking hold of me as we descended, reminding me of the way my little guidebook described life in Italy under the barbarian occupation.

But my sour mood didn't last long after reaching the ferry at Horseshoe Bay on my way home. It was a lovely spring day and the mountains across Howe Sound looked stunning in their crisp blue and white. The sky seemed so big and somehow bright compared to Europe. Hope returned to the landscape, but it was clouded with sadness. We spend our lives in one of the most favoured settings on the globe, just like they always say. But our public life is bleaker than the weather in Newfoundland. We should be getting so much more out of it.

THE YELLOWHEAD

In my family we never believed in recreation as a regular part of life. We never took holidays. Only once do I remember Dad shutting down the logging camp and declaring an official day off. It was May the 24th and we all climbed into Parky Higgins' fishboat and went to Egmont for a picnic. We kids didn't know how to take it. We were bewildered. I kept asking Dad what broke down, thinking it must have been something really big.

"This is just once in a blue moon," he said.

I was a very literal child and phrases like "once in a blue moon" didn't help me. I couldn't figure out what a blue moon could have to do with something we were doing in broad daylight, or how the moon could ever be blue, unless he meant the way it looked when it came out during a sunny day, and looked almost transparent like a thumbnail trimming held up against the blue sky, except that was probably just one of those many things which seemed to appear to my eight-year-old eyes and nobody else's. I didn't know. But I did know Dad didn't have room in his overworked life for all my questions — I had proved this already beyond a shadow of doubt — so I let it ride. I think I was about twenty-five before I finally figured out the trick of metaphors.

The more usual way of sneaking a little relief into our workaholic lives was to camouflage it. My dad never actually took time off to take us for a fling in town — the Big Smoke that is, Vancouver — but he would often take one of us kids along when he had to fly down for yarder parts. Then, once we were out of the camp's grip, he would become a little more playful, and we might sneak in a side trip to a touring roadshow of *Showboat*, the PNE or more likely, some of his elderly relatives out in the Fraser Valley. He couldn't bring himself to set free time aside, but he was good at goofing off on the way back. This, as I understand it, fits with the clinical definition of the workaholic: he's not a guy who necessarily gets a lot done, he's just a guy who never officially lets himself off the hook.

The only times we ever took holidays consciously and openly were when my parents were driven to it by desperation. These therapeutic trips were often brief, unplanned car dashes to the interior of the province undertaken in an atmosphere that was anything but jolly; nevertheless, they invariably worked. A day or two away from disaster centre amid the inspiration of the BC landscape and their spirits would revive.

My own adult life has followed in the same pattern. In twenty years together Mary and I have rarely given ourselves an official day off, let alone a week. We have continued to sneak relief in the ways I learned from my own parents.

The rationale for our 1976 road trip to Prince Rupert was a combination of the latter two excuses described above: we had a new book out we wanted to distribute through the northern interior, thus providing the essential job-related tie-in, and we had to get away from ourselves and take a look at things. We'd been ploughing along in much the same rut for six years and our lives had taken on a settledness I found unsettling. Where we had started out together in the early seventies as a try-anything-once, live-life-one-day-at-a-time-team, we had by this time fallen into a pattern of working every day at our book publishing projects, doing the same thing month after month, not changing and not rightly knowing how to change. We thought of trying new things, making moves, but every move we considered seemed too major, too hard.

After six years together we didn't have any children. We were having the classic war of wills; she wanted children but I didn't. Or rather I did, but not then. Never then. Always there was some major objective to get out of the way first—write my book, build our house, establish a secure income. The situation was becoming a little desperate. I knew it had to break one way or the other, but

I just couldn't face up to it. I was wonderfully articulate about why no abrupt moves should be attempted *at that particular time*, while so many other things were hanging fire. Mary was too dispirited to do anything but sulk, and weep silent tears at unexpected times. There was a stiffness developing between us that lasted past the arguments. I knew something had to change, but I felt powerless to take the situation in hand.

It was into this context my parents' old behaviourism asserted itself, and I began advancing the notion that a serious car trip to establish our books in the interior, something we had spoken of doing off and on for several years, was now shaping up as a priority. Mary responded without enthusiasm, as she did for most things at that juncture, and dismissed the notion as an unnecessary waste of money we didn't have. I came back with the fact we had just invested twenty thousand dollars in new titles and the pressure was on to squeeze out every sale we could; the interior sales were the tail end of the market, but we couldn't afford to ignore any opportunities and we had the coast pretty well looked after. But the capper was that Mary's parents had a new factory-camperized Dodge van they had been urging us to make use of. All we would have to do was buy gas and groceries; the rest of the trip would be free.

This camper was an attraction in itself. It was all deep pile carpets, chrome fixtures and teak panelling. We lived in a soot-stained pink house trailer with buckled birch veneer at this point and the gleaming new camper had more modern conveniences than we did at home. In fact it was just the sort of stainless-and-formica luxury we were fond of ridiculing as it paraded past during summer months on the Sunshine Coast Highway, and to that stage we hadn't seriously considered taking the offer up. Now that the idea hatched, it took on all the temptation of a forbidden pleasure. It also scared us. We weren't used to being responsible for anything that expensive and fragile and we wondered if Mary's dad knew what he was doing offering us free run of it for ten days. He probably wondered too, but like the good parent he was he didn't let on and handed the keys over with a smile.

It drove sweeter than our car. I was unused to being in a vehicle where everything worked. The deep-pile comfort made me feel illegitimate, jaded. Now we were part of the great American consumer class that was destroying the world for its own bored pleasure. Was this where we were headed? Is this what marriage, middle age, parenthood, must inevitably lead to? Languor possessed me, and I felt sick for the vigour of my lost lean youth. I placed all my hope in the cleansing process of travel and pressed down the accelerator, wanting to have the fat Lower Mainland behind us.

The Fraser and Thompson canyons reeled by without raising a flicker of interest. Once they had caused me infinite wonder, now they left me unmoved in my cocoon of ennui. Mary sat silent in the passenger seat. Kamloops rolled out before us. I headed through town and across the river, stopping briefly at the home of a cousin I'd once driven to Mexico with in a spur-of-the-moment, drunken spree of wild-oat sowing. He'd been the brilliant wastrel, throwing away his opportunities like a madman lighting cigarettes with twenty-dollar bills, and I'd looked to him for inspiration. Now we found him in a suburban bungalow, married-with-child, worrying about keeping his lawn green. We resisted their entreaties to stop over, eager to push on into unfamiliar territory that might peel back the pall. Somebody told us to go up the North Thompson and take the Yellowhead route through the Big Bend country west into Rupert, and that's what we were doing. I'd just read *Tay John* by Howard O'Hagan and his grotesque rendition of the Yellowhead legend had ignited my interest. The "Yellow Head" or "Tête Jaune" in French, originally referred to a half-Iroquois mountain man who had been cast out by his people for having blond hair and came to trap in the Yellowhead Pass area before the building of the railroad. His real name was Pierre Hatsinaton and he gained a Paul Bunyan–like reputation for wrestling grizzly bears and that sort of thing, except there was a spiritual dimension to it I didn't quite understand. He became a symbol of hope to the local Shuswap tribes in their retreat before white civilization, and also to the white and part-white mountain people in their search for identity.

O'Hagan developed the legend of the blond halfbreed into a preposterous fantasy but he knew the Rocky Mountain country well and I wanted to see the landscape that radiated through his words with such feral mystique. It was the kind of thing I thought we needed to peel the scales off our souls.

The North Thompson is a pretty mountain river, blue and cold and of many changes—pinched and writhing, pooled and placid. It dominates the valley. There isn't much land, a few sidehill bits of ranch, the people mostly sustained by sawmills. The road and railway run on opposite slopes, restlessly trading sides. We recognized one of the depressing, broken-down towns, Avola, from the story of Pat Lane's life. Pat is now one of the reigning Canadian poets, but then he was a friend down the road who told over and over again the story of his bleak beginnings in adult life, a teenager from Vernon shackled by a shotgun marriage and working in the Avola mill without a hope of ever knowing the world. It was in the fifties during bomb scare times and at one point the men of the area formed a vigilante defence group to mow down all the townies they expected to see barrelling up the road escaping lower mainland fallout, hungry for the larders of Avola's rickety house-trailers. Pat captured the purgatorial mood of the place in a couple of short poems like "Mill Cry" and "Thirty Below" but never completed any of the various stories and novels he started about it. He always got so mired in depression thinking about it, I don't know why he even tried. What draws a person back?

From what we could see, Pat's depression was well founded. Of the mill that is eternally closing in his poems we could find no trace, but there was a little railroad shed, Avola Black Diamond Mill or somesuch, to prove the truth of it. The trailers that cause his memory such pain still clung to the hillside punctuated by a one-room school, gaunt-windowed, made of logs. Car hulks in every yard, and the ubiquitous yellow backhoe. No town is so betrayed and broken down, it seems, as to be unable to sustain at least one yellow backhoe, hunching scorpion-like in the back yard beside the clothesline. Above the highway was the only sign of ongoing life, a newish tourist palace in the fake Spanish mode. Below town by the river we found the fallen-silent mill. Fallen silent, fallen flat, carried off, willow growing over. What a place to have in your past.

At Valemont we stopped to see my young brother Don. He was twenty-three then and I was proud to see how he was developing into a serious construction worker. He was a mechanic for one of the companies hollowing out the centre of the province for powerline right-of-ways and he booted his pickup around town like he owned the place. He had been passed over for foreman because of his youth, but he ran his department anyway. Waitresses fawned and brought him what he wanted without his asking, while he made barely a grunt of acknowledgement—which seemed enough to please them. Everybody treated him with respect, except some of the punks on the crew who didn't know enough to. They didn't care, they acted so above it all, as if they belonged to some new supergeneration that had seen through the value system of the working scene and figured out how to live beyond it. I knew they hadn't though, I'd seen enough like them brought into line after a few hotshot years.

Valemont was a bustling place in those heady days of the last big construction boom, as lively and cocky as Avola was ghostly and feeble. We stopped the night in an unpaid parking slot behind the company motel, running our power cord in through a window on the sly. I worried about getting the boys in trouble with their landlord but they all chorused together, "Fock him!"

Of course, I thought. Fock him. What kind of an old hen was I becoming? I became one again the next morning when Don announced he was skipping his morning shift so he could take us down to the Mica logjam, which was the big sight to see in the area.

"Won't somebody notice if you don't show up for work?" I asked him, worried that perhaps he hadn't quite understood how damaging a tendency to even occasional unreliability could be to the reputation of a young construction worker marked for big things.

"Jesus, I sure hope so, How." he said. "It'd be a hell of a thing if a guy could be off the job and nobody missed ya." It was a danger signal when Don started adding the How. It meant we were falling into the old big brother-little brother thing, an emotional morass from which there was no logical path out. But I couldn't help myself.

"I know but won't somebody be pissed off?"

"Somebody? Like who, How?"

"Well you must have some kind of a boss. A foreman or something."

"Oh, I don't think so. I've covered his ass enough times."

"Yeah, but there's got to be somebody above him keeping a eye on things."

"Yeah there is, How, but he would be so worried I was off talking to one of the other outfits he'd probably give me a raise."

In the old days he would have flown off the handle and told me

not to treat him like a kid, but now he was toying with me instead.
It was a breakthrough in the history of our relationship — a
breakthrough for him — and it made me feel small. I shrugged. It
was no doubt a good thing for a man to know his worth, but I still
thought it was a bit cheeky, not just to goof off for half a day, but
to do it in the company four-by-four.

The Mica dam had just flooded a ninety-mile-long stretch of
the Rocky Mountain Trench without clearing the forest and all
manner of floatable matter, mostly fully-limbed trees that had
ripped themselves out of the ground by their own buoyancy, roots
and all, and had drifted up to the top end, filling a bay four miles
deep with jumbled wood. Looking down from the top of the
mountain it seemed a clot of minute fibres felted together into a
pulpy mat, but as you got closer the vastness of the mess hit
you — miles and miles of trashed timber, big logs layered a hundred
deep. Enough pulp to print the LA *Times* into the next century,
tossed away because some politician was in hurry to get employ-
ment stats up before an election call. Don told us the people of
Valemont were pretty sore because this huge new lake courtesy
of BC Hydro had raised the humidity, created a wind funnel and
changed the whole region's weather. Windstorms rumbled down
the valley, blowing down hundreds of acres of forest. A few nights
earlier some of Don's friends were making a shaky late exit from the
beer parlour when a gust tore the big plank door out of their hands,
ripped it off its hinges and sent it cartwheeling across the parking lot
into a Camaro where it did three hundred dollars damage.

"Eighty-nine," Mare intoned.

"Good," I said. "Very good."

We'd been working away at that number ever since Kamloops.
It had started out at 3-something, 354 I think and it had taken the
longest time to get it down to 300 or anywhere you could start to
see around it. It was in the 200s all the way through Little Fort,
Blue River, Vavenby, Avola. Even when we got it down to the
hundreds, around Prince George, it didn't seem to get rid of as
fast as it should. But now, eighty-nine, we felt we were getting
somewhere at last. The numbers appeared every ten or so miles
on signboards carrying a stylized image of a youth with long yellow
hair. We weren't sure where we were supposed to be when the
Yellowhead Route zeroed out, Prince George or Prince Rupert.

It officially went all the way to Rupert, but these numbers appeared to be counting down for Prince.

This was Big Bend country. It reminded me of the Yukon around the South McQuesten, thick stands of pipecleaner trees, sedgy swamps and mountains jabbing up. The open spots were

The Yellowhead Highway

warm and bright in the sun, but in shade the ground stayed white with frost all day.

As the miles spiraled monotonously away and the countryside rolled by like an endless home video projected on the windscreen we both began to be affected by a weird sense of artificiality. All that country going by but we couldn't touch it. There was no interaction between us in our hermetically-sealed perambulating living room and it out there. Occasional "fill 'er ups" and "nice days" exchanged with pump jockeys were our only contact with the people of the country and we began to feel trapped. This was not the feeling I'd hoped to get out of this trip. Where was the old inspiration of the BC landscape? I began turning on the CB radio to see if we could get anything that way. We didn't hear much that made sense until Mare got us stuck between two semis just outside of Valemont. The two drivers were jawing nonstop and we listened to them for an hour.

One guy had his own rig. They talked about the various establishments they could buy to get off the road, and other guys who'd done good and bad, mostly bad. One guy who bought the Husky at Blue River lost $120 a day all through the strike.

"Yeh well, cottonpicker, it wouldn't take too many days like that to clean a guy out, over."

"Yeah, 10-4 on that, that's for sure."

"Yeh, that's a 10-4 alright. Hundert, hundert twenty clams a day and that cottonpickin' strike went on for jus' about three weeks. I was kinda glad I didn't go for that place when I heard that."

We passed a chunky-looking crewcut guy tearing along the shoulder on a horse at full gallop. There were huge poofs of hot breath bursting out into the cold air, gravel flying up, and he was beating on the horse's ass with a piece of rope. It was a startling apparition, way out in the middle of nowhere. And oddly, even from that brief glimpse I was certain I'd seen that same guy twice before, at widely disconnected junctures in my life. The first was ten years earlier at a gymkhana I'd ended up at in Oliver on one of those desperate car forays with my parents. The second was at the Mount Currie rodeo in 1973. Both times I'd had only glimpses of the guy and I didn't know why I even remembered. It would seem more likely to have been three different guys, but his burly crewcut belligerence, like one of those surly agents who guard the US president, except with this dash of horsiness thrown in, made a lasting impression.

The truckers giggled for the next ten miles.

"Yessir cottonpicker, looked t' me like that fella wants a new set of injectors cut down on that exhaust there, that exhaust looked t'me like she was burnin awful rich ten-four."

"Ten-four alright on that for sure, ha ha ya that fella had the hammer down and that's for sure."

"Roger there conpicker, mercy me, I think maybe he should get a compression check when he gets into Blue River Motors. The way those stacks a his was blowin' he could have a bad headgasket conpicker."

They keep this up until they've said everything they can think about it five times. The one who keeps saying mercy me and cottonpicker is the motor mouth and the other guy keeps trying to sign off but the ratchetjaw won't let go. The only thing that distracts him is when another truck goes by.

"That eighteen-wheeler jus' pass us, yuh on?"

If he was, they'd go through the whole routine, where's he outta, where's he goin', what's he packin', where's smokey holed up.

"Well maybe see you down Keremeos then cottonpicker."

"Yah, 10-4 Bluestreak, see ya Monday." Then after a decent wait to let the passer pass out of range he's back at his first friend.

"That fella, he's been working for the Public six years I hear tell, mercy me, I don't know how a man can do it." "The Public" was Public Freightways, a big trucking outfit notorious among the independents for its regimentation of the free-spirited truckdriving life. It has since fallen victim to free trade and vanished.

"10-4. Yeah, not too many guys stay with 'em that long. I guess he likes the way they do it."

"Well 10-4 to that, conpigger, they got so many rules and that kinda thing, mercy me, a fella don't know if he's comin' er goin'."

"Yeah, 10-4. Too many rules kinda gets a guy down."

"10-4, you said a mouthful there conpigger. Why, ah tell ya now—a lotta guys won't believe it—but it's true now conpigger when I worked at that Public type outfit they gave you another driver's licence, and this was a company-type licence just like your goverment licence there, and anything you did against the rules, like you let your hair get within a quarter-inch of your collar, you let your sideburns get an eighth of an inch below your earlobes, you get caught wearin' shitkickers, well then, conpigger, they put points on your company licence. Well, mercy me, there's so many rules, half the time you're breaking one you don't even know it, and you get so many points on this conpiggin' company licence there they call a fella up and put a fella under two-week suspension. Conpigger, this type fella couldn't put up with that there Public type stuff."

"Rrrrrrrrrrroger there, Bluestreak. I guess in that outfit you'd be on the Speed-o-Graph pritneer all the time."

"Oh mercy me yes, 10-4 on that conpigger, you don't turn a wheel without you got it on the clock and every time you break the ol' double nickels they're marking you down for it, mercy me—one time Ed Ogle and me we kinda passed some time in the Exeter Arms there on a run outta Prince so we jus' left the clock off and hoofed 'er straight home in nine hours. Said we forgot. Well conpigger down the Public dispatch he got out his calclater and sez that averages out to fifty-three miles per hour steady and what with all those towns and what not, there's no way you can average fifty-three steady without you do a lot of seventy-three and eighty-three, and that's how I came to leave the Public 10-4."

We left them behind on a long grade and I was sorry. I was dying to pick up the mike and say something but I couldn't dare. For miles I felt the urge to just speak into it to see if anybody answered but couldn't bring myself to. I wasn't sure how to run it. You pushed a button or something. Mare probably knew, her pop was a radio ham and she grew up with CB in the front room, but she'd think I was foolish.

We rolled into Prince George in the late afternoon and managed to locate my sister Cindy and her new boyfriend Ken, who was an accountant and had a whole different set of values to what I was used to. They were into VSOP cognac and belonged to a gourmet cooking circle. We were into herbal tea and homemade granola and found this a bit hard to take. He was the first person of our generation we'd met who openly admitted to having investments. Then I was appalled; now I wish I'd got some tips.

We tolerated each other's peculiarities and had a comfortable break from the road. They begged us to stay over for a deluxe brunch the next morning but at ten we'd been awake for two hours and they weren't stirring so we decided to leave a note and hit the road. Just as we reached the end of town I noticed we were out of gas with no filling station in sight, so we swung around and went back. By this time the bookstore in the Bay was open, so I paid a call. The manager was thrilled to meet a living writer and urged me to drop by the local TV station, who would certainly give me a shot on the afternoon show to push our books. I followed her advice, reeled off my spiel to some impatient airhead, and they decided to do a VTR if I could make it back at three. We doodled around town looking for the other bookstore and got an appointment to see the manager there at five. Then we doodled around some more.

I wanted Prince George to impress me but I couldn't make it. From afar it was an explosive mix of loggers and cowboys bent on mayhem, up close the only way you could tell you weren't in Richmond or Surrey was the number of four-by-fours. Every second vehicle was one, plastered with mud all up the back although you couldn't find any sign of dirt roads in the town itself. There was the odd character walking around in a Roy Rogers outfit, and they did tend to drive their cars like cutting horses. I was ambling along in a crosswalk one place when a four-by came screaming right at me at about fifty miles an hour, swerving to pass by inches at the last minute. I dove for the curb, being more accustomed to the Vancouver system where vehicles waited demurely on the other side of the intersection until the crosswalk was clear, but the driver appeared to know what he was doing, more or less.

The streets were of a generous width to begin with but the whole downtown was a bottleneck owing to the town's strange policy of barricading off each curb lane and using it for angle parking. This left only one lane each way for traffic, but even that lane was slowed to an ooze by parkers backing out and others waiting to take their places. Ken said it was even worse when there was snow because the steep crown on the roadway left you with your front wheels down in a rut and your rears up spinning on the ice. It was hard to believe how anything could be so screwed up. It took us ten minutes to go one block and that was on a Thursday evening in clear weather. There was a great tension throughout the whole northern interior because the snow was so late. Not that they like it, my sister said, they just wanted to get on with it.

It was dark before we got back to the place on the highway where we'd turned back at 10 AM.

The TV spot had been one of those ninety-second encounters with futility which could have done no one any good and we had less than fifty dollars worth of book sales to show for our lost day so I was determined to get somewhere before we plugged in for the night, even though it meant missing some sights in the dark. I could sense the landscape changing around us as we reeled forward into the blackness, flashes of roadside bush our only clue. A few towns, a few mills off in the woods lit up like cities. Fort Fraser, Topley exist. Burns Lake proved to be a run-down place the road twisted through, like Greenwood. Houston was bright and open. We came to a stop finally in a government rest area beside the Morice River, in great doubt as to what surrounded us.

Daylight revealed a dry sort of valley such as you might see in Cariboo country, small pine and spruce and grass, dry grass, wherever the trees cut away. There was a low range of mountains about five miles to the south and another right beside us. It wasn't much, not enough to justify the reputation that had come through to me of a great valley. A few steps down the bank the Morice River slurped by, not nearly so clearly as I imagined it in our headlights the night before. I went down in shirtsleeves to clean the dishes from our Mexican supper, the ground crunchy with frost and the water so icy two plates were all I could stand, rubbing a paste of dirt and mudwater into the cold fat. I came back gasping.

The rest area had recently been vandalized, garbage drums all overturned and the handsome, heavy-plank tables thrown into the river where they drifted downstream and hung up in shoreline snags. It was the kind of thing that made you despair for humanity. In my mind I went through a little Mighty Mouse scenario of coming upon the vandals in the act: spotting the three hooligans down the bank in a frenzied struggle to heave the last three-hundred-pound table into the river, I would reach into the camper for my single-bladed splitting mall and proceed to reduce their parked four-by-four to a pile of broken glass and punctured metal. It would take them a while to believe what they were seeing and start scrambling up the bank howling bloody blue murder, whereupon I would calmly administer the coup-de-grace to their distributor and hop in our idling chariot, zooming off with a confident sneer as they waved their arms helplessly and flung their Cat caps into the dirt. But wait—I didn't notice the Harley parked in the bushes. Now it screams down the yellow line like a Howitzer, I try to sideswipe it, the black-sheathed figure leaps cat-like onto our runningboard, wrenching at the door handle as Mary stares out in stark terror...

Even in my fantasies I couldn't win. I resolved if we came across any real hooligans to keep driving.

Then on into the Bulkley Valley. It did get bigger and better. A bit further on, the road went over Grouse Mountain at five thousand feet and you could see lots of soft hills all poplar and birch and widely spaced pine with grass showing through and lots of open meadows high up on the hills like a drybelt Switzerland. The Bulkley itself appeared, a middle-sized river about on par with the Similkameen or Squamish, and jumbled greenly along on a clean gravel bed, twisting into rapids at Telkwa, where the

road also twisted and went bumpy. Telkwa was tilted, hills on both
sides, houses peering over the highway, a novelty in this relatively
open country. There's something about towns built on hills.
Definitely gives them something over the flat kind. I made a
mental note, in case I ever had need to found a town. Oddly, we
later ran into a guy, a dropped-out city planner from the States,
who was starting a town, or trying to restart one. He'd bought a
ghost town just above Terrace called Pacific and was trying to
figure out what to do with it. In the mid-seventies the woods were
full of people doing things like that.

Telkwa had log cabins downtown, a big old building that served
as a combined store and museum and closed-up filling stations
flaking cream paint, offered for sale by our friend the Yellowhead.
Some entrepreneur with a sense of history had lifted him from
the roadsigns and put him to work as the namesake of a real estate
firm. Thus mighty legends endure in the time of the
entrepreneurs.

Farms, barns. Silver roofs, dry grey wood and lumpy brown
fields, here and there a steer. It is not a fat country and not exactly
lean, the Bulkley, but right in between. Coming into Smithers
there was a market garden or two, with rows of winter cabbage.
Back at Houston we had stopped to see the local historian, Elnora
Smith, who said flatly that agriculture in the Bulkley Valley was
a bust, although that was what the government laid it out for in
the first place. It's not the soil, she said, it's the weather, which is
not severe so much as flukey. There can be as many frost-free days
in November as July, and no month is safe.

Smithers was a bright place, almost prosperous with new Snap-
Loc aluminum buildings shouldering out the wonkier wooden
ones, but most construction in the Bulkley was wooden and old.
Log barns were common, and once we passed a house of ancient
axe-hewn logs sporting a bright new shingle roof. Mare drew my
attention to a house covered all over with birdhouses—in the
shape of churches, log cabins, schoolhouses, firehalls. Nice. A bit
of eye candy put out for passers-by, but it wasn't enough, none of
this was enough. We were travelling but we weren't being trans-
ported. We were still in the same stolid mood we'd started out in.
I wondered if it was the rig. Its comfort seemed to insulate us from
the countryside. Maybe if we were humping along in that old
listing Pontiac I took to Mexico, sleeping under trees and scroung-

ing parts in garbage dumps and running into weird characters, you'd have more of a sense of going somewhere, of being on foreign ground. At the time I had hated the insecurity of never being sure you'd still be mobile by the end of the day, but maybe that was what you needed to bring out the adventure. This dream home on wheels made everything so unreal.

The first place that really struck sparks was Moricetown. Indian village with old white-spired church, lots of battered new maroon and turquoise bungalows, spacious new community buildings with lumberyard labels still bright but aluminum windows already busted, twisted, hanging out of their frames. One of the new buildings housed a fire department with two truck bays and the band administration office overhead. The other appeared to be a community centre or meeting hall of some sort. And there was a meeting taking place, but down the road, at the old church. Cars, several dozen of them, blocked the narrow gravel road in front and overflowed from a vacant lot next door, where the charred remains of a burnt house poked up. We were thinking of going in, checking around for what signs or relics we might find of old Father Morice, the legendary scholar-priest who explored the whole northern interior and wrote one of the best histories ever

Moricetown

done on BC, but there were backs against the windows, backs blocking the door, and only one face turning to see who'd come to intrude. It was Sunday, but two or so, late for an regular church service. Must be some sort of secular gathering I thought, but funny they would jam up in the rickety little church instead of the spacious new community hall. Guess they just felt more comfortable with the old place.

The river, though, was the thing. The river and the rocks. Nine times out of ten when you get off on a place it's the rocks that make the difference and here it was the spectacular black rock twisting out of the ground, taking over the landscape, pinching the tough little river into a frothing jet that squirts over a ledge into a knotted green pool, walled around by jagged cliffs overhanging several hundred feet up. This was the storied Moricetown Falls. A bit further down, toward Hazelton, was a different sort of rock show as the river cut into some red sandstoney stuff that was all kind of sloping and melted-looking, seeming half stone and half dirt.

New Hazelton is about ten miles down the highway, Newtown the locals call it but there was nothing there but a few motels and gas stations. Four miles down a side road from Newtown is Old Hazelton or Oldtown and that's where the big reserve is, with stores and the big Indian art museum they call K'san. On the way to Oldtown you go over Hagwilget canyon, which is the other big viewpoint in the area. It's a knockout. Little skinny canyon like an alley between two skyscrapers with the most graceful wispy miniature suspension bridge spider-webbing across. In the old days the Indians had a suspension bridge of their own in the same spot, woven out of wire scrounged from the abandoned Collins Overland Telegraph. Looking down through the openwork deck of the present structure you could see the river shooting through the canyon like a firehose. This was the Bulkley's last show before slumping into the Skeena at Hazelton.

The K'san art centre was on a cottonwood flat below town. There was a group of northern type long-houses made from sawn lumber and a collection of poles in that narrow Skeena style with small complex figures. Some were finished and standing, others were still on the ground being carved. Downtown was a building shaped like a paddlewheeler at the site of the old riverboat dock, housing the museum and municipal office. Beside that was a weathered old pole with three little guys wearing a tall, tall hat, a

Moricetown Falls

famous pole we had a photo of on our bedroom wall. It delighted me to see it, like being lost in Europe and stumbling onto Michelangelo's *David*. So *this* is where I am, you say. It put the whole visit in context.

We needed gas, but instead of going to the slickest joint on the highway the way we'd been doing ever since we found ourselves trapped aboard this pleasure barge, I did what I usually did with my own rusty pickup and looked around for the smallest, grimiest street-corner station that looked like it needed our business most. A greasy old character crawled out from under something and staggered over to serve us, and immediately we got talking. It turned out he was the uncle of a kid who'd been my best friend all through school in Pender Harbour. A further coincidence was that the friend, who I'd lost track of years before, was now living on the same road as my sister in Prince George. It took away some of the feeling of unconnectedness and I began to think there might just be some hope for this trip after all.

Ever since we started out we'd been ignoring hitchhikers. Normally I'd pick up the odd one but there was something about it not being our motorhome I suppose, and being a bit out of our own element. People didn't really expect to get picked up by an RV, was another thing. They didn't work on your guilt the way they would in an old car. But I was feeling a bit more myself now and surprised Mary by stopping to pick up two teenage boys who wanted to go somewhere that sounded like "Saltdown" but turned out to be the third Hazelton installment, South Hazelton or "South Town." Then back on the highway I gave the wheel to Mary so I could do up my journal and just out of Moricetown she pulled over for a little Indian kid with unusual mulatto-yellow hair.

"He's probably only going two blocks," I speculated. "If he is I'll give him a kick in the pants." He looked about eleven or twelve and I rolled down the window to explain how to get the side door open, but he was already in.

"Where you guys goin?" he asked brightly, plopping his skinny body into the plush settee as if he never travelled any other way.

"Well, we're going all the way to Prince Rupert eventually," I said. Prince Rupert was over two hundred miles and still seemed in another country.

"Good."

"Where are you going?"

"Rupert." He said it matter of factly. "Are you writing a book?"

"No," I tell him, "I just keep a journal."

"Yeah?" he said doubtfully. "You look like Farley Mowat."

"Thanks a lot," I said.

His name was Silas George. I asked him what his parents thought of him hitchhiking all the way to Rupert by himself.

"They don't know," he said.

"They don't?" I said, suddenly alarmed. "How come?"

"My dad was passed out so I couldn't tell him, and I couldn't find my mom so I just split. I've got to be back in Rupert tomorrow morning for a game with CanCel."

"What kind of game is that?"

"Hockey. I play goal and the team doesn't have a spare so I have to be back. CanCel's got some good shooters."

I wondered what we were getting involved in. If home was in Prince Rupert, why were his parents in Moricetown? Was he a runaway or something? There was nothing suspicious about the way he acted. He seemed perfectly sure of himself. In fact he was so self-assured I held my concern in check, out of respect. In case everything was as normal as his manner suggested, I didn't want to seem overly fussy. When I was a kid there was nothing I hated worse than grown-ups who came around and made a fuss about me doing stuff I did every day.

"What will your parents say when they find you gone," I asked.

"Nothing."

"What were you doing in Moricetown?"

"My mom was already up there visiting my auntie and Dad wanted to go up and see her but he just retired from his job running the lightplant at Rupert airport on Friday and went on a big drunk and we didn't want him to drive himself so we tried to get my big brother to take him because he's fifteen but he was drunk too so I had to do it."

"*You* drove your dad from Prince Rupert to Moricetown?"

"Yeah."

"By yourself?"

"Yeah."

"What kind of a car did you drive?"

"His. It's a pickup. A '76 Cheyenne with those real thick tires, you know? My nephew picked it out. Whenever we get a new car we always get my nephew to pick it out. That way we know it's okay. He never picks a bad one."

"How old is your nephew?"

"Seven."

"Why did he pick the Cheyenne, did he say?"

"The tires. He liked the thick tires."

I was still trying to decide if we were doing the right thing or if we should turn around and take this kid back to Moricetown. But he acted so calm and matter-of-fact he was hard to doubt.

"Did you have any problems driving up here?"

"Yeah. Just out of Cedardale I hit a squirrel. I tried to swerve but the tires mashed it. I wasn't used to them, they're so thick. After that, every time I'd see one of these dry leaves jumping along and I'd think it was a squirrel and go off the road nearly."

I had to laugh. Every once in awhile I mistook one for a hopping frog.

"How long did it take you?"

"Just under four hours, but we stopped at Terrace for a burger. My brother has the record. He did it in two hours and twenty-seven minutes but that was in a '73 Cutlass. I don't like going too fast in the truck. Those big tires kinda shake if you go over eighty miles an hour. I found a smooth place between seventy and eighty and just kept it there most of the time."

He'd been driving since he was eight. When he was younger they lived in Thornhill—you know, in Terrace there, he said, realizing we didn't know much—and they had the biggest house in Thornhill, but it burnt down.

"That's too bad," I said.

"Yeah, my little brother got killed when our house burnt. That was last year."

"That's terrible."

"I'm the youngest now. Unless my mom adopts my nephew. My really big sister she's left her husband and she lives with all sorts of different guys and my mom, she doesn't like it."

Leaving Hazelton we had a glimpse of huge mountains, the Seven Sisters, rearing up to the south and far off in the west a breathtaking white-fanged range visible just for a minute. The Skeena is alive at that stage, green and full of sinister rolling boils, occasionally flaking into whitecaps as it gets wedged between bars. Couldn't have been too relaxing running those two-hundred-foot sternwheelers up. Mare was still at the gear and I was still scribbling down my amazement over Silas George the infant Sterling Moss. He had undertaken to provide us with a running commentary on the passing countryside, pointing out Usk and

Skeena Crossing, where his dad once parked a truck for three months and when he came back found nothing but the frame.

"They'd took it all for parts, the people that live there," he explained awkwardly. He knew we weren't too swift, but he wasn't sure just how much he needed to talk down to us.

Thornhill turned out to be an ill-defined area sprawling for miles east of Terrace. There was a sizable school but he said he had never gone to that one. He was only three when they left Terrace.

"I thought you said it was last year your house burnt down," I said. I figured I'd caught him bullshitting for sure this time.

"No, that was a different time. The one in Terrace was quite a few years ago. We all got out of it. The one where my little brother died was last year, in Rupert."

"Oh, I see."

"It started in the wiring. My great big sister got woken up by the fusebox popping and ran upstairs and got us all out except my little brother. The fireman got him, but he was dead. He suffocated. He didn't get burned."

"Why didn't he wake up and get out with the rest of you?"

"I don't know."

Terrace is approached by two bridges, an old one and a new one just like Silas told us it would be. Mary, being cautious, at least when driving an expensive new RV, followed the bulk of the traffic over the new bridge while the kid struggled to relate some complicated tale of land speculation affecting the approach development. I tried to imagine myself being aware of such a thing at such an age. There were bookstores, newspapers and a radio station to see in Terrace but without discussing it Mary and I had both silently decided the important thing was to get our boy home in time for his game with CanCel. Terrace could be dealt with another time. We took the bypass and began circling around the town with its smoking riverside chimneys.

"Aren't you going to gas up?" he said.

The gauge was just a bit under half but there was something in the way he asked the question that made us go straight to the nearest gas station. We'd come to accept his road knowledge completely. He got out and bought a can of pop and offered me a drink from it. A stiff wind blew the garage's sign board down and clattered empty oilcans across the lot.

"Is it always like this here?" I asked.

"No," he said.

I took over the wheel as the rain began and the darkness thickened. The road started off bravely, new and wide, but soon dwindled to a bumpy track piggy-backed along the railroad grade, often separated only by a concrete barrier with signs warning drivers to stop in their tracks and hang on if they saw a railway snowblower coming. Mountains had closed round on either side, and the Skeena had spread out to fill the space between them, looking more like a broad coastal inlet than a river. The Skeena canyon isn't a cut canyon like the Thompson or the Fraser, but a found canyon between two sloping sets of mountains, what obviously would have been an inlet if the river hadn't laid prior claim. The hard light of the interior with its crisp yellows and browns was now displaced by the diffuse, smeary blues and greys of the coast. The road ran only few feet above the water all the way, rising just at Kitselas Canyon, which isn't a big league canyon like Hell's Gate or the like, but must have given the paddlewheel skippers a few grey hairs just the same. The roadbed was set on fill well out into the soft rivermuck, the ashphalt cracked and broken from continual settling. It hopped back and forth from one side of the tracks to the other, slowing to twenty, turning at right angles, humping over rickety wooden bridges that barely passed two cars. It was by far the worst driving of the trip. I worried my way through at thirty and forty and only a few cars tried to squeeze past. The kid peered over my shoulder, telling me more than once when I left my lights on high beam, and warning me to slow for some particularly bad potholes. He announced that we'd soon turn away from the river and find the going better, which proved true, but my nerves were shot and I kept crawling along in the pelting rain.

"There's no cops here," he advised, thinking maybe that was what held me back. "I'll tell you when we get to the places the cops hang out." A few miles later, he pointed out the exact sideroad they liked to haunt.

"Get behind another car," he advised. "Then if they got radar on they'll nail him and let you go. That's what my brother does."

I had to keep looking at him to reassure myself he was really only a small boy and not a grown man with a squeaky voice. I had been a bit precocious, growing up in logging camps and running boats and boom winches, but I'd never seen anything to beat this guy. Mary and I were by now both completely in awe. I wondered what his future would be and whether his remarkable confidence would lead him to great things, or whether he would get beaten down by prejudice and despair like so many of his race.

"Do you think you will stay in Prince Rupert when you grow up?" I asked.

"Quite likely I will," he said matter of factly, as if he had long ago given the matter all the thought it needed and put it forever behind him. He preferred to talk about hockey. He had been a high-scoring winger but broke his leg go-kart racing and lost his speed so they moved him to goal and he had to buy all new equipment. I asked him if he thought he would go into professional hockey.

"No, I'm not good enough."

None of this "I dunno" stuff for him.

He pointed out the road to Point Ed just before the bridge onto Kaien Island and urged us to go see the Buntze Rapids. "They're *beautiful*," he said.

Then we were into Rupert and he pointed his house out to us, but offered to show us the way to a good seafood place. When we got there it was closed.

"Darnit," he said. "Oh well. Try the Commodore. Thanks for the ride."

And with that he was gone into an alley and out of sight.

I felt like running after him and saying I wanted to keep in touch, saying we wanted to take him home with us and help him become a great man. We were both quite deflated by his sudden departure.

Driving back over the road two days later everything we saw reminded us of him—the Port Edward turnoff, the side road where the highway patrol like to set up their radar and the railway tunnel where he said his dad used to stop the car and let them run through, him and his little brother before he got killed and his big brother and sister and maybe even his really big sister, screaming and hollering at the tops of their lungs, while their dad drove down and waited for them to come out the other end. I couldn't understand how Indian kids, who I knew often had that kind of attention and indulgence, could go so wrong. So much love and so much experience, so much raw life poured into them so early, so much learning and toughening you would think it would build character so powerful they could walk up to the nearest bottle-fed, hothouse-bred whitey and just blow him over with a breath. Maybe they would yet, when Silas George's generation got its turn.

We talked about him all the way home. I still think about him all the time, thirteen years later. He would be twenty-four now. I'd give anything to know what he's up to, and to be able to tell him what he did for us.

We got home five days later fully prepared to start our lives over. We decided that all our publishing gambles were going to pan out just fine—which they did—and bought a real house with a gorgeous view over Malaspina Strait and left the pink house trailer behind forever. The following July Mary delivered a handsome son we named Silas.

He's twelve now and watching him make one of his end-to-end rushes for a cheering crowd at the Sechelt hockey arena gives Mary and I a bigger thrill than anything we ever did in those long-ago years of our own youth.

Did I mention that he has a fine head of bright yellow hair?

ACKNOWLEDGEMENTS

"Oolachon Grease" previously appeared in *New Catalyst, Ruebsaat's, Event*, and *BC Bookworld*.

"The Bomb that Mooed" previously appeared in *Raincoast Chronicles #10, Raincoast Chronicles Six/Ten, Vancouver Magazine*, and *The Nelson Island Story*, by Karen Southern (Hancock House, 1987).

"The Day Joey Came" previously appeared in *Raincoast Chronicles #6* and *Raincoast Chronicles Six/Ten*.

"Tides" previously appeared in *Raincoast Chronicles #5* and *Raincoast Chronicles First Five*.

"Metlakatla" previously appeared in *Heritage Canada, Raincoast Chronicles #4* and *Raincoast Chronicles First Five*.

"The Handkerchief Angle" previously appeared in *Ruebsaat's*.

"Minstrel" previously appeared in *Raincoast Chronicles #11*.

"Hubert Evans Meets the Cadborosaurus" previously appeared in *Raincoast Chronicles #10, Raincoast Chronicles Six/Ten*, and, in part, in *Mysterious Canada: Strange Sights, Extraordinary Events and Peculiar Places*, by J.R. Colombo (Doubleday Canada, 1988).

"Bill Sinclair at 90″ previously appeared in the *Peninsula Voice*.

"How It Was with Trucks" previously appeared in *Vancouver Magazine, Trucklogger, Raincoast Chronicles #3* and *Raincoast Chronicles Six/Ten*.

"The Men There Were Then" and "Those Bloody Fishermen" previously appeared in *The Men There Were Then* (Pulp Press, 1983) and in *The New Canadian Poets, 1970–1985, edited by Dennis Lee (McClelland and Stewart, 1985)*.

"What a Way to Go," "I Kill Myself and Maim Myself" and "The Third Stiff" previously appeared in *The Men There Were Then*.

"Codfish and Cappuccino" previously appeared in the *Coast News* and the *Powell River News/Town Crier*.